Harry Pearson was born in 1961 in a village near Middlesbrough. He was educated by kindly Quakers. An early attempt to become a journalist foundered because his spelling wasn't good enough. After many years spent working in jobs that required overalls or paper hats, his life was altered for ever by reading an article about Alan Foggon in the football magazine *When Saturday Comes*. Since then he has written seven books, including *The Far Corner*, and contributed to a dozen more. He has written for *When Saturday Comes* for twenty years and is a weekly columnist for the *Guardian*.

Praise for *Slipless in Settle*

'Deftly mixes observation, history and affectionate appreciation of the North's people, landscapes and idiosyncrasies'
Huw Richards, *Guardian*

'I doubt there will be a funnier cricket book published this year'
Richard Whitehead, *Wisden Cricketer*

'There's no funnier sports-writer in the language'
Frank Keating, *Oldie*

Slipless in Settle

A Slow Turn around Northern Cricket

Harry Pearson

ABACUS

ABACUS

First published in Great Britain as a
paperback original in 2010 by Little, Brown
This paperback edition published in 2012 by Abacus

A CIP catalogue record for this book
is available from the British Library.

ISBN 978-0-349-00010-7

Typeset in Baskerville by M Rules
Printed and bound in Great Britain by
Clays Ltd, St Ives plc

Papers used by Abacus are from well-managed forests
and other responsible sources.

MIX
Paper from
responsible sources
FSC® C104740

Abacus
An imprint of
Little, Brown Book Group
100 Victoria Embankment
London EC4Y 0DY

An Hachette UK Company
www.hachette.co.uk

www.littlebrown.co.uk

For Catherine, always the loveliest girl in the room

Acknowledgements

For beer, lifts and illuminating chat my thanks go to Paul Rocca, John Cleary, Cec Wright, Dave Edmundson, David Morrison, Peter Smith, William Pym and my dad.

Fuller histories of league cricket can be found in *League Cricket in England* by Roy Genders and *Cricket in the Leagues* by John Kay. For more information about specific leagues I can heartily recommend *See the Conquering Hero*, Dave Edmundson's wonderful history of the Lancashire League, Cotton Town Cricket by Roy Cavanagh, *Over the Hill by way of Highmoor* compiled by Phil Taylor, *One Hundred Years of the Ribblesdale Cricket League* by Alan West, and *The Centenary History of the Bradford League* and *In The Big League* edited by Ray Baker. Other books that happily filled many train and bus journeys were Gerald Howat's biography of Learie Constantine, *S. F. Barnes – Master Bowler* by Leslie Duckworth, *We Don't Play it for Fun* by Don Mosey and various works by J. M. Kilburn. Bill Alley's first autobiography, *My Incredible Innings*, is worth picking up for the anecdote about the dance-hall fights with the red-headed Scotsman alone.

A Note about the North

Where exactly the North of England begins is a matter of debate. For the purposes of this book the parameters of the North are those defined by My Dad's Law of the North. My Dad's Law of the North is named after the man who invented it – my dad. It states simply that when a straight line is drawn between the mouth of the Mersey and the mouth of the Humber, then everything above that line is the North and everything below it isn't. Clearly this will raise eyebrows in some quarters as it means a large chunk of Yorkshire, including Sheffield, Barnsley and Doncaster, is not in the North of England and therefore its citizens are not Northerners. You may find it hard, for example, to consider Geoffrey Boycott a southerner. Though I think you will agree that this offers the only plausible explanation as to why he supports Manchester United.

Introduction

'Oooh Learie Constantine,' Mrs Jessup said.

Mrs Jessup had false teeth so pickled in dental whitener that in the twilight of a winter's afternoon they seemed to emit an apocalyptic glow. The teeth had a life of their own, clattering together whenever she opened her mouth to speak so that when you were in conversation with her it was like watching a badly dubbed film. Mrs Jessup had fierce eyes, a firm set to her jaw and hair that from a lifetime of chemical marshalling was shaped like a mob cap and as rigid as steel.

Mrs Jessup worked in the stillroom of a hotel where I was barman. When I locked the doors at ten past three in the afternoon, she'd come and sit by the fire with a pot of tea and a plate of pink wafer biscuits, while I finished washing the glasses and putting the lemon slices and cocktail cherries in the fridge behind the bar. For the first few months Mrs Jessup totally ignored me, but then one day she gestured me over when I pulled down the shutters, and when I looked over to the table I saw that there were two cups on her tea tray and a couple of extra wafers. I went and sat down. Mrs Jessup poured me a cup of tea. 'Miss Maynard says you're a hard worker,' she said without looking up.

Miss Maynard was Mrs Jessup's best friend. She worked all over the hotel doing any job that needed doing. She could unblock a toilet and make a plate of roast beef sandwiches, though she never did them at the same time, obviously. Miss Maynard was a tiny woman of indiscernible age, who wore her dark hair scraped back and had a face the colour of a kipper, nicotine-stained by the untipped Capstan cigarette that was slotted permanently into a groove in her lower lip. To be described as a hard worker was the highest praise you could expect from Miss Maynard and Mrs Jessup. They came from a generation of working class people for whom laziness and greed were two of the most despised vices, because laziness meant more work for others and greediness less food for everyone else.

Mrs Jessup lived in one of the boondock villages of East Cleveland, the sort of place where the kids threw stones at strangers. Before settling there though she'd lived a busy and interesting life. She'd been out in Berlin when the Nazis annexed the Sudetenland, in the East End during the Blitz, Kenya during the Mau Mau crisis, all the while maintaining a strict attitude to the correct disposition of doilies and seeing off an array of husbands, all of them diligent, well-mannered martyrs to a bewildering range of chronic gastric ailments.

One November afternoon when Mrs Jessup and I were having our tea, she told me that she had been born and brought up in the Lancashire cotton town of Nelson. To the Northern cricket fan Nelson was synonymous with one man – Learie Constantine.

'Ooooh, Learie Constantine,' Mrs Jessup said when I mentioned the great West Indian and an odd look came across her face, which after a while I realised was a coquettish smile. The tone in her voice had changed too, and her eyes had taken on a distinct sparkle. The only time I had ever seen Mrs Jessup like this before was after she and Miss Maynard had been on a coach trip to the London Palladium to see *The King and I* with Yul Brynner.

Mrs Jessup had been quite bowled over by the shaven-headed star and the following evening after service and a medicinal bottle of barley wine she'd recalled his performance, or at least one aspect of it, in the stillroom surrounded by silver coffeepots and the remains of Melba toast. 'He just came to the front of the stage and stood,' she said and mimicked Brynner's pose, feet planted far apart, hands on hips, head tilted back, eyes narrowed, an arrogant curl to her lip. 'Oooh,' she'd said, after she'd sat down and readjusted her dental plate, 'Yul Brynner!'

Oooh Learie Constantine had created a sensation when he'd come to England with the West Indian tourists in 1928. He'd hit 1381 runs and taken 107 wickets in just twenty-six matches. It was the manner in which he'd done it, though, that had caught the public imagination. The Trinidadian had bowled ferociously fast, fielded with feline grace and smacked the ball around with amazing power. Against Middlesex at Lord's he'd smashed a century in fifty-nine minutes, including one blow off the back foot that flew over cover point and ricocheted off the Old Father Time weather vane on the roof of the North Stand.

The news that Constantine had signed a two-year contract to play as a professional in the Lancashire League for Nelson during the 1929 and 1930 seasons created an even bigger stir than that shot at Lord's. The Trinidadian's contract was said to be worth six hundred pounds a season plus bonuses and collections. In an era when the maximum wage was in force in football it was a salary that by common consent made Constantine Britain's highest-paid sportsman.

Hiring professionals to play alongside the amateurs had been a tradition in Northern cricket that dated back to the Victorian era. Over the years great names from across the world had come to the region to play in obscure towns and villages. Kapil Dev, Bobby Simpson, Fazal Mahmood, Martin Crowe, Eddie Barlow, Mohammad Azharuddin, Abdul Qadir, Michael Holding, Steve Waugh, Polly Umrigar, Dennis Lillee, Mohinder Amarnath – it was quicker to name the great Commonwealth cricketers who hadn't played as northern pros. Don Bradman and Keith Miller. There you are. Oh, and Sunil Gavaskar.

On summer Saturday afternoons after I'd locked the bar I'd leave Mrs Jessup to her copy of *Reveille* and walk along to the local cricket club to watch a game in the North Yorkshire South Durham League. One afternoon the burly New Zealand test all-rounder Lance Cairns belted a drive clean out of the ground and across the bus station, scattering a crowd of teenagers heading to the Carlton for the early evening showing of *Footloose*, on another the future West Indies spinner Roger Harper took a diving catch in the covers so extraordinary even the batsman it dismissed stood and applauded.

An added attraction of visiting the cricket club was that for a couple of pounds you could buy a ticket for a cricket tea, which you got to eat *in the same room as the players*. This is not something that happens at Lord's or the Oval. Many English cricket fans saw Desmond Haynes dismantle an opening attack, but I think there will be few who can claim, as I can, to have watched the great man getting stuck into a cheese savoury bap and a slice of sandcake.

The clubs hired the biggest-name pros to increase their chances of winning and to bring in the punters (three thousand watched former Yorkshire and England all-rounder

Johnny Wardle's debut for Lancashire-League Rishton in 1958 – not a bad turn out in a village with a population of around seven thousand). The system also gave the local amateurs a chance unique in sport – playing with and against the game's greatest talents. When Viv Richards signed for Wardle's old club in 1987 it was the equivalent of your local Saturday afternoon amateur football team securing the services of Kaka or Cristiano Ronaldo.

Mrs Jessup had been a pupil at Whitefield Elementary School when Constantine and his wife Norma arrived in Nelson one rainy April evening. After the last bell, she said, they'd sometimes go across the road to Howard Street where the West Indian couple lodged. One of the older lads would form them into a queue outside the Constantines' home and then, for a farthing apiece, he'd allow them to step forward and peer in through the window for a few minutes. Learie and Norma were the first black people Mrs Jessup and her schoolmates had ever seen. The chance to watch them engaged in their domestic chores, lighting the fire perhaps, or eating their tea, seemed improbably exotic and astonishing.

Learie and Norma bore the intrusion with stoicism. They were intelligent and resourceful people and Constantine saw their role in England not only as an exercise in financial self-improvement, but also as an opportunity to do something for the people of his island home. He wanted to show the British that he and his fellow West Indians were as capable of self-governance as the white dominions of Canada, Australia and New Zealand. When not playing cricket or studying for a law degree, he toured the north giving lectures in town halls, mechanical institutes and working men's reading rooms.

Constantine battled prejudice and ignorance with charm and dignity. He taught Northerners about the West Indies, and

the North taught him about England. The Trinidadian's experience at home had led him to believe that all white people
were rich, powerful and well educated. Even in the sixties that
was a common misapprehension. Cec Wright, a Jamaican
who'd come to play at Colne in the Lancashire League in 1961
told me that when he'd travelled up on the train to Manchester
from London Airport he'd pointed to the rows of red brick
buildings he could see out of the window and asked the man
sitting opposite him what they were. 'They're houses,' the man
had replied curtly. 'They are where *we* live'.

And Cec Wright had been taken aback, 'Because this was
the Mother Country,' he said, 'and we thought everything
here was beautiful. It was where our Queen lived. And
although really you knew not all English people lived in a
palace like the Queen, in the back of your mind was the idea
that they did.'

In the tough, grimy, depression-busted cotton and coal
towns of East Lancashire Constantine learned the brutal truth
about the Mother Country. 'When I was a young boy in
Trinidad, going to school and picking fruit and vegetables
from the garden,' he would later write, 'Hargreaves the captain of Nelson, my exact contemporary, was working in a
cotton mill.' Until he moved to Lancashire, 'I never knew the
extent of poverty.'

Off the field Constantine worked hard on his degree and
his lectures, on the field he played, sensationally. In nine seasons for Nelson he hit 6363 runs at an average of 37.65 and
took 776 wickets at less than ten apiece, displaying all the
while a showman's eye for the dramatic gesture, the grand
flourish. When Constantine fielded, a simple catch in the deep
would be transformed into a piece of magic when he
appeared to over run the ball and then at the last second stuck
out a hand and caught it behind his back. Slip catches were

grabbed and tucked into a pocket with such adroit swiftness spectators thought the ball had vanished. 'This, surely,' one thrilled observer noted, 'was cricket that heralded the atomic age.'

During his years at Seedhill, Connie's legend grew so great that, even fifty years after he had left the Lancashire League and entered the House of Lords as Baron Constantine, he remained the measure by which all other professionals were judged. To paraphrase Joseph Heller, Constantine was so amazing that even those who had never seen him play could remember him vividly.

Mrs Jessup *had* seen Constantine play, but only once. Her father was a tradesman and didn't like her going to watch Lancashire League cricket, which attracted a partisan and often rough and drunken crowd. But he'd taken her to a nearby village where Constantine had played in a charity match for the local church. And Mrs Jessup remembered the huge crowd that had gathered and how the children had been sent to the schoolhouse to bring more chairs for the lady spectators. Constantine had batted and bowled and laughed and joked with the people on the boundary, 'and when that ball come near him,' Mrs Jessup said with just the same throaty growl she'd used to describe Yul Brynner, 'he just . . . swooped'.

'Oooh Learie Constantine,' Mrs Jessup said. She poured herself more tea, shovelled four spoonfuls of sugar into it – she was on a diet – took a sip and pointed a pink wafer at me. 'And I'll tell you something else,' she said. 'He was as black as the ace of spades, but . . .' and she looked me straight in the eye for moment so that I got the message, '. . . he was a proper gentleman and a hard worker, you make no mistake about that.'

*

If you grew up in the North of England and loved cricket, Constantine was one of the legends you lived with. Another was S. F. Barnes. Barnes's given name was Sydney, but the great bowler was such a forbidding figure it's hard to imagine anyone ever calling him by it, even his own mother. S. F. Barnes was tall and raw-boned, his hands huge and gnarled as rootballs. His face was drawn and lupine, eyes deep set. In photos he stares straight at you with the humourless, mocking glare of a man who relishes a punch-up.

S. F. Barnes was born in Smethwick in 1873. He bowled medium pace with a high arm action and cut the ball off the pitch both ways and swung it through the air too. He extracted alarming bounce from even placid wickets and though he wasn't particularly fast, the thought of facing him unnerved the bravest batsmen. Barnes rocked to the wicket with the rhythm of a metronome and was as accurate as the time signal. One young Bradford League batsman announced that he would play Barnes by 'defending the good balls and waiting for the bad ones to hit'. 'You'll wait all year then,' came the reply.

In twenty-seven test matches S. F. Barnes took 189 wickets at under seventeen apiece. Even more remarkable, he did it while hardly bothering with first class cricket at all, turning out in just a handful of county matches for Warwickshire and Lancashire. Instead he honed his skills as a professional in league cricket, for Rishton, Burnley, Church and Rawtenstall, Saltaire and Keighley, and St Annes, as well as half a dozen sides in the Midlands. His career as a club pro ran from 1895 until 1940 and in that time he took over four thousand wickets at the meagre cost of 6.08 each.

Despite Barnes's long association with clubs such as Saltaire, he remained an enigma. The great bowler was so laconic that he made the average Spartan look like Foghorn

Leghorn. When Saltaire had placed their advert for a new professional, Barnes had replied by telegram. His job application read simply, 'Will I do?'

The only known occasion when he made a joke was during a Lancashire League match when somebody shouted from the boundary that at Lord's Australia were 400–2 and Barnes shouted back, 'Who's got all the wickets?'

Barnes was feisty and awkward, a craftsman with a keen sense of his own worth. His manner offended just about everybody in the hierarchy of the English game. When Lord Hawke, the autocratic captain of Yorkshire and the MCC, angered by Barnes's refusal to go on a tour of South Africa snapped, 'We cannot understand you. You only play when you like,' Barnes snapped right back, 'And that is what I will keep on doing.' For once Lord Hawke was rendered speechless.

S. F. Barnes played cricket with a remorseless, grim tenacity that endeared him to Northern supporters. 'He was entirely dedicated to getting batsmen out,' the Glamorgan captain Wilfred Wooller noted. 'He had little use for anything or anybody that stood in his way.' In a festival match Barnes was bowling when a new batsman, a fashionable, dashing amateur came out to the wicket. The great bowler's skipper drew him to one side. 'This chap was at a party last night. Didn't get to bed until four o'clock. Go easy on him for a few overs, will you?' Barnes scowled, went back to his mark, ran in and knocked the fashionable amateur's off stump out first ball. That was S. F. Barnes. He might not have been born in the North but he was a Northerner in spirit.

It was that spirit that was a cornerstone of Northern cricket, that marked it out as different from the game in the South. As Basil D'Oliveira, who began his career in England playing as a professional for Middleton, noted of his time in the leagues, 'Everything runs second to winning.' When Don Mosey, the

Keighley-born *Test Match Special* commentator wrote his history of Yorkshire cricket he called it *We Don't Play it for Fun*. Brian Close, who'd begun his career at Rawdon in the Airdale and Wharfedale League, produced an autobiography entitled *I Don't Bruise Easily*, David Lloyd, who'd started at Accrington Cricket Club and was still turning out for them in his sixties, called his book about coaching *Anything But Murder*.

Back in the eighties a friend of mine reckoned you could tell if someone came from the North or the South just from his or her attitude to David Gower. 'Then with the first wicket down,' the rubicund Tony Lewis would say during the test match highlight programmes of that decade, 'we were treated to a typically lovely cameo from David Gower.' And up would come film of the left-hander hitting a series of nonchalant drives through the covers before being caught at the wicket for thirty-seven.

At times Gower's habit of getting out just when he ought to have been settling in may have frustrated fans and selectors, but in half-hour highlight package terms he was worth a dozen Hansie Cronjes and a hundred Geoffrey Boycotts. Indeed, at times the Leicestershire batsman's innings' seemed almost purposely contrived so that only minimal editing was required to produce a pleasant two-minute segment of stroke play ending with that familiar waft outside off stump that con-jured images of an eighteenth-century fop shooing away a persistent beggar with his scented handkerchief.

Southerners loved Gower. They praised his elegance, the delicacy of his stroke play, his cavalier approach to the game. Northerners hated him. To hear my friend tell it Gower had less guts than a kipper and was so lacking in spine his team mates had to carry him round in a bucket.

Gower's curly hair and demeanour put many Northerners

in mind of Basil Fotherington-Thomas, the poetry-loving prep school weed from the Molesworth books. During a John Player League match at Scarborough one year the bloke behind us greeted Gower's arrival by bellowing, 'Hullo clouds, hullo sky, hullo caught at second slip waggling at a wide one.'

Gower's autobiography was called *With Time to Spare*. 'Look at him,' my dad would snarl whenever the England number four strode out to the wicket. 'Feckless blond-haired little pillock.'

In the South, cricket had been organised in much the same manner as the largely middle-class game of rugby union. It was all friendly matches where winning and losing had no lasting consequence. In the North, cricket had been organised like the predominantly working-class association football.

In the South people talked about village cricket as if it was some separate entity. In the North village cricket, club cricket and league cricket were all one and the same. Many of the most famous clubs in the region were villages. Lascelles Hall near Huddersfield had a population of around three hundred, but it had once had five players in the Yorkshire first eleven. Marske-by-the-Sea, where both my parents grew up, was a fishing village of no greater size than those that dot the coasts of Devon or Cornwall, yet the cricket club had thought nothing of hiring the England and Yorkshire batsman Doug Padgett to come and play for them, paying his wages with the profits from the bar and fruit machines in the clubhouse.

In the North all cricket, whether it was the high-end stuff played by Constantine and Barnes, or the Wednesday evening games set up for shopkeepers and farmers, was played in leagues. There were, at a conservative estimate, just short of a hundred in Yorkshire alone. Here all cricket was competitive, often ferociously so.

In the South cricket's gentlemanly image was bolstered by the MCC and the hallowed ground of Lord's. In the North cricket was a sport for everybody. In the eighteenth and nineteenth centuries church ministers and factory owners had actively promoted the game among the working class as a means of keeping them out of trouble. In the church Burgesses' account for Leeds in 1757, for instance, there is record of a sum of fourteen shillings and sixpence paid to professional cricketers 'to entertain the populace and take them away from cock fighting'.

When the Ten Hours Act was introduced in 1847, reducing the average working week from seventy hours to fifty-five and a half, the need to keep northern factory workers from cock fighting and other unhealthy pursuits was even greater. Haslingden Cricket Club was set up in 1854 largely to address the problems, creating a place within the Rossendale cotton town where men could go and find that 'there was no drinking or gambling but simple pure and wholesome cricket'.

The game took hold faster than anybody could have guessed, its popularity helped by the fact that the local workers proved to be pretty good at it. In areas like East Lancashire and the West Riding of Yorkshire most were employed in cotton or woollen mills and working with shuttles and looms required swift hands and excellent hand–eye coordination. The locals were good at cricket because it required many of the skills they used in their jobs.

The idea of introducing cricket into the industrial North was that it would keep men away from vice and at the same time teach them gentlemanly virtues. In the latter case, however, things didn't quite work out as planned. Fierce local rivalries were fought out on the field of play. In Lancashire the clash between Haslingden and Bacup was often marred by insults and scuffles. When Church played neighbours Accrington, supporters of the winning team would sneak out after dark and whitewash the scores on a wall that marked the boundary between the two towns. The scores would stay there until the next meeting, a reminder of parochial triumph and humiliation. Across the Pennines cricket matches in Pudsey – the spiritual home of Yorkshire cricket – were played out in an atmosphere of 'frequent uproar, confusion and . . . fighting'.

By the end of the Great War things had calmed down considerably, but cricket in the North never quite lost its edge. As Roy Genders writes of the Bradford League in his 1952 book, *League Cricket in England*, 'Here was cricket in the raw, not the spit and polish county stuff, but the real "blood and guts" warlike cricket which delighted these tough Yorkshiremen reared on the windswept moors and who wanted some action for their money.'

Genders took the whole thing with grim relish, but many outsiders were not impressed with the Northern attitude to the game. In 1951 the great John Arlott – born in Hampshire – wrote a piece in his book *Concerning Cricket* called 'The Case against League Cricket', in which he attacked the way the game was played in the north of England, which he felt damaged its artistry and compromised its grace.

Arlott was not a snob, not by any means, but comments such as his only aggravated the North's permanently simmering sense of grievance. All cricket fans in the North grew up with a deep-rooted mistrust of Lord's and the cricket establishment. Everybody you met could tell you of 'a lad from down the road who was ten times better than any of this lot in the England team'. But did they give him a chance? Did they heck as like. Hasn't got the old school tie, has he? Hasn't got the right crest on his blazer.

Mostly this was nonsense. Players from George Hirst to Jimmy Anderson, via Len Hutton and Brian Statham, had emerged from Northern club cricket to enjoy successful careers with England. S. F. Barnes and Cec Parkin had toured with the MCC when playing in the Lancashire League. In the thirties Leslie Warburton had piled up so many runs and wickets for Littleborough in the Central Lancashire League he'd been invited down to Lord's to play in a test trial. As Mr Warburton went south a Manchester journalist asked Mrs Warburton if her husband would be journeying to Australia with England that winter. 'Certainly not,' she replied. 'He has his work to attend to and his other hobbies – knitting, playing the violin and the piano – to keep him occupied.' Fortunately for the sake of marital harmony Warburton got a duck, bowled poorly and was not selected.

It was nonsense, more or less, but the feeling that the game's authorities looked down on the club cricket of the North and were biased against its players persisted. Coupled with bloody-minded provincial pride, this paranoia created a singular mindset. Sitting on the boundary benches at Radcliffe (where the great Barbadian Gary Sobers had once suffered the ignominy of seeing a local batter, Alan Stuttard, clobber him for five sixes into a nearby duck pond) the author and former Lancashire League player Dave Edmundson said, 'In East Lancs people look for the scores of their local league club first, then Lancashire's, then England's. That's the order of priorities.' Despite all the foreign stars it was a proud and self-contained world. If you called someone parochial round there they took it as a compliment.

It was this that made the leagues the embodiment of Northern cricket. The county game was influenced from the outside, its rules and conventions dictated by Lord's. If it had once been an embodiment of regional pride, that feeling dissipated through the nineties. During that decade Yorkshire abandoned its county-born players only policy and whittled down the number of grounds the team played at. They'd stopped appearing in Hull in 1990, in Middlesbrough, Bradford and Sheffield in 1996 and Harrogate in 2000. Once Yorkshire County Cricket Club had come to visit Yorkshire, now Yorkshire had to go and visit it. The England players' central contract system further weakened the appeal of county matches. Michael Vaughan scored almost as many hundreds for England as he did for Yorkshire, Andrew Flintoff managed only a handful of appearances for Lancashire in the last three seasons of his test career, and if you wanted to see Paul Collingwood playing at Chester-le-Street you might just as well wait for an England game there.

The leagues no longer attracted the large crowds they had once done – though local derbies in the Lancashire League still drew more people than a midweek County Championship match at Old Trafford – and they still churned out top players (Vaughan had first played cricket at Worsley in the Manchester and District Association, Collingwood at Shotley Bridge in the Northumberland Senior League, Flintoff at St Annes in the Northern League) and despite the encroachment of the England and Wales Cricket Board, by and large, they remained steadfastly independent. They were little republics of hardcore Northernness.

I decided to pay them a visit. I'd go to one game each in all the north's most illustrious and celebrated leagues to see if the game was still the raw-boned, red-blooded affair that had thrilled Genders and appalled Arlott, the one that Constantine and Barnes had brightened in their singular ways and that I had watched thirty years ago on Saturday afternoons while Mrs Jessup was dozing by the fire, her teeth clacking in time to her breathing.

If writers like Don Mosey were to be believed, Northern cricket was a tough game, played in tough towns, by tough, sometimes awkward men. It was certainly no place for a feckless blond-haired little pillock. Luckily I'm six foot five and my fair hair turned grey a decade ago. And besides, maybe things had mellowed since then. Even in Haslingden.

Intent to Murder

Workington

The train rattled on towards the Gilsland Gap and Cumbria. At Haltwhistle Cricket Club a man in a blue anorak and wellingtons was marking out the pitch with what I could only hope was indelible chalk. It was barely spring in Northumberland. Icy, damp winds blew from the Borders. The leaves on the trees were present but seemingly reluctant to unfurl, clutching themselves tightly like a woman in a sixties farce whose towel has been blown away by a freak wind. The only creatures in white that looked comfortable running around on the greensward were the lambs. Yet at Lord's the first test against the West Indies was almost over.

It seemed a bit early for international cricket to me. In the past, the tourists traditionally spent early May gazing at a small lake in Worcestershire under which, or so officials would assure them, lay a pitch. After that they'd spend a week huddled beneath northern skies that had gone beyond glowering and turned downright abusive, before moving on to the south coast to take on D. H. Robins's XI (because back then the tourists played so many games there weren't enough actual counties to keep them occupied. They had to make teams up, or they'd have run out of opponents by mid-August) while wearing so many sweaters they looked like marshmallowmen and had to invite umpire David Constant to blow on their blue, benumbed fingers for them before they could hold a ball. Back then, until the visitors had sprinted from the field in at least a couple of hailstone showers at Chesterfield they weren't considered sharp enough for international cricket.

Times move on. For decades people have been complaining that the football season encroaches ever further into the cricket season. Now the summer game, splendidly marshaled by the ECB chief executive and pet-shop magnate Giles Clarke was mounting a counter-offensive. It had marched slap-bang into football's domestic and European climax, all blazers blazing. It seemed that if everything went to plan the next time New Zealand or Bangladesh came to England they would be playing a series of one-day internationals in mid-March. And if that doesn't make the Premier League quake in its hand-tooled unicorn hide loafers, then what will?

Times move on, but as the train headed westwards and clouds the colour of oil slicks and the texture of sputum coagulated above my destination, I couldn't help wondering what Mr Griffiths would have made of this ludicrously early start to a test series.

Mr Griffiths was a fixture at Headingley when I first started going to matches in the mid-seventies. Yorkshire's HQ, it should be said, was a more decorous place in those days. The Western Terrace was far from the Viking-helmeted, gorilla-suited, false-breasted transvestite Bacchanal it is today. Back then a broad-beamed, Crimpelene-clad matron occupied every other bench and the air was filled with the scent of lavender or apple blossom cologne and the clicking of knitting needles. The presence of the floral legion ensured a certain decorum on the Western Terrace.

Not that the old ladies in the flowery dresses were entirely without their own moments of noisy ribaldry. As dusk began to settle and a day of Thermos-flask coffee and Gypsy creams took its inevitable toll, they would often lay aside the baby's bed jackets on which they had been busy to call noisily on the England selectors to pick Richard Lumb, point out that Rodney Marsh looked like a bulldog chewing a toffee, or bellow, 'Thomson, tha' couldn't hit a cow's backside with a banjo.'

But that was as far as it went. At the close of play they would wander off in rustling groups, back to their homes in Pudsey and Pateley Bridge with the sculleries that smelled of scones, and the bowls of sugared almonds on the sideboard, and husbands who had to clean their hands with Swarfega before they were allowed in the front room.

Mr Griffiths was very much at home in this well-mannered company. An immaculately dressed West Indian who worked on the trains, Mr Griffiths would lean against the rail of the main stand and his calls and imprecations would fill the day, mingling with the cries of the newspaper seller ('Eee-Ark-shuh Parsssst') and wandering, blue-coated ice cream man advertising his 'Ah-Yuuuuum-ee, Ah-Yuuuuuum-ee choc ices'. (The choc ice man attended all of Yorkshire's matches, his skin gradually becoming more weatherbeaten as the season went on until by the time of the Scarborough Festival he was the colour of a conker.)

Leaving aside the phalanx of tattooed numbskulls with literary agents, not many spectators achieve fame. Over the years only a very few have gained widespread public recognition: Manolo the drum-banging Spaniard, Sheffield Wednesday's Tangoman, the Tour de France's Teutonic Satan, and the elderly couple who turn up at Holland's international fixtures wearing wigs made from carrots.

Arguably the most famous spectator of all was Stephen Harold Gascoigne, better known to the world as Yabba. In the inter-war years Yabba would finish his shift selling rabbits from a cart and appear on the Hill at Sydney where he'd berate wayward bowlers with his catchphrase, 'Oh for a strong arm and a walking stick.' He was held in such affection that when Sir Jack Hobbs played his last game at Sydney he made a point of going over to the Hill and shaking his hand. A statue of Yabba was unveiled at the SCG in 2008.

Mr Griffiths was Leeds's Yabba. Only he didn't hurl insults, he shouted tactical advice and always in the most polite terms. 'Captain, it is time to bring Mr Underwood on,' he would call in his deep and sonorous Caribbean voice. 'An extra slip fielder might be in order when Mr Old is bowling, Mr Greig.' Soon Mr Griffiths was so well known that it was hardly a surprise when one morning during the 1975 Ashes test he walked out into the middle before start of play to inspect the wicket with Australian captain Ian Chappell.

Mr Griffiths's great idol was Geoff Boycott. He was the first person I ever heard call the Yorkshire opener 'Sir Geoffrey'. Boycott is still with us – indeed, I am listening to him as I type this – but his biggest fan fell silent some while ago. I'm not sure what became of him. I'd dearly love to have heard his voice again, though. Even if it meant attending a test match in February.

'Bit bleak, Workington,' a friend of mine had remarked when I'd told him where I was headed. Since my friend came from Middlesbrough and worked in Easington, setting of the film *Billy Elliot*, that wasn't an assessment from a member of the sneering London-centric, metropolitan elite (not that there's anything wrong with them, obviously). To be honest, even the most patriotic Northerner would find it hard to disagree.

Workington is one of England's forgotten corners, a part of Cumbria you're unlikely ever to find yourself in unless you get lost when leaving the Lake District. The only time I have ever been here before is when we took a wrong turn coming away from the World Gurning Championships in nearby Egremont.

The town's bleakness was really why I'd chosen Workington CC v Furness CC at the Ernest Valentine Ground as the starting point for my journey. There was nothing more likely to dispel any notion of cricket being all cream teas and chaps in straw boaters than Workington playing their local arch-rivals from a nuclear-submarine-building town in the top flight of the Carlsberg North Lancashire and Cumbria League, Premier Division. Well, not unless there's a game between fish-processing workers in Murmansk.

The train from Carlisle had trundled along the fringe of the Solway and down the coast, rain the consistency of tapioca splotting against the windows. We'd passed vast industrial dairies and rows of houses rendered in a colour that squatted grimly in the no man's land between grey and brown. The Irish Sea looked like the contents of a slops bucket. At Flimby, estate agents' signs flapped forlornly in the wind and one bungalow still had an illuminated Santa Claus balanced on the chimney. 'Leaving Flimby – Please Call Again' read a plaintive sign on the outskirts of the village as the road headed off into a landscape of allotments, light industrial sheds and the Iggesund chemical plant.

I arrived in Workington ninety minutes before the start of play and, during, an aimless time-killing walk around the town, got lost and ended up in an area of derelict allotments and scrapyards. 'Danger Razor Wire' read the signs, and 'This property is alarmed'. Behind sharp steel fences large dogs barked. In a nearby stream the wheels of drowned shopping trolleys poked up from the sludge and a lone and grubby swan stared miserably about as the wind turbines on the harbour side thrummed in the icy southerly wind. All in all it's no surprise that, back in the thirties, west coast Workington's football team played in the semi-pro North Eastern League alongside Blyth, Spennymoor and Horden Colliery. The town might be Cumberland but it's coalmining and shipbuilding country, definitely more Catherine Cookson than Beatrix Potter.

Another of my reasons for coming to Workington was New Zealand pro Simon Beare. Or rather it was Beare's absence. Workington had won back-to-back league titles thanks in part to the Kiwi's efforts with bat and ball. Beare had arrived at the Ernest Valentine Ground in 2005 and quickly made a name for himself, hitting a league record 215 off just 117 balls against Keswick, an innings that included fifteen sixes and eighteen fours. Workington's total that day, 397–7, was the highest in the North Lancashire and Cumbria League's 113-year history.

Beare had also endeared himself to his team mates by mucking in with the upkeep of the ground, picking up a paintbrush on one of his first days at the club and whitewashing the sightscreens. In this the New Zealander was a throwback to earlier times: when pros had first been employed by northern clubs their job hadn't just been to play the game. Hedley Verity's 1929 contract with Middleton of the Central Lancashire League hung on the wall of the clubhouse. It laid out very clearly what the great spin bowler was expected to do for his pay: organise net practices, bowl to members four evenings a week, mow the outfield, prepare the wicket and effect all necessary repairs to equipment and buildings.

When Australian Bill Alley arrived at Colne in the Lancashire League in 1948 he found himself doctoring the batting strip with the help of a veteran groundsman: 'If the opposition pro was a spinner, you'd be watering the ground until the grass started to sprout up. On the other hand, if you were up against a first-class seamer you'd be down there chewing the bloody grass with your false teeth.' Not that Alley minded. He looked on manual work as the ideal fitness regime for a cricketer. In *My Incredible Innings*, the all-rounder reveals the arduous regimen that ensured he went on playing top-class cricket until well into his forties – gardening. 'I have two acres of land,' Alley writes, 'and while I could turn the soil over quicker with my rotary hoe, I prefer a spade.' In case anyone hasn't cottoned on yet, the future umpire adds that, when it comes to preparation for sport, 'Exercise is the great thing'.

In league cricket up until the late fifties the pro was not just a player, but also coach, groundskeeper and caretaker. As a consequence, many of the early professionals were chosen for their knowledge of loams and rollers as much as of away swingers and late cuts. They were journeymen. The first genuine international talent to be tempted into the leagues was the Yorkshire and England all-rounder Bobby Peel.

Peel was a pitman's son from Churwell near Leeds. He worked down the mines himself before cricket provided an escape route. Peel bowled left-arm spin and batted high up the order. He took over fifteen hundred first-class wickets and scored eleven thousand runs, including a double hundred against Warwickshire. Archie McClaren described him as 'the cleverest bowler of my time'. He was also one of the most awkward to handle.

Peel was the *enfant terrible* of Yorkshire cricket in the last decades of the nineteenth century. And that was not a title you came by easily in those days. A man had to really work at it. In the late Victorian era Yorkshire had a reputation as a hard-drinking, wild living crew – the Lynyrd Skynyrd of cricket. 'Ten drunkards and a parson' was the common description of the White Rose eleven of Peel's day. The parson was lay preacher, teetotaller and sometime skipper Ephraim Lockwood.

Bobby Peel was the star of this dissolute side and when it came to excess, he exceeded all his colleagues. Peel stood five feet six inches tall – he was a gallon of bother in a half-pint pot. Or as the august *Yorkshire Post* cricket writer J. M. Kilburn put it: 'He was immensely talented, firmly independent in character and susceptible to temptations in the way of life of professional cricketers of his time.'

The stories about Peel's brilliance and boozing are legion, but a couple will suffice to make the point. England versus Australia at Sydney in 1894. At the end of the fourth day the home side were apparently cruising to victory. Peel had five teeth extracted and celebrated his survival of the ordeal by getting blind drunk. He arrived at the ground for the final day of the test expecting to stand on the boundary nursing a hang-over as the Aussies knocked off the runs. Instead he discovered it had been raining overnight, the wicket had turned sticky and his services were required. His team mates put Peel in a cold shower to sober him up and he staggered out on to the field. Observing the dampness of the wicket he called to the England captain, A. E. Stoddart, 'Give me the ball, Mr Stoddart, and I'll have the buggers out by lunch.' Peel took 6–67 and the last Australian wicket fell two minutes before the break to give England an unexpected victory by ten runs.

In 1897 Peel was banished from Yorkshire by the omnipresent Lord Hawke – who as county skipper was impos-ing much-needed discipline on the players – after an incident in which the all-rounder turned up at start of play so plastered that when he bowled he mistook the sight screen for the stumps and when he was removed from the attack, urinated on the wicket.

Turned out by his native county, Peel signed as a professional for Accrington in the Lancashire League. His arrival in East Lancs made newspaper headlines. So, predictably, did his departure. Peel took eighty wickets but had two-thirds of his salary withheld by the committee because of unspecified 'trouble'. He was not re-engaged. Instead he returned to Yorkshire and pro-ed for Morley. Morley had begun life in the 1840s playing at Fish's Field under the unlikely title of Throttlers Off CC. By the time Peel arrived they had relocated to their present ground in Scratcherd Lane and changed their name to something less alarming.

The prevailing feeling now is that Bobby Peel's waywardness was connected to depression. 'He took no pleasure from the game,' noted Lord Hawke sadly. Yet Peel went on playing until well into his sixties and lived to the age of eighty-four. Commenting on his notorious final appearance for Yorkshire, he categorically denied drunkenness, saying, 'I had two small gins with water before the start and nothing whatsoever at luncheon.' Sinking gin at breakfast-time was apparently normal in Yorkshire in those days.

Asked about Lord Hawke's involvement in his dismissal, Peel commented, 'He put his arm around me and escorted me off the field and out of Yorkshire cricket. What a gentleman.' Which was either very gracious, or exceedingly sarcastic.

The excitement that had surrounded Peel's arrival at Accrington showed clubs across the North the benefits that could accrue from signing professionals who were more than just cricketing handymen. Soon more high-class players were following in Peel's slightly wobbly footsteps. And so, in a perhaps appropriately circuitous and wobbly manner, we return to Simon Beare.

Beare had played half a dozen games for Otago, which under the ECB's restrictions on the hiring of overseas players meant he didn't qualify. So Workington had employed him as a player–coach. In autumn 2008, however, the ECB had closed what they saw as a loophole in the regulations and declared that hence forwards any imports could be employed as player, or as a coach, but not as both. Beare hadn't played enough first class games to qualify as a player, so Workington would have had to employ him as a coach and bring in another overseas player as pro. The idea of a double salary didn't appeal and so they decided to dispense with a pro altogether.

Today's opponents, Furness, would soon find themselves in a similar position. The visitor's professional was an experienced Pakistani batsman, Majeed Jehangir (at least that was what he was called in 2009, up until the autumn of 2007 he had been listed as Majid Jahangir). Jehangir had scored four first class hundreds playing for Sialkot, Gujranwala and the Agricultural Development Bank of Pakistan. He'd started out in the North Lancs and Cumbria League with Keswick, switched to Dutton and was now in his fourth season with the Barrow-based side. Jehangir had scored runs freely and bowled effectively too. However, like Beare he'd been beset by visa complications. Whether he would arrive in England in time for today's match was open to doubt – he'd already missed four games. As it turned out the workings of the Department of Employment and PIA were immaterial.

I was walking past Passions Bar and Nightclub when the first rain drops, as big and sloppy as Bambi's tears, began to fall. By the time I'd passed the Theatre Royal with the billboards advertising *Intent to Murder* it was pelting down. I arrived at the steps down past the Lady Walk Brewery over-looking the Ernest Valentine Ground in a swirling storm, just in time to see the last of the Workington and Furness players slamming their car doors and driving off. Deep-throated yells were coming from the rugby league stadium and speedway track.

I splashed down a side street where the words 'Chavs R Scum' were sprayed on a derelict house, and turned the corner into a vicious headwind, overtaking boys with crimson mullets whose shellsuit bottoms clutched their ankles like man-acles and girls in skinny jeans or tubes-of-mince bare legs. Cars droned past filling the air with dirty spray and the smell of burning vegetable oil. By the time I had gone another thirty yards my jeans were stuck to my legs like Elastoplast. Another thirty and the rain had turned lumpy on me, pinging off my face with a sting like the flick of a wet towel. I ducked under the awning of the first shop I found, teeth chattering.

And so it was, soaked to the skin, scourged by the hail, chilled to the bone and huddled in the doorway of a tattoo parlour opposite a Roman Catholic primary school in Oxford Street, Workington, that my cricket season began.

On the train home I dried myself in the toilet with tissue. Several bits of soggy paper got stuck in the stubble on my chin. Broken by the day, I gave up trying to remove them and walked down the carriage sodden, bedraggled and blotched with papier mâché, looking like someone who has forgotten to take his medication.

At Carlisle station two steam trains had arrived, the *Scots Guardsman* and the *Princess Elizabeth*, great beasts, their glossy sides gleaming like those of thoroughbreds. The presence of the pair had sent a gathering of trainspotters insane with excitement and they galloped from one platform to the other, arms waving, yelling frenetically. Anyone watching would have thought it was some sort of pre-arranged fight between groups of particularly geeky football hooligans.

By the time the Newcastle train rolled in I was almost dry. Four jolly Northumbrian women stood in front of me waiting for the doors to open. One said to the others, 'Do you think ten is too young to wear a thong?'

Without Simon Beare, Workington failed to retain the title for a third year. Majeed Jehangir eventually got his visa. Despite missing the first month of the season he scored 729 runs for Furness at 45.66 and helped his side to the championship and victory in the final of the Higson Cup. A month or so later Furness announced they would not bring the Pakistani back for 2010 because of the visa complexities. Instead they opted to sign a young South African, Cameron Delport. Delport didn't have Majeed's experience or proven record in league cricket, but did possess something that was almost more valuable – a British passport.

Two Klingons and a Gorilla

Horden

That Friday the first swallows had appeared skimming over the Tyne. They must have regretted making the journey from southern Africa. The weather was still bitterly cold, the sky spitting a blotchy rain. Heavily laden coal wagons sprinted past bringing salvation to chilled pensioners and blue-cheeked tots. At Chester-le-Street the second day of the second test against the West Indies had been abandoned without a ball being bowled. Nobody protested.

In the newspapers it said that the ECB was calling for a clampdown on ticket touts. This seemed a bit superfluous since any scalper who'd invested in tickets for the West Indies series would have been filing for bankruptcy. The first day at the Riverside had been watched by a crowd so tiny Andrew Strauss would likely have attracted a bigger one by collapsing in the street.

To sit and watch cricket all day in County Durham in early May required dedication, toughness and enough fleece to swaddle the Grand Duchy of Luxembourg. A friend who had been to the first day telephoned. 'I'm not saying it was cold,' he said, 'but they brought the covers on with huskies.' One of his party had gone to the toilet midway through the afternoon and never returned. 'Either he'd gone home, or a yeti had got him,' my friend said.

Saturday looked more promising. The temperature had risen to the underside of tepid and blue sky peeped out shyly from between porridge-coloured clouds. At Newcastle Central Station the combination of the regular Saturday night stag and hen parties and the Durham test match meant I was the only person not wearing a novelty hat or a designer T-shirt with my nickname – Cider Sponge, Streaker, Gashmonkey – on it.

Men so big that when they stood in the road traffic treated them as a roundabout, passed by the coffee and pasty stands at a brisk clip in transit for merriment. Women on hen nights tottered by on towering heels, wearing white miniskirts and crop tops in Mekon death-ray green, one wearing a bridal veil and a wire headdress featuring a bright red arrow pointing at her forehead, another had a T-shirt bearing the legend 'Sperm Donor Wanted'.

The new castle to which Newcastle owes its name was built by Henry II in the second half of the twelfth century. On the roof of the keep a sloping seventeenth-century sundial bears an inscription that might serve as the motto for the Saturday crowds: 'Times tide doth waist, therefore make hast, we shall die all'.

Things were a good deal quieter when I arrived in Horden. It was raining too, not a heavy rain, just the sort of fine rain that hangs in the air, all-enveloping like an unfinished and bitter argument. The bus from Peterlee dropped me off at a stop next to a spiritualist church. Down the road towards the North Sea was a medical centre named after Manny Shinwell, the Labour minister who nationalised the mining industry. Outside the Comrades Club a mother and a ten-year-old girl in a shimmering pink party frock unloaded a chocolate

fountain from the back of a Renault Clio and scurried
indoors. A poster in the window advertised a night of entertainment featuring 'Donna, Promising Young Vocal Artiste'.

Horden Welfare Park – with its football, cricket and rugby
grounds, its bowling green and flowerbeds – is an enduring
monument to community spirit. Paid for by the miners
through subscription back before the Great War it's as neat
and tidy as a front parlour when the vicar's due. On the backs
of the benches that line the paths are little plaques telling the
history of the town – how many cinemas it once had, when
the railway station closed, the tonnage of coal the pit once
produced and the number of men who died digging it.

In Horden 80 per cent of the workforce were once
employed in the mining industry. The streets run up from the
headlands above the sea to the hill where the pithead stood,
as if that was the only direction the population would ever
expect, or need, to go in. The colliery closed in 1986. Since
then the population has dropped by several thousand and
local business seems almost entirely devoted to the North-
East's new boom areas – tattoos, tanning and taxis.

Unlike Tan-Tastic! and The Naughty Needle, the National
Union of Mineworkers and British Coal were paternalistic
organisations. They looked after the workforce and their families, providing them with a whole network of support from
pensions to sports fields to medical care, discounted TVs and
subsidised beer. The industry that supported that has gone,
but the welfare grounds remain, dotted across the coalfields,
a tiny reminder of what once was, like the hat of a dead man
hanging behind the door in a widow's bungalow.

I'd come to Horden because the strength of league cricket
in Durham – the Durham Senior League in which Horden
played and the North Yorkshire South Durham League in
particular – had been key evidence in the campaign to grant

the county cricket club first class status. The leagues had produced a steady stream of top class cricketers, Jim McConnon, Maurice Tremlett, Dick Spooner, Nobby Clark, Harold Stephenson, Geoff Cook and Peter Willey among them. More recently, Gateshead Fell had given a grounding in the game to England's Graham Onions. During the course of the 2009 Ashes summer Onions would gain nationwide fame less for his bowling than for the fact that on Twitter pop star Lily Allen confessed to fancying him.

For most older cricket fans it was a huge shock to discover that a hard-living and glamorous female pop star had a crush on a north-country pace bowler – a clear indication that either cricket has become crazier or pop music much, much tamer. Looking back over previous decades it's hard to imagine anything remotely similar happening. Picture Janis Joplin telling the crowd at Woodstock about her eagerness to 'Get in on with Ken Higgs', or Marianne Faithfull telling the *NME* 'I fantasise about not entirely straightforward sexual high jinks with Lancashire's Peter Lever' if you must. Or indeed can.

Whatever, the Durham leagues' list of former players was enough to impress any observer. 'Surely the time is now to hand when Durham . . . could take her place in the first class league,' Roy Genders wrote in 1952. Naturally Lord's thought otherwise and Durham had to wait another forty years to play in the county championship.

Horden were batting when I walked in through the gates by the clubhouse. Boldon's fast bowler running in from the football ground end was pretty sharp and beat the bat repeatedly. He was a wiry man, with rolled-down sleeves buttoned at the wrist, and he looked vaguely familiar. This is because his name is Jonny Wightman and I had seen him playing football several times for South Shields.

*

Football and cricket are closely linked in County Durham. Back in the days when the sports' two seasons didn't encroach on each other as much as they do today a number of top footballers turned out in the Durham leagues. Alf Common, the world's first thousand-pound footballer, used to delight the crowds at Darlington with what the *Northern Echo* called his 'dashing Jessopian displays'. Billy and Jack Smith of Whitburn both played in the 1934 FA Cup final with Portsmouth, Raich Carter who captained Sunderland when they won the League Championship played for Hendon. A year after winning a league championship medal with Manchester City, Colin Bell hit a club record score of 160 in 103 minutes for Castle Eden, taking part in a stand of 111 for the fourth wicket to which his partner Peter Hewitson contributed a cautious three runs.

In the fifties Horden had come close to securing the services of Welsh international centre forward Trevor Ford as their professional. Ford eventually decided to rest instead, but his Sunderland team mate, the England inside forward Len Shackleton, did play as a professional in the Durham Senior League. The mischievous Shackleton was nicknamed the Clown Prince of Soccer. In photos he stares out with a lopsided grin, as if he is enjoying a private joke with himself. He was a master of ball tricks and deflating one-liners. Shack came from Bradford and was a cricketer of some ability, playing minor counties for Northumberland and Durham.

Boldon had tried to secure his services by offering him a hundred pounds for the season. The Yorkshireman turned that down and signed for Wearmouth instead. His renown as a footballer guaranteed money on the gate wherever he played. Early on in a game at Whitburn a big crowd of Sunderland fans turned up to cheer him on. 'Good old Shackleton. Come on Shack. Away Len!' they called as the footballer walked out to bat. When their hero arrived at the wicket the Whitburn wicketkeeper took off his glove and stuck out his hand, 'Good afternoon,' he said sarcastically, 'my name's Emmerson. What's yours?'

Jonny Wightman hasn't the same level of fame as Shackleton but he bowled quickly enough and had the Horden opener caught at second slip within a minute of me taking a seat in the lee of the pavilion. The wicket brought in a burly man with a big face – Steve McCoy, the Horden skipper. He took guard, surveyed the field cautiously as if expecting to encounter an ambush at mid-off, adjusted his cap, nudged his box, spun his bat, settled in the crease and was clean bowled first ball.

As McCoy trudged back to the pavilion two small boys playing football along the boundary looked up. One said excitedly, 'Hey, your dad's out already!' His friend shook his head in amazement. 'Crikey, this is going to be a short game.'

The boys went back to their football. The skipper's son shot goalwards and yelled, 'I'm Ronaldo, man.' At least I think there was a comma. It could be that he was imitating a new superhero: Ronaldoman, pledged to fight crime with his special powers of hair gel, tumbling over and sulking.

I went into the pavilion to take a leak and buy a strip of raffle tickets. I'm not sure why I bothered with the latter. I knew I wouldn't win. At Northern League football matches they always have a raffle. The traditional prize is an array of meat from a local butcher. Down the years I must have entered at least a hundred such competitions and I've never won a sausage, literally.

When I came out of the clubhouse the home side were 16–3 and Kelbert Walters was striding out to the wicket. Walters is an eighteen-year-old Anguillan who was pro-ing for

Horden. There's quite a tradition of West Indians playing in Durham. Lance Gibbs turned out for Whitburn in 1964, the league's first thousand-pounds-a-season profesional, and took 124 wickets at 8.53 each. Richie Richardson played for Gateshead Fell and one of his successors as test captain, Jimmy Adams, at Eppleton. Horden's finest pro had been Leeward Islander Derick Parry, who'd helped them win five titles in the nineties.

The first West Indian to play in Durham had been one of Learie Constantine's fast-bowling partners, George Francis. The short, stocky Trinidadian was taciturn and shy, Connie's polar opposite, but he was quick and so accurate that during one famous spell against Australia he wore a hole the size of a plate in the wicket. Francis had been employed by Seaham Harbour in 1929 and stayed on the north-east coast for five years. Bowling very fast indeed, Francis took 104 wickets in his second season and seven thousand people paid to see him in action in a game against Durham City. In 1933 he went off to play for Radcliffe, then in the Bolton League. Later in the season I met an old chap there who'd been to watch him play. 'He didn't have much trickery,' he said, 'but he were quick. By, he were quick'.

Walters, said to be one of the fastest young bowlers in the Caribbean, made his debut for the Leeward Islands when he was seventeen and was picked as a member of the thirty-two-man Stanford Superstars squad for the controversial twenty-million-dollar match with England. He's a regular in the Windies under-19 side. Walters has a nest of dreadlocks poking out of the back of his helmet, but his batting is nowhere near as exotic. The bowler at the Rugby Ground end, Phil Shakespeare, was not as lively as Wightman but he moved the ball around through the air enough to bamboozle the West Indian. Walters prodded and swished so much that watchers might be forgiven for thinking his bat is spectral. Egged on by the slip fielders, Wightman fired down a series of bouncers, which seems like the height of foolishness given the West Indian's reputation.

A quicker, fuller delivery whisked past Walters, clipping his pad on the way through, and the bowler and fielders went into a wild, whooping dance of delight. The umpire – who had bristly white hair and a Zapata moustache, and generally looked like the sort of bloke who might turn up on *Rock Family Trees* talking about the time he played bass in Judas Priest – wasn't impressed. Neither was the man in the Asics warm-up coat leaning against the back of the red-roofed football stand. 'How, Boldon skipper,' he bellowed. 'Get these to play fair.'

In an effort to make some progress Walters started shuffling down the pitch towards the bowler as he moved into his final strides. It's a tactic Brian Close famously adopted against the quicks, but whereas the bald-headed Yorkshireman was belligerently decisive, the Anguillan was tentative, like a man in his pants approaching a strange and savage looking dog. It's hard to know how effective the tactic might have been because the second time he advanced he was clean bowled. 37–4. Walters bats at eleven for Anguilla, and it's hard to avoid the conclusion that it's only because there's no vacancy at number twelve.

The new batsman was the first man who put willow to ball against Wightman. Twice he flicked him off his legs for four, but then he was caught at the wicket. And Horden were 51–5.

Across the road members of the bowling club in uniforms of pale grey slacks and white fleece pullovers were loading their woods into the backs of cars and preparing to set off for an away fixture in Haswell. From the clubhouse came excited

yells and bellows of triumph as the 20–1 outsider Alexandros
won the 2.40 at Newbury. Through the metal grilles that cover
the pavilion windows to protect it against vandals and arson-
ists, I could see women in pinnies laying out rows of paper
plates and filling bowls with bags of Hula Hoops and Kit
Kats.

After a brief break for rain, Horden's number three, Jon
Minniss, who battled away merrily (mainly by avoiding facing
Wightman), was out for forty-six and returned to the pavilion
smacking his bat against his right pad, irritated by missing a
half-century.

I wandered round the ground trying to find somewhere that
was out of the wind, which had turned nasty. Years of following
non-league football have taught me that if you want to be
warm you should go and stand where the locals have congregated. Admittedly this is not as easy as it sounds at Horden
since there are only twenty spectators, but since twelve of
them were sitting within five yards of one another over by the
back of Horden FC's clubhouse I figured that must be the
place. 'I thought it might be warmer over here,' I said to a man
in a warm-up coat with a Sunderland FC badge on it. 'It is,'
he replied. 'Marginally.'

An optimistic ice-cream van went past playing 'Popeye the
Sailorman'. 'My dad told me that when an ice-cream van
played "Greensleeves" it meant he had nothing left to sell,' a
bloke sitting in a tartan fold-out chair said to his mate. 'And
you believed him?' his mate asked. 'Of course I did. He was
my dad. The bastard.'

The Durham Senior League was founded in 1902. Boldon
joined in 1905 and Horden came in as the replacement for
Raich Carter's old club, Hendon, in 1940. The League's reputation for nurturing talent – one of the most celebrated of

the League's former players, Colin 'Olly' Milburn, had, at the age of seventeen, scored 156 and taken 7–4 playing for Chester-le-Street at Horden – had led to calls for Durham County Cricket Club to be given first class status.

Ironically, Durham's entry into the County Championship, and gradual rise to become a dominant force within it, came at a time when the Senior League itself was in decline. In 2000 the new ECB-approved North-East Premier League started up, sucking away three of the League's biggest teams, Sunderland, Chester-le-Street and Gateshead Fell. By that time attendances were already plummeting faster than a bungee-jumping Mike Gatting. Once four-figure crowds turned up to watch the likes of Gibbs, Richardson and Adams. Now, on many Saturdays the aggregate gate for the entire league was less than three hundred.

More damaging than the lack of spectators was the shortage of players. In 1999 Wearmouth had closed down because they could no longer put a team out. Every autumn the local and regional newspapers were filled with appeals for anyone who could hold a bat, or turn his or her arm over to get in touch with this or that cricket club or see them slip into oblivion. In West Yorkshire and Lancashire they didn't have the same problem. That was partly because both areas were more densely populated than Durham, and also because they had a greater number of citizens of Pakistani and Indian descent. The sons and grandsons of people who'd arrived from the subcontinent still played cricket, but more and more it seemed that those who ticked the box marked 'White British' didn't have time for it.

When Wightman took his fifth wicket, the cover fielder diving high and to his right to pluck the ball out of the air with the practised flourish of a magician pulling a coin from behind a schoolboy's ear, Horden had been reduced to 87–7. Still seeking warmth, I went into the clubhouse to get a pint.

Back in the early seventies, if you said you didn't much care for the latest LP from Gong or Hawkwind, champions of such bands would likely reply, 'Have you listened to it on acid? You have to drop some acid, man, then it all, like, makes total sense.'

For many years I took a similar approach to cricket. When people said it was boring I responded, 'Have you watched it after eight pints of still cider? They were on cider when they created cricket. If you don't drink cider, you'll never get it.'

This had come to me when I suffered an epiphany at Worcester (and yes, I'm still trying to get the stains out). What occurred was that I travelled up to watch the West Indies play the opening three-day match of their 1984 tour with my friend Demon Bob, and on the way we detoured through Herefordshire and bought a good deal of the sort of farmhouse cider that comes in those plastic containers you normally get petrol for the lawnmower in. There is of course a good reason for this, which is that a lawnmower can run quite merrily on cider. Although after the first gallon you struggle to get it to go in a straight line, obviously. And when you put it back in the shed it tries to pick a fight with the strimmer, before getting all maudlin and singing Patsy Cline ballads to the hoe.

Anyroad, once inside the county ground we took up position on some benches at square leg and watched the cricket in the sunshine and drank our cider. Some time shortly after lunch Gordon Greenidge smacked a half-volley from Richard Illingworth that sailed right over my head. With my cider-heightened faculties it seemed I could discern rich harmonies in the whirring noise the ball made as I followed its flight, pick out every stitch on its intriguingly gnarly seam and see a reflection of my loved ones in the polished leather John Inchmore had been rubbing on his loins all morning.

For several minutes afterwards I watched the game unfold with a beatific grin on my face, mesmerised by the way the fielders in their whites seemed to have assumed shifting amorphous shapes, while the outfield had taken on a new and beautifully rich celestial hue. It was only when a steward appeared and kicked me gently on the shoulder that I realised that while watching Haynes' shot fly over my head I had toppled over on to my back and was now looking up at the sky.

After I eased up on the cider I rarely fell over at cricket any more, nor did I ever really enjoy the game quite so much. Frankly the antics of Paul Allott, Chris Tavare and Derek Pringle (described as 'a modern cricketing legend' in the brochure for the recent Woodstock Literary Festival, incidentally) seemed altogether more fascinating and heroic when they were completely out of focus.

I drank my pint indoors and, fortified, went and sat outside again. It was a long time since I'd spent all afternoon at cricket and I'd forgotten the discipline and training required to stay awake for long periods in the open air when you are sitting comfortably and nothing much is going on to disturb you. By twenty to four I had started to nod off. 'Heavy night, eh?' an old fellow remarked as he walked past and saw my head sagging. I chuckled in what I hoped was a gruff and manly fashion. Actually I hadn't had a heavy night at all, but somehow I felt that the truth – 'No, actually, I just had a small glass of Manzanilla before dinner' – was worse. There are places where a man might reasonably announce himself as a sherry-drinker, but somehow I didn't think Horden was one of them.

The home side battled on, thanks in the main to a couple of youngsters, Scott Birks and Adam Dixon. Dixon played boldly,

riding his luck. A snick through the slips zipped to the boundary to bring up the hundred. Point dived but narrowly missed
another slash that skips cheerily through the off for another
four.

During the second rain break of the afternoon I stood in
the clubhouse watching the half-time scores coming through
on Sky. A couple of tattooed lads leapt to their feet punching
the air when the news comes in that Fulham have taken the
lead at Newcastle. 'You're going down with the Smoggies /
Down with Smoggies' they chanted at the screen. Horden,
midway up the Durham coast, was Sunderland territory.
There was little love here for the Magpies or Middlesbrough.
Or indeed anyone else. When the report came in from the
Britannia Stadium a man sitting near me muttered, 'Stoke
City versus Wigan – that'll be one for the connoisseur, that.'

Back on the field Dixon was caught at mid-on for twenty-two
off a new bowler, a young medium pacer who runs to the
wicket with his knees pumping like he's riding an invisible
bike. An equally youthful slow left-armer named Bittlestone
replaced Wightman at the football stand end and quickly
snipped off the tail. Horden are all out for 139, far more than
they looked likely to make at one stage. Wightman finishes
with 5–55 in fifteen overs.

After tea Boldon came in to bat. The wind had switched
from the south to the west and it was bitterly cold. Kelbert
Walters, numbed perhaps by the conditions, struggled to work
up as much pace as Wightman. He bowled ineffectually and
far too short. The ball had been skidding through all day.
Hardly any batsman had played a shot off the back foot.
Trying to extract bounce from the wicket is like pouring water
on lard. Back in the eighties another promising West Indian
teenager, Ian Bishop, had been pro at Tynedale in the

Northumberland Senior League. A friend of mine played against him. I was impressed that he'd survived, because I'd seen Bishop play for Derbyshire at Lord's a few years after that and he was a very nasty proposition, popping bouncers off the batsmen's ribcages with such regularity it sounded like somebody playing the glockenspiel. I asked my friend how fast the Jamaican had been then. 'Not as quick as I thought he'd be,' my friend said. 'Mind, he could barely turn his arm over with all the jumpers he was wearing. Looked as if he'd got the local plumber to lag him like a boiler.'

In the face of Walters and some equally poor bowling from his team mates Boldon knocked off the runs in just twenty-one overs. Afterwards I walked up Eighth Street, past Geordie Pizzas and Menace Taxis to the bus stop.

Perhaps it was the weather, but the cricket I'd seen at the Welfare Ground had hardly been the gritty stuff of Northern legend. In 1952 Roy Genders had believed that the Durham Senior League 'for efficiency and as a cricket nursery . . . its enterprise in engaging the very best of professionals . . . the attractive cricket played and ever increasing gates . . . perhaps takes pride of place of the cricket leagues of the British Isles'. If that was still the case, then I feared that, on the evidence of what I had seen at Horden, this was going to be a long and disappointing summer.

The bus back to Durham was crowded. An old man sat down next to me. He wore a blue anorak and exuded a vague smell of Pot Noodle. His grey hair had been cut by somebody who had plainly run out of time or patience and left half the back undone, so that one long strand on the left hung down over his collar. 'Bobby Carter died,' the old man suddenly said to me as we turned into Shotton Colliery, past the Comrades Social Club and William Morris Terrace. I expressed surprise and sadness at the news. 'Aye well,' the old man said, 'I tell you something: he were seventy-eight years old, yet not a fortnight afore he died – he had a woman.'

He got off in Peterlee, at a stop where a tyre centre stands next to a bridalwear shop. And we juddered on through the clustered villages of County Durham with their Salvation Army halls, primitive Methodist chapels and bulky brick social clubs; skid-risk signs, piebald horses, four-wheel-drive pick-up trucks and St George's flags fluttering over pigeon lofts. Rape plants were coming into flower in the fields around the ruins of Ludworth Tower.

The clouds had cleared by the time we came to the outskirts of Durham City. Outside the Top Ten Bingo Hall a cluster of chunky women with home-dyed hair sucked the life out of cut-price king-size cigarettes, tilting back their heads and blowing the smoke heavenwards.

Play had finished for the day at Chester-le-Street and on the train back north I shared the carriage with seven FBI agents, two Klingons and a gorilla.

Boldon finished the season in fourth place, Horden in seventh. Jonny Wightman took forty-three wickets at 15.13 each, his opening partner Phil Shakespeare thirty-five at 15.05. Jon Minniss scored 510 runs at an average of 36.42. In June, Kelbert Walters was recalled to the West Indies to play for the Leeward Islands in an under-19 competition. He did not return.

A Palpable Sense of Bannister

Guisborough

The train chuntered down the Durham coast, along head-lands where cars were queuing for a moto-cross event and fields of static caravans where kids flew kites and dads leaned on door frames in their vests. The last time I'd been on this train it had been a midweek evening and a middle-aged woman and a man in his twenties had been arguing over the price of cannabis. 'He's phoned me up and went "I'll sell you an ounce for fourteen quid",' the woman said. Her companion, however, was sceptical: 'He'd never have been selling it for that,' he said. 'He might,' the woman countered, 'if it were somewhat by way of a loss leader.' The conversation might have passed from my mind had it not been for the fact that a few moments later the man addressed the woman as 'Mam'. Nice to see parent and child sharing a common interest, I suppose.

At Middlesbrough I caught the Saltburn bus. We left the town to the east past a shop called Hump It and Dump It, the advertising line of which proclaimed 'We don't just talk rubbish, we shift it!' and on through Brambles Farm which, as anyone familiar with the tradition of British urban nomenclature will already have surmised, is a vast post-war council estate of baleful aspect, up Ormesby Bank, the sort of long, sharp incline which slows the bus down to such a pace you start to feel you are actually going backwards and on into the outer suburbs, mile after mile of seventies housing estates, once aimed at the sort of ambitious young Northern executives exemplified by Rodney Bewes in *The Likely Lads*. Indeed, it's hard to pass them even now without imagining that behind the curtains a young couple is drinking Mateus Rosé and reading the instructions that came with the fondue set.

I felt cheerful and uplifted by the view from the window because, though Laurence Sterne might not have recognised it as such, this was, for me, a sentimental journey.

At the start of the new millennium an old school friend I had not seen for close to two decades called round. I was delighted to see him, not least because he had lost considerably more hair than I have. When you are in your forties there's nothing so heartening as finding that a contemporary has aged worse than you have.

As he prepared to leave, my friend handed me a large manila envelope. 'I thought you might like this back,' he said. Inside was a A5 hardback notebook – my cricket diary of the 1984 season, a journal containing an account of every day's play I attended along with my wise thoughts on selection, captaincy and myriad other aspects of the game.

Naturally I could barely contain my eagerness to read about my past. No sooner had my long-lost chum stepped out of the door than I was slamming it behind him with a perfunctory 'Right, yeah, see you' and racing off into my office with the expectant cackle of a missionary spotting a non-believer in an iron lung.

I sat down with the notebook, thrilled at the thought of getting reacquainted with my younger, livelier and more vigorous self. However, it soon became obvious as I dipped at random into the diary's hundred-plus pages, that when I was younger I was not lively or vigorous at all. Nor was I myself. I used phrases like 'not yet blooded at international level' and 'accrued a not inconsiderable advantage', referred to India as 'the subcontinent' and put inverted commas round any word I considered to be in the slightest bit 'with it'. It was hard to avoid the conclusion that twenty years ago I was Jack Bannister.

Later my partner Catherine came into the room. 'Is it good?' she asked. 'Mmm,' I replied, 'Well, it's . . . interesting. I mean, I selected my World XI to play the West Indies and I saw Courtney Walsh play when he was a youngster and noted that, erm, "though tall and spindly and presently not much above fast medium pace his model action certainly bodes well for the future".'

'What are the lists at the top of the page?' Catherine asked.

'They're the two teams that were playing, in this case Northamptonshire and the West Indies.'

'Why are some of the players' names underlined in red?'

When you have been in a relationship with somebody for two decades you get so you can sense when a conversation is heading in a direction that will do you no favours. I held up my hand for quiet, 'Listen,' I said, 'isn't that someone at the door?'

Catherine listened for a moment. 'No,' she said, 'it isn't. Now about these red underlinings, what are they for?'

'Test caps,' I said briskly. 'They indicate players with test caps. That's why all the West Indian side is underlined with the exception of T. R. O. Payne (wkt) and C. A. Walsh.'

If I didn't know Catherine better I'd consider that in response to my comment she sniggered. 'Oh I can see you,'

she said, 'sitting in the stan   it   where was it, Bletchley? –
with your felt tips and your ruler.'

'I didn't do it when I was in the ground,' I snapped, 'I'm
not a total twat. I did it before I set off.'

Catherine flipped over a page of the diary. 'Well these two
teams must have been rubbish because none of them is underlined.'

'That,' I replied with the kind of withering sarcasm I
thought might regain me the upper hand, 'is because it is Eton
versus Harrow.'

'Oh very posh. Is that why they have the initials after their
names? OB – is that Order of the Bath?'

'No,' I said, 'those intials are   '

I used to have a Norwegian friend who had been a ski-
jumper in his youth. I asked him once if he didn't ever feel
frightened when he was jumping. 'Oh yes,' he said, 'but of
course when you get most frightened is when you have set off
and by then it is much too late to stop.' Now for the first time
I appreciated what he had meant.

'. . . tapabowler,' I mumbled in the vain hope of slowing my
downhill trajectory.

'What?' Catherine said.

'Type of bowler. Those letters are the type of bowler. OB
is off breaks, RFM is right-arm fast medium and . . .' I would
have continued but it was impossible to make myself heard
above the laughter.

Later in the week when Catherine had finally wrested herself from the ticklish fingers of Mr Mirth she became
consolatory. 'Don't be embarrassed,' she said. 'We all do stuff
like that when we're adolescents.'

'Thanks very much,' I said, 'I was twenty-three.'

'You obviously weren't getting much sex, then.'

I shook my head. If only this perfectly reasonable

explanation had been true, then I might have laughed off my serial underlinings, my list of Centuries Seen this Season (10 in total. Highest 144*, M. A. Lynch, Surrey *v* Leicestershire. The Oval. June 11) and my habit of recording the time I arrived and left the ground in brackets as the product of frustration and despond. But alas it wasn't. The reality was far more painful.

From the style of the diary and the number of references to bright young prospects (Junior Clifford, winner of the Find A Fast Bowler competition, C. Gladwin of Essex, George Ferris) it is clear I thought that – like the work of Samuel Pepys – my own diary would be pored over by future generations in fascination and wonder. Well, I was half right, because should anyone else ever stumble across it they will certainly wonder.

One of the games I had been to see in 1984 was Guisborough against Blackhall. On that occasion the two teams had . . . Oh, but let my younger-older self tell you about it:

Sunday afforded the opportunity to see the new Blackhall professional Clayton Lambert play (see p. 13) [*p. 13 records a conversation with two 'old men from Stockton' in the pub at Lord's during a rain break in a Benson and Hedges Cup match. 'They told me that West Indian Clayton Lambert, who has succeeded Desmond Haynes, has scored over three hundred runs and has not yet been out. Local opinion rates him more highly even than his Caribbean compatriot'*] in a match with Guisborough. The game proved to be an entertaining one with Guisborough 'pro' Shastri making forty-seven while tail-enders Russell and Pennock slogged merrily at Blackhall's rotund attack. A total of 174 did not seem formidable as Lambert opened the batting and peppered the legside boundary to the tune of thirty-five or so runs. When he was out however Blackhall collapsed to Shastri who picked up five wickets with his slow left-armers to cap a good all-round display.

Now, twenty-five years later and freed from the shackles of my younger self, I had gone back to Fountains Garth to see the same fixture again.

Guisborough is much changed since I last visited it. Burton's Shirt Factory is now a housing estate and the Blackett Hutton foundry has been knocked down and replaced with a B&Q. The town has changed and so have I because when I walked down the high street I noticed for the first time that it is full of what I now recognise as 'fine and substantial Georgian properties'. 'Some money's worth here,' I thought. The new library, which when I was at infant school had seemed gigantic and space age, was now revealed to be really quite small and angular and seventies – the sort of place you could imagine a Scandinavian geography teacher living.

The cinema where I'd once watched Elvis Presley double bills and the entire series of Magnificent Seven movies (including the one that, if memory serves, was called *Second Cousins Twice Removed of the Magnificent Seven Ride Again for a Third Time*) was now an expensive-looking gym.

In one of Mark Twain's best-known tales Tom Sawyer gets his friends to help him whitewash Aunt Polly's fence, not by appealing for their help but by charging them for the privilege. 'He had discovered a great law of human action, without knowing it,' Twain remarks of this event, 'namely, that in order to make a man or a boy covet a thing, it is only necessary to make the thing difficult to attain.'

The strange transformation of the gymnasium has been

worked by Twain's rule of exclusivity. At one time the gym
was, in most peoples' minds, a place of horror filled with alu-
minium climbing apparatus, rubber mats besmirched with
ancient and mysterious stains in the manner of a vagrant's
vest, vindictive PE teachers and spotty-faced boys hanging off
the wall bars scratching their fetid armpits and making gibbon
noises. This abysmal scene was rendered all the more ghastly
by the powerful odour of fear and municipal boiled cabbage
that hovered for ever in the stagnant air, and the terror that
you might be forced to climb up a rope thus affording teenage
girls the chance to see up the leg of your shorts and giggle. No
adult in his or her right mind – i.e. not a PE teacher – would
willingly enter so dismal a place.

Then, one day some entrepreneur hit on the brilliant idea
of making the gymnasium members only and charging vast
sums of money to enter it. Bingo! Suddenly it was all 'I've just
joined a gym', 'Oh, how super. I love the gym. What gym are
you in?', 'I must pop out to the gym at lunchtime' and 'I
haven't been to the gym all week and I feel absolutely ghastly,
darling.' Nowadays if you want to swing on the wall bars
while scratching your armpits and making gibbon noises you
have to wait in line behind dozens of barristers and junior
solicitors.

At Fountains Garth, Guisborough were batting. Blackhall's
fast bowler Stuart Lobb was galloping in against a backdrop
of the jagged Cleveland Hills, which poke sharply upwards as
if they have the aspiration to be mountains but not quite the
height. A big burly fellow, Lobb banged the ball into the
greenish-looking wicket with a mighty snort of effort, but the
surface gives nothing back, absorbing all his energy like a
black hole swallowing light. As this strip and the one at
Horden had demonstrated, the dampness of the North in the
early part of the summer offers little encouragement to raw

pace. Kelbert Walters had struggled at the Welfare Park and when Michael Holding had played for Rishton in the Lancashire League wickets in May had been so slow he'd halved his run up and suffered the indignity of being clobbered for four sixes in a couple of overs by an amateur, Ian Osborne of Church.

In his comments to the local newspapers afterwards Osborne was noticeably sympathetic to the great West Indian. In the Lancashire League teams played each other home and away. There was no point antagonising 'The Whispering Death', when you might end up batting against him a few months later in poor light on a bumpy track.

I took a seat on a bench along the eastern boundary. This side of Fountains Garth was once the site of the notorious Moors Yard, a rough area of the market town whose inhabitants would watch the cricket from their back yards, barracking opponents so roundly and in such rude terms that the committee of the North Yorkshire South Durham League had ordered Guisborough to erect canvas sheets to block the miscreants' view of the field and spare the players further indignity.

The men sitting along the wall that separates the ground from a footpath were more grizzlers than hecklers. They complained that OAPs were clogging up the high street. 'They've all blessed week to do their bloomin' shopping,' one said, 'so why do the whole lot of them leave it for Saturday morning?'

Guisborough got off to a good start though it was extras that did the bulk of the scoring. An opening no-ball flew straight past the wicketkeeper's outstretched glove for four byes and of the first twenty-five runs, the two opening batsmen managed just six between them. The outfield didn't help. It was as spongy and soggy as Aintree. After eight overs the fielders were bringing on buckets of sawdust to fill Lobb's mighty footmarks.

Tariq Aziz, Guisborough's Pakistani professional, was one of the openers. He's a short, compact batsman from Lahore with seven first class centuries to his name. Now turned thirty-eight, he'd spent several seasons in the North Yorkshire South Durham, scoring a truckload of runs, and had just joined Guisborough from Redcar, who had been relegated at the end of the previous season.

Tariq was the first of the batters to show any intent. He cracked one delivery from Lobb off his pads for four and glanced another deftly to the long leg boundary. In an effort to get his line right, Lobb overcompensated and Aziz thrashed the ball through the gully with a swashbuckling flurry of wrists.

The other opener, Martin Hood, is a tall elegant player who has a habit of lifting his back foot off the ground after playing his shots, like a man pulling his foot out of something unsavoury. The pair knocked up fifty inside fourteen overs. The home side had been put in to bat after losing the toss. The latter is business as usual, apparently, local statisticians claiming that Guisborough haven't won the toss at Fountains Garth since Spring Bank Holiday 2008.

Guisborough's pavilion and clubhouse is a seventies brick block that puts me in mind of a municipal care home for the elderly, which given the age of most people who attend cricket matches these days is maybe appropriate. The bowler from this end is named Sargeant, though the fielders call him Zammo. A wiry bloke with a beaky face, he bowls medium pace. His run up is business-like and culminates in a light hop, as if he's avoiding an unexpected puddle. When he came down to field near me on the boundary he pulled a rueful face. 'It's going to be a long day,' he said, 'a long, long day.' It certainly was for him. He bowled remorselessly from one end while all manner of people chanced their arms from the other.

The first of them was a grey-bearded man named Fariq Iqbal who bowled brisk off-spin and gets thumped around until he's replaced by another spinner, with Guisborough seventy-five for no wicket. The new man was tall and came in off a short run that began with a quick hustle, followed by a sudden stop as if he has forgotten something and then culminated with a leisurely step and a slow twirl of the arm. His deliveries were slow and looping, but they didn't do much to suggest a breakthrough was in the offing. Tariq continued to cut and flick, while his taller colleague thumped the ball straight and through midwicket with a great clonking noise, as if his bat were hollow.

Fountains Garth is in a natural bowl, with grassy banks. Parallel to the square is a small vegetable plot with neatly tended cabbages, onions and potatoes. Behind it is a privet hedge through which elderly bowlers could be seen making their serene way around the green. Perhaps because of the drainage from the surrounding banks the outfield is so marshy that it took real power to strike a four. Blackhall fielded tenaciously, hardly missing a stop, but the score kept clicking upwards and Guisborough reach a hundred in twenty-six overs.

The clouds had darkened and a stiff westerly breeze that seemed to herald a rainstorm snaps the flags on the pavilion roof. 'Where's this summer we were promised?' one of the grumblers snaps. 'They haven't a ruddy clue,' the man next to him growled back. 'It was supposed to be the hottest summer on record.'

'They haven't a ruddy clue, I tell you.'

After a drinks interval Tariq was unexpectedly trapped LBW by Owen Gwyn, a young fast bowler who wears a Durham

Cricket Academy shirt and beneath it a T-shirt that says 'I'm so fast you won't believe your eyes'. Though actually, I do.

The new batsman, Neil Russell was wearing a Twenty20 top with his nickname on the back. He's Guisborough's home professional. At one time, in line with clubs on the west side of the Pennines and in County Durham the North Yorkshire South Durham teams were only allowed one paid player, but four years ago the league relaxed the laws to allow sides to field two pros, one from overseas and one from Britain. It was a pragmatic decision. Sixty miles south in the Bradford League they could pay as many players as they wanted to. No decent amateur was going to hang around and play for nothing when he could pick up four or five grand a season by getting in his car.

The question of what constitutes an amateur is a bit of a vexed one. In the Durham Senior League the amateurs had traditionally all been paid expenses and compensation for the loss of working hours. In the Lancashire leagues such payments were forbidden, and so the amateur players effectively paid – through lost wages and expenses – to play cricket. In Durham they didn't.

Russell, as befits his status, is a bit tasty with the bat. He quickly settled in at the crease and thwacked the ball around like a man with a train to catch. He reached fifty in next to no time, completing his half century with a big heave over midwicket for a six that flew over the metal railing and bumped into the housing estate beyond. It was five minutes before the groundsman managed to find it.

Lobb returned and, thundering in like a warhorse, trapped Russell LBW for fifty-three. Guisborough were 214–2 after forty-six overs. The wind snapped more seriously. 'It's supposed to be blinkin' May,' one of the grognards remarked, pulling on a Berghaus anorak. Another wicket fell in a slog as the overs ran out. Zammo's earlier prediction to the grumblers of a Guisborough total of 270, proved an overestimate and they fell short at 244–3, Hood completing a patient century with a push into the offside.

It was an impressive total, but the grumblers were unwilling to let it pass without a mitigating clause. 'If Neil Killeen had been playing for them it would likely be a different story,' one said, and his chums murmured in agreement. Killeen is Blackhall's English pro, a tough looking veteran who bowls combative medium pace. Killeen also plays first class cricket for Durham. He'd been slated to turn out for Blackhall, but on Friday had taken five wickets on the last day of a Championship match and the county had kept him on as a result.

I bought a £2.50 tea ticket off a couple of primary-school girls and their mum. 'It's a full tea,' the mum said, 'a full tea.' You take the tea in the upstairs lounge with the players. The little girls are in charge of the tea urn. Ticket holders get a big plate full of grub that includes a ham bap and several different types of cake.

As I sat and munched my way through a slice of Battenberg, the Blackhall skipper called for a whip round to pay for the scorer's tea. The umpires, meanwhile, sat silently on their own square table away from the teams, as if asking a player to pass the sugar might compromise their neutrality

I was glad of the tea. When I started the season I'd resolved not to bring food with me, but instead to forage for local delicacies to add a certain gastronomic flourish to my travels. Unfortunately so far I'd not managed anything of note. In Workington I'd had to forego food altogether due to financial irregularities. I'd gone to the cash point near the Hub (a modern sculpture in the town centre that looked like a giant cyberpunk hand grenade) to find that some evil stranger had been taking money out of my account. And the evil stranger was, of course, the bank itself, which despite having been saved from financial ruin by the British taxpayer continued to slap its customers with punitive charges every time they went two pence over their overdraft limit. The bastards.

In Horden, Geordie pizzas had been closed (I was hoping for a ham and pease pudding deep dish) and the nearest thing I could find to local produce was a packet of Phineas Fogg crisps, which had been flavoured with exotic tastes of the orient thirty miles or so to the west in Consett. In Guisborough I imagined I would fare much better. I was hoping to indulge in one of my favourite adolescent feasts – a cheese slice. A cheese slice was a big slab of pastry with a mix of egg, onion and cheese slathered through the middle of it. The cheese was traditionally the same rich orange as Robert Kilroy-Silk's cheeks and just about as tasty as them too. Sadly Guisborough proved to be yet another corner of the kingdom that has been subjected to Greggsification and all the independent local bakers had been obliterated. I can remember when Greggs were pretty much confined to Tyneside, but now they have spread their gospel of lardy snack foods across Britain and the globe. There is even one in Antwerp in Belgium. I imagined that the local fashionistas such as Dries Van Noten and Ann Demeulemeester called in for a bacon-and-cheese turnover and a carton of Ribena Light whenever they'd designed a spiffy new frock.

The North Yorkshire South Durham League was formed in 1893, though matches had been played in the region all the way back in the 1750s. One of the founder members was Ironopolis, the original name of Middlesbrough. Guisborough joined the league in 1895. Cricket in the town had had an inauspicious, indeed almost criminal, start; records from the 1820s show payments to parish constables to 'assist in the detection of players at cricket on a Sunday'.

Like Horden, Blackhall are a colliery team. They'd joined the North Yorkshire South Durham League in 1933 from the Durham Coast League. The club's star turn in the early years was a local all-rounder named Jack Carr. Taken on by Blackhall in 1931 as professional, coach and assistant groundsman, Carr was often described as 'Durham's most popular cricketer' and receipts from clubs that Blackhall visited during the decade he played for them indicate that his presence could put as much as a hundred pounds on the gate – a considerable sum in an era when the entry charge for adults was two and a half pence. Carr took 1398 wickets for Blackhall at 9.75 apiece, but it was his batting that drew in the punters. Striding out to the middle at number five, holding a piece of willow which by all accounts weighed the same as a railway sleeper, Carr played a mighty straight drive at practically every delivery, swinging the bat with such force that even edges flew away to the boundary. His most famous innings was a score of 110 – including six sixes and nine fours – from a total of 162. He belted seven thousand runs for Blackhall in nine seasons and it was largely down to his prodigious efforts that Blackhall won the North Yorkshire South Durham title in their first season and also took the Kerridge Cup – the league's knock-out trophy, which was played to a limited-overs format long before anyone else had thought of such a thing – into the bargain.

Of Carr's successors at Blackhall, Desmond Haynes had hit nine centuries in two seasons as a pro, Roger Harper had briefly succeeded him and then Clayton Lambert had come in. Lambert was the dominant figure in the North Yorkshire South

Durham during the eighties and early nineties, hitting thirty centuries for Blackhall and Redcar. The day I'd gone to watch him play in 1984 his opposite number in the Guisborough ranks had been Suresh Shastri. The Indian spinner took 153 first class wickets for Rajahstan and later became a test match umpire.

Suitably fortified by cheese savoury sandwiches and sly pie, the two teams returned to the field of play. Blackhall's opening bat, John Darby, a left-hander, didn't bother with a helmet. He is a sturdy man with slicked-back hair, a generally old-fashioned air and the classic cricketer's broad-beamed build. He took a dim view of Guisborough's opening bowler smacking the first delivery straight down the ground, pulling the next through midwicket and depositing the third over the boundary at long on.

Darby slapped another delivery through the covers with the sharp snapping noise of good timing. He seemed determined to win the contest by a knock out. 'Nice to see somebody batting without a helmet,' I remarked to one of the grumblers. 'Oh aye,' he responded, 'it looks very pleasant . . . until they get hit in the mouth'

Blackhall's other opener, Warren Swan, is the club's overseas pro, a South African who plays for Boland. He was out for a third ball duck, caught off Russell at mid-off from a checked drive that spooned gently to the fielder. As he trooped off I thought of what Bill Alley said about being a pro in the Lancashire League: 'They wanted to see the ball hit and they hated you if you got out cheaply. If you made a hundred, however, you could walk down the street on Monday morning and kick the bishop up the backside!'

Guisborough's opening bowler from the Pavilion end, Paul Goodchild is shaven-headed and worked up a lively pace. He had the number three, Hardy, caught brilliantly at square leg, the fielder diving full length to grab a firm pull off a long hop.

Fariq the bearded off-spinner came in. He was struck on the front and rear pad first ball and given out LBW, a decision he reacted to with total incomprehension. 24–3 and now the bare-headed opener's urgency seemed to have method to it – he simply couldn't rely on whoever is at the other end keeping him company for long. Goodchild was on a hat-trick. His next ball struck the batsman on the front pad, producing a mass chorus of shrieks. The umpire, who stood hunched and moribund like a wet crow, slowly raised his finger. The fielders went mad.

Zammo Sargeant came to the wicket wearing a cap, his shirt collar turned up in the manner of Geoffrey Boycott or Tony Greig. His first ball from Goodchild struck him on the thigh-pad, but despite the psychotic appeals he survived. Not for long, though: in the next over he attempted a drive and was caught in the covers. Blackhall were 28–5 with Darby on twenty-two. He was as feisty as when he'd started, and clouted another boundary over long off. Eventually he was out chancing his arm once too often, for thirty-eight. Stuart Lobb, the Blackhall pace bowler, puffed out his mighty chest and livened things up even more by whacking a fifty in twenty-four balls that includes six huge sixes. It was never going to be enough though and Blackhall were eventually bowled out for 166, Goodchild finishing with 5–29.

As the two teams left the field I noticed one of Guisborough's players was wearing a knitted wool hat. It was a cold day, a lazy wind whipping across from the North Sea coast, but even so this seemed like the very antithesis of tough Northerness to me. What next? Mittens? Polonecks?

I commented on the hat to the grumbler who'd made the remark about helmet-less batsmen getting hit in the face. He grimaced, 'Way,' he said. 'It's these modern people. They've all gone soft, haven't they?' and he wiped a dewdrop off his nose with the back of his hand and stomped off into the club-house for a half of bitter.

At the end of the season Guisborough were third. Tariq Aziz scored 1196 runs at an average of 38.58. Neil Killeen took sixty first-class wickets for Durham, which was little consolation to Blackhall, who finished bottom of the division and were relegated.

All Roads lead to Rhodes

Lascelles Hall

That Saturday I'd woken to a second successive day of the
sort of baking summer stillness the weathermen had been
promising us since April. The sky was a lively Swedish blue
and lacking in even the tiniest hint of the prospect of malice.
It seemed we had gone from winter to summer with nothing
in between, as if the weather gods had decided that in the current economic climate they could no longer afford an item as
blatantly frivolous as spring.

The cricket pages of the newspapers were filled with pro-
files of the Australian touring party. There was predictable
consternation in some quarters because the visitors had only
seen fit to include one spinner, the widely derided Nathan
Hauritz, in the squad. The fuss about Hauritz reminded me
of Albert Padmore.

Back in the mid-seventies the Barbados and West Indies off
spinner Albert Padmore was the cricket club professional in
the seaside village where my grandparents lived. I'd see him
striding down the street on weekday afternoons, past the off-
licence, sweet shop, and old-fashioned haberdashery that
pasted yellow cellophane over the windows so the perennial

display of sturdy foundation garments didn't fade in the
pitiless North Riding sun. Padmore was tall and angular, and
invariably clad in an ox-blood thigh-length leather trench coat
and a suede bakerboy cap. In an environment of coconut
mushrooms, Emva cream and winceyette nightdresses he
appeared improbably hip and exotic. It was as if Samuel L.
Jackson had turned up in *Heartbeat*.

Padmore came to England with the West Indians in 1976.
He took fifty-nine wickets in the tour matches. Watchers compared him to Lance Gibbs. But Clive Lloyd's side was based
around pace, pace and more pace, so the Barbadian only got
to play in one test. Disillusioned, he signed up for the Kerry
Packer World Series and was later banned for life for playing
in South Africa. These days he lives in Florida where I'll
wager he draws far less attention than he did in Marske-by-
the-Sea three decades ago.

Traditionalists didn't like the way the West Indians
ignored spinners, and not much had changed. On Radio
Four Long Wave the fact that Ricky Ponting's team was
making do with Hauritz provoked predictable tutting. It's
unlikely – even allowing for reception on long wave, which
is so filled with fractured percussive hissing it often sounds as
if Tony Cosier, Vic Marks and co are involved in a marathon
spitting contest – that we'd have heard such noises if, for
example, the Aussies had chosen to come here with only one
naggingly accurate medium pacer whose deliveries just do a
little something off the wicket. Likewise there'd be no
laments for a total absence of a bits-and-pieces man who
bowls little wobblers and can get valuable runs at number
seven. This is because spin bowlers occupy a special place
in the hearts and minds of cricket lovers. They are a bit
like branch line railways; people campaign to preserve them,
not because they have any intention of actually using one,

but because it is strangely comforting to know they are still there.

Back in the eighties, when Padmore had turned over the task of thankless Windies spinner to Raphick Jumadeen or Derick Parry (the man who'd done so well at Horden) it briefly looked as if wrist spinners might disappear from the game altogether, a situation that prompted *TMS* stalwarts Brian Johnston, Henry Blofeld and Christopher Martin-Jenkins to take up the leggies' cause with genuine fervor. Nobody actually said that purveyors of leg breaks and googlies were an integral and vital part of the ecosystem, or talked up the importance of biodiversity, but the phrase 'I believe you need to field a genuinely balanced bowling attack' pretty much amounted to the same thing. You can bet that if a Japanese factory ship had ever menaced Abdul Qadir, Blowers, Johnners and CMJ would have been straight out there to insert themselves between the whirling Pakistani and the threatening harpoon.

The fact that so many people regard spinners as something that must, alongside the corncrake and the natterjack toad, be preserved at all costs makes them quite unique. In other sports positions and styles come and go. No one in football makes a concerted appeal to the government to order the reintroduction of half-backs. And during the Olympics Stuart Storrie never launches into a heartfelt peroration on the topic of pole-vaulting and the fact that 'nobody seems to be using a length of bamboo these days and I can't help feeling the field events are altogether less rich as a consequence'.

As an example of how a spinner can survive in a pace-heavy team, Nathan Hauritz would do well to study Ashley Mallett, a world-class off-break bowler who, like Padmore, suffered during the speed-obsessed seventies. In his first twenty-three tests the South Australia player took a hundred wickets. In his next fifteen he got just thirty-two. By then Dennis Lillee and Jeff Thomson had appeared on the scene and his role had gone from attacking the batsman to keeping the ball warm while one or other of the quick men stood down at third man for a spell chewing on the inside of his mouth and ignoring all the kids who were walking behind him making v-signs while pretending to scratch their ears.

Most of the time when Australia were fielding, Mallett squatted down in the gully staring at the striker and projecting an air of dark foreboding. Because it has to be said that even in a team that contained Ian Chappell, Rod Marsh and Lillee, Mallett stood out when it came to exuding gum-chewing, hard-faced malevolence. He made Jack Palance look like one of the Fimbles. At Headingley in 1975 he came down to field near the boundary and I made the mistake of momentarily catching his eye. It was like a flash premonition of a fractured skull. Mallett took just nine wickets in that series, but if there'd been a set of averages for psychologically unsettling the opposition I bet he'd have topped it easily.

I set off to Huddersfield on the 9.08 train. It was York races and the train south was packed with Geordies decked out in their blinging best. A group of four gay Tyneside men in linen suits sat across the aisle. One said, 'The service in the hotel was absolutely *scandalous*. We had to check out at seven to get our flight home. The receptionist said, "You'll get no breakfast at that hour." Well, I didn't like *her* attitude. I said, "Don't worry, darling. We'll be in a rush. Tell the kitchen to nail a kipper to the wall and we'll lick it on the way past." You should have *seen* the look.'

The sun was baking down on bright yellow fields of rape,

silver-green wheat and buttercup-freckled meadows. It was so hot the tarmac was melting. At York station even the train-spotters had taken off their anoraks.

From York I got the Trans-Pennine Express. The conductor was a Mancunian with such a strong accent that he announced the final destination as 'Manchester Air-paw' the final syllable sounding like he was blowing a kazoo. Mancunians swallow so many consonants you can't help feeling that if they ever ingest any vowels the outcome could well spell disaster.

Beyond Leeds we passed through narrow valleys jammed full of terrace houses, brick factory chimneys, four-storey mills, canals and engine sheds and discount carpet warehouses. The pale yellow brick of every building was rimmed with black and ancient grime. Even in the seventies, as Martin Wainwright records in his book *True North*, twenty-five tons of soot fell each month on every square mile of Leeds south of the River Aire.

The last time I had been in Huddersfield was in one of those summers of rioting. There'd been unrest in Bradford and when I got a taxi on Saturday night that took me to my hotel the driver had predicted blood on the streets with that tone of cheeriness men can't quite keep out of their voices when proclaiming that the worst will happen. 'There'll be anarchy,' they say. 'It'll only take one incident and the whole country'll go up', and there's a glint in their eye that is as close to punching the air with glee as makes no difference.

This summer everything in the North was calm and peaceful. At Huddersfield I left the extraordinary Palladian railway station (surely the grandest in the land) and walked past the George Hotel in time to hear a man tell his son, 'That there is where rugby league was invented,' a sentence that it was more or less compulsory for at least one citizen of Huddersfield to utter every ninety seconds.

The split in rugby had been over broken time payments, the same issue that would lead the Football Association to boycott the first three World Cups. Oddly enough, although cricket had a reputation for being archly conservative the crusty old buffers who ran the game had never been as twitchy about the supposed evils of allowing amateurs and professionals to mix. Possibly this was because many of the greatest amateurs of cricket's golden age – W. G. Grace among them – had harvested small fortunes from the game. As Harold Larwood once remarked of his nemesis Don Bradman, 'I was a professional and he was an amateur, but he made more money out of cricket than I ever did.'

Cricket had begun life as a gambling game. It presented more opportunities for betting than just about any other sport you can think of. Despite its fusty image it had actually had a far faster and more rackety past than rugby and had more in common with boxing and horse racing than it did with football. Take a look at the cricketers of the Golden Age, the late Victorian and early Edwardian era, when England quite literally ruled the world. They include a pair of suicidal batsmen (A. Shrewsbury and A. E. Stoddart); Bobby Peel; a record-breaking all-rounder who attributed his success to neatsfoot oil (George Hirst); a strokeplayer who was photographed naked for 'a medical study' (C. B. Fry) and another whose career was ended when he allowed himself to be locked in a heat-treatment box for too long (G. L. Jessop). Hardly a collection of the dull and the morally upright.

Publicans funded the early teams, and the swell mob of high rollers, crooks, pimps and playboys filled the crowd with the pungent scent of expensive tobacco and easy money. The involvement of Bollywood gangsters and Sharjah bookmakers might have alarmed some of the game's administrators, but they were part of a centuries-old tradition, a return to the style of Victorian days.

The bus dropped me off near a pub called The Tandem. Lascelles Hall cricket ground is a short, steep haul, a hundred yards off the main road. As you turn into the gravel drive that runs along to it you suddenly leave the Huddersfield suburbs and enter a rural world of high meadows, fringed with dog roses. The Highfield Lane ground is lovely, edged with a ditch of white painted boundary stones, an old-fashioned scoreboard above the mowershed, wooden benches tucked under copper beeches. To the front is a view out across the valley and beyond the hills rise up through farmland of rich meadows to a flattened scarp topped by a nineteenth century folly. You can't write about cricket in the North without coming to Lascelles Hall, the Hambledon of Yorkshire. And even if you're not, it's definitely worth a trip.

The ground was once in a field nearby with a well in one corner. Lascelles moved to the new site just after World War Two, buying the land with money raised by subscription. In the clubhouse there's a wooden board bearing the names of the benefactors – it's a roll call of Yorkshire cricketing greats.

'If you look over that way you'll see Kirkheaton's ground. Or at least you could if the pavilion wasn't in the way,' the man at the gate told me. Kirkheaton is where George Hirst and Wilfred Rhodes started out. Just as you can't go to Huddersfield without hearing that the George Hotel is the birthplace of rugby league, so you can't go to any cricket ground in Yorkshire without hearing the name of Wilfred Rhodes. Wilfred Rhodes is to cricket in the White Rose County what Jesus Christ is to the Gospels.

Hirst was highly respected. A stocky man, built like a front row forward, he was said to have invented swing bowling and is the only player ever to have scored two thousand runs and taken two hundred wickets in a first class season. Rhodes though is something else, a source of wonder. Rhodes was venerated, spoken of with awe. He had bowled slow left-arm with numinous brilliance and batted so well he had sometimes opened for England alongside Jack Hobbs. In retirement he had coached youngsters and as an old man blinded by cataracts he was still so filled with wisdom it was said he could tell which shot a batsman had played just by the sound the ball made on the bat. There had been many new Len Huttons and new Fred Truemans, but nobody had ever suggested that anybody was the new Wilfred Rhodes. It was simply unthinkable that anyone should even be compared to him.

When Hirst and Rhodes played for Kirkheaton the village team was the best side in Yorkshire – including Yorkshire. And even when they were both established test and county cricketers they still came back and played in the Huddersfield League whenever they could. In 1904 the pair, bowling in tandem, dismissed Slaithwaite for 9. You might wonder why men of such international renown would come back and play in the local league. The answer is that both felt they owed Kirkheaton a debt and playing was their way of paying it off.

At Lascelles, opponents Armitage Bridge were batting. The home side's professional was a Sri Lankan, Ranga Godage, who played over sixty first class games for Galle Cricket Club. He now lives in Australia where he plays for Orchard Park Red Backs in Victoria. The Red Backs are named after a spider that is said to be the fourth most poisonous animal in Australia, the fifth if you count Steve Waugh. Godage has turned thirty-five but he's still a handy performer. The previous week he'd snapped up nine wickets for nineteen runs as Lascelles – who hadn't won a match for nearly twelve months – romped to victory.

Godage is a tall, barrel-chested, straight-backed man with
a look of Kapil Dev about him. He bowls with a high arm
and he was clearly quicker than most batters were expecting,
making them hurry into shots as the ball scurried on. He was
accurate too, rarely deviating from a good length on off stump.
He epitomised the old 'If they miss I hit' approach and is so
consistent he seems likely to wear a George Francis-style hole
in the wicket.

Godage was the first of many Sri Lankan pros I'd see over
the next few months, all of them following in the footsteps of
Alfred Holsinger, 'the fastest bowler in Ceylon', who had
become the first of his countrymen to earn a living from the
game when he was employed by Eppleton in the Durham
Senior League ('The first coloured gentleman to play in the
district', as one old history put it) back before the Great War.

It is a sign of the way the power in world cricket has shifted.
At one time the bulk of pros came from the West Indies. Such
was the wealth of talent in the Caribbean that cricketers who
could barely get a game for their island side in the Shell Shield
could come to England and walk into a job with a top northern club. Cec Wright, who'd pro-ed for two decades in the
Lancashire League and Central Lancashire League had only
managed to force his way into the Jamaica team on one soli-
tary occasion. The days when the West Indies could more or
less dispense with the services of men like Cec, Roy Gilchrist,
Sylvester Clarke or Clayton Lambert had long gone, however
Now it was Sri Lanka that had a surplus of good players.

Godage was Lascelles's overseas pro, but that didn't mean
he was the only player on the field who was getting paid.
Further north and to the west the committees may have set a
limit on the number of professionals a team could field, but
there was none of that squeamishness about cash in parts of
West Yorkshire. Even at this level – the Drakes Huddersfield

Cricket League, Frank Platt Conference One (effectively the league's second division) – some clubs were laying out twenty-seven thousand pounds a season in wages, with the best of the non-designated pros picking up eight grand for what amounted to a summer weekend job. It's a lot of money and, as one spectator observed, 'You'll never get it back.'

The trouble is that unless you pay them your best players will go to a club that will. Raising the money for such extravagance isn't easy. At one time gate receipts and raffle ticket sales might cover it, but not any more. These days the clubs are reliant on sponsors and benefactors, successful local men for whom the pride of seeing their local village cricket team lift the regional knock-out trophy will match the thrill Roman Abramovich might feel if Chelsea won the Champions' League.

The Northern leagues fed on this sort of parochial pride, off the sort of tribalism that still existed in villages and small towns. All the teams in the Bradford League came from within a twelve-mile radius of the town hall, yet early on a couple of the clubs had quit because they felt the league wasn't quite local enough. 'Hitler's biggest mistake was that he never bombed Blackburn,' people from Burnley would tell you. And some of them weren't joking either.

There were about sixty spectators watching the game at Highfield Lane, many of them connected with the club in some capacity or other. There was a lot of good natured banter and private jokes. When a man sauntered in wearing a purple vest and white Bermuda shorts, somebody sitting near me yelled: 'Is that suitable attire for a member of the committee? In my day you only showed your varicose veins in the back garden.'

An ancient man with an upturned collar and the round rosy face that suggested G. Boycott at ninety-seven said,

'Every morning since I were a lad I've had a slice of bread and beef dripping for breakfast.'

'Aye,' the man sitting next to him responded, 'and you'd never guess he's thirty-two, would you?'

Despite the outlay of money many older spectators are downcast by what they are witnessing. 'This is the worst team we've had here for fifty years,' the bread-and-dripping man said, though the cricket we were watching was far more competitive and of a much higher standard than the previous two matches I'd seen.

Lascelles Hall is not Horden or Guisborough, however. It was once one of the genuine powerhouses of the English game, arguably the oldest cricket club in Yorkshire with a history stretching back to the 1700s. Lascelles could justifiably claim to be the cradle of the game in the county: they'd been famous long before the Huddersfield and District League was formed in 1891.

In 1873 Lascelles had taken on and beaten the Yorkshire first team by 143 runs. In 1877, perhaps to head off further humiliation, six of Yorkshire's first XI came from the village. One of them, Ephraim Lockwood – the teetotal preacher – scored eight thousand runs. Another, John Lockwood – who hit eight centuries for Yorkshire despite an inauspicious debut when he'd arrived without his kit and been forced to field in a red, green and black rugby jersey – went on to be the groundsman at the Oval, preparing the wicket on which, in 1902, Hirst and Rhodes would famously 'get 'em in singles' to help England defeat Australia by a single wicket.

Allen Hill, the first player to take a test wicket, played for Lascelles. So did the first man to take a test hat-trick, Billy Bates (the Australians gave him an ostrich egg to commemorate the feat). Bates was a snappy dresser whose sartorial

elegance earned him the nickname 'The Duke'. Hill bowled
with a highly praised round-arm action, generating a fair pace
off just a few steps. He was beset by injury problems and a
combination of a damaged knee and a broken collarbone
ended his cricket career prematurely. Disaster, it should be
said, seemed to follow Lascelles's golden generation. When a
journalist from the *Yorkshire Evening Post* wrote to Headingley to
inquire as to the whereabouts of another of them, opening
batsman John Thewlis, he received a curt reply: 'Think dead.
If not Manchester.'

On the field Armitage Bridge battled well, but whenever they
seemed on the verge of taking command Godage nipped in
with a wicket. Of the visitors, only the poetically named
Dimbleow got in, striking forty-six. The Sri Lankan was the
star of the show, but Lascelles's wicketkeeper was good too,
standing up to the medium pacers, taking a few sharp ones
down the legside, and narrowly missing out on a couple of
stumpings.

Midway through the innings there was a big appeal for a
caught behind off Godage's bowling. The wickie was so sure
about it that when the umpire shook his head he chucked the
ball down in disgust. An over later Godage clean bowled the
batsman. 'How is that, umpire?' extra cover called sarcastically, before adding a word of congratulation to the bowler.

'What did you just say?' the umpire barked.

'Er, "Well bowled, Ranga",' the extra cover said.

'No, not that. Before that. The remark before that,' the
umpire replied, taking several steps in the fielder's direction.

'I never said owt before that.'

'You are a liar!' the umpire snapped back and began stamp-
ing towards him. For a moment it seemed we were going to
see a match official finally crack and lamp a badly behaved

player. Discretion got the better of the umpire, however, and he stopped after a few paces, but he carried on glaring at the extra cover every chance he got. 'First time that lad gets hit on the pads he's LB for sure,' a man sitting nearby remarked.

Armitage Bridge finished on 185–9. Godage taking 6–46 and Lascelles's twelfth man came round with a hat for the pro's collection. Taking up a collection was a great tradition of club cricket in Yorkshire and Lancashire. When a player got a fifty or achieved certain bowling figures (five wickets for less than forty, say) then the crowd would show their appreciation by chipping in. That was the sort of reward men like S. F. Barnes approved of.

And unlike in most other sports   golf for example – amateurs were allowed to pocket their winnings. This was another reason cricket had appealed to the working class in Lancashire and Yorkshire – they could earn money from it. Often quite a lot of money. The great England centre-forward of the thirties and forties, Tommy Lawton, had been a very good cricketer. He'd played for Burnley in the Lancashire League. As a teenager he'd scored 91 in a Worsley Cup match against a Colne side that included the Indian test player Amar Singh. A hat was passed around the crowd and Lawton got a little over twenty pounds 'in pennies, halfpennies and farthings'. At the time, Lawton was playing for Everton where he earned six pounds a week. For workers in the cotton and woollen mills, hitting a fifty on a Saturday afternoon might bring them the equivalent of three months' wages.

The crowds weren't always generous, however. When Australia's opening batsman Sid Barnes signed as a professional for Burnley in 1947 he came to Lancashire with great expectations of making his fortune.

Ray Robinson, the great Australian cricket writer – the best after Cardus, my dad always said – called Barnes the 'Artful

Dodger'; another Aussie journalist, A. G. Moyes, described him as 'the problem child of Australian cricket'; his team mates knew him simply as 'Bagger'. Barnes was cocky and arrogant. He was the flashiest dresser in the Australian side, wearing Savile Row suits and Argyll socks. He married the daughter of a theology professor, drove a Humber Snipe and 'signed' autographs with a rubber stamp. At the wicket he had a taste for old-fashioned japes that often landed him in trouble. He once slapped Alec Bedser across the buttocks with his bat after cutting him for four, and taunted the slip cordon when he came into bat, "spect you bastards are hoping to catch me out'.

Barnes arrived at Turf Moor with his usual flashiness, driving a swanky car and wearing a fashionably cut sports coat. He knocked up a fast, and to his mind entertaining, fifty but when the collection came in it was pitiful. Barnes – who like many pros had been expecting to bank his salary and live off his collections – remarked on it to one of his team mates. The man shrugged. 'Serves you right turning up like that. You should have come on the bus, in a shabby suit.' Barnes dressed down and travelled by public transport from then on, but the word had got around. No matter how well he performed, his collections remained meagre.

Maybe Barnes was bitterly disillusioned at this situation, because in July he punched a team mate during a dressing room rumpus. Burnley fired him and the Lancashire League committee put him on their blacklist of professionals who were never to be re-hired. The man from New South Wales returned to England the following year with Don Bradman's Australian team (still regarded by many people as the greatest side of all time). In the Old Trafford test he was fielding in close at silly mid-on and was struck in the ribs by a shot from Lancashire's Dick Pollard. According to Jack Fingleton,

Barnes 'dropped like a fallen tree' with a bruise on his chest the size of a soup plate. He was carried from the field by four policemen. No doubt a few people in the crowd felt Bagger had got what he deserved.

During the interval between innings, I found a place under a copper beech and unpacked my tea. In Huddersfield covered market I'd managed to find an independent bakery. They didn't have anything savoury, but I did get a Manchester tart. A Manchester tart is basically a bakewell tart with meringue on the top, because everything from Manchester is a bit showy.

Armitage Bridge was the club of Schofield Haigh, who had once formed part of a brutally effective three-pronged attack for Yorkshire. Since the other two members of it were Hirst and Rhodes, Haigh doesn't get much of a mention these days. He bowled medium pace with a slinging action and took most of his wickets clean bowled. Lascelles Hall's nicely produced programme made mention of Haigh, but my attention was more taken by a sentence on the history of the visitors that read: 'The 1984 installation of ladies and gents toilets replaced the antediluvian outdoor cesspits which had bedevilled many social functions at the club.' Welcome to West Yorkshire, a place where even the programme sledges the opposition.

Bridge had a decent opening attack. From the pavilion end, a young lad with blond hair and an earring that twinkled in the sun bowled at a sharp pace, moving the ball away from the right-hander. 'Nice areas. Good areas,' the slip cordon shouted. His opening partner approached the wicket in a tearing hurry and bowled with a mad flurry, like an octopus falling off a stepladder. I got the impression he delivered the ball off the wrong foot, but the whirl of limbs was so convoluted that even after careful study I couldn't be quite sure.

On the boundary nostalgia was breaking out. 'We had a heck of a team twenty years ago. One time our opening attack was Garth le Roux and Arnold Sidebottom. Allan Lamb was playing over the hill at Holmfirth then,' one man said. He had that West Riding trick of tucking his chin in so far when he spoke it looked as if he was trying to pop it out through the back of his neck and as a result his voice came out as a low, gravelly rumble. 'When Lamby played here one time he hit five consecutive sixes and they all landed halfway up that meadow there.'

'Before Lamb, Holmfirth had that Derbyshire fella. Ashley Harvey-Walker. Bit of a character. Had false teeth and a metal bat.'

I remembered Ashley Harvey-Walker from his days playing county cricket. I'd seen him often on the TV on Sunday afternoons, playing in the John Player League. 'He had a moustache too,' I said. 'A long, wolfish face. He was a bit like Lee Van Cleef. He had the look of a Wild West badman.'

'Aye well, when he immigrated to South Africa somebody shot him dead,' the chin-tucked man replied, 'so mebbe appearances weren't deceptive in his case.'

Lascelles were 50–1 when I left to catch the last train that would get me home before Sunday. As I passed out through the gate the bread-and-dripping man wandered over and shook my hand. 'Thanks for coming,' he said, 'I'm glad the weather's been good for you.'

'It's a really beautiful ground,' I told him.

He smiled, 'Aye, you never come up here when the larks aren't singing.'

I walked off down the gravel drive, through a foaming avenue of cow parsley. Ash trees were releasing their seeds with little pops, showering the ground with round, flat brown pods like wholemeal confetti, and skylarks ascended into the baby-blue sky, twittering as they went.

Lascelles went on to win the game by five wickets, Ranga Godage getting his second collection of the day with an unbeaten sixty-one. At the close of the season Lascelles were sixth and Armitage Bridge seventh in a division that included just eight teams.

Freezing Cold and Sheepshit
in the Garden

Carlisle

The previous Saturday in Huddersfield the hot summer weather had seemed unbreakable. I'd imagined a summer like 1976, all hose pipe bans, rock hard wickets, fast outfields and Michael Holding whistling the ball past the batsmen's ears. In fact it had lasted less time than Andy Lloyd's test career. The walkers were wearing waterproofs when the train passed through Gilsland and the covers were on in Haltwhistle. I'd planned to go to Settle to see the home side play Blackburn North but when I phoned Settle tourist office for a weather forecast the lady was reluctant to commit herself. 'It's not as bad as I thought it would be,' she said. 'It could fair up. It might not. It's hard to tell, really.'

Settle was a three-hour trip, so I decided not to risk it and to go and watch Carlisle play Vickerstown in the Carlsberg North Lancashire and Cumbria Cricket League Division One instead. A trip to Edenside Park hadn't been part of my itinerary, but the game at Workington had come to nothing and I felt Cumbria deserved a second chance. Besides which I was very fond of Carlisle. There were parks that ran along the river Eden, a massive second-hand bookshop, an independent

coffee roaster and generally something pleasingly old fash-
ioned about it. Possibly that was because the Great Border
City was a bit of a backwater. This had not always been the
case. At the start of the industrial age Carlisle had been a real
powerhouse. In the early 1800s Percy Bysshe Shelley had set
up home in the Lake District because he was convinced that
when England's answer to the French Revolution came its epi-
centre would be either Manchester or Carlisle and he wanted
to be near to both when the fun started. As it was nothing
much happened at all in either city so Percy went off to
Europe with his mate Lord Byron (himself an accomplished
cricketer). Since then the only really radical thing that had
happened in Carlisle was the nationalisation of the pubs in
1948.

I liked Carlisle, but not everyone felt the same way. When
Stan Bowles, the quintessential seventies football geezer, had
played for the local team he'd summed up his time at Brunton
Park with the memorable words, 'Freezing cold and sheepshit
in the garden – that's Carlisle.'

I had an hour to kill before play started so I sat in a department store café opposite the red stone cathedral reading the
papers. The cricket sections carried the tale of poor young
Reece Topley. The teenager had been struck on the head by
a Kevin Pietersen drive while bowling to the England team in
the nets at Loughborough. You didn't have to have witnessed
the incident to know it would have featured a sound like a
coconut being struck with a croquet mallet.

When I'd attended my first test match Alan Knott and
Tony Greig were in the process of setting Australia a run
chase at Headingley and the ball was flying all around the
ground. I was very nervous about being hit by one of Knotty's
strange pick-up shots, or a Greig pull, but my dad reassured
me that I was totally safe because, 'there are hundreds of pairs

of good Yorkshire hands in front of you'. The fact that most of them were holding pints of beer they'd be reluctant to drop just to save a beaky teenager from getting smacked in the gizzard, didn't enter his thoughts, or mine.

I'd got away with it that day, but ten years later I suffered a Topleyesque blow when a batsman thick edged a wild swipe in my direction at second slip. The Velvet Underground sang that between thought and expression lies a lifetime. Something similar may as well have elapsed between me seeing the ball flashing towards me and raising my hands to catch it because by the time my palms were in position, I was lying on my back with a bruise in the centre of my forehead and the ball had gone first bounce over the boundary rope for four.

When I came to I had a bigger crowd around me than there is at most county championship matches. Everyone offered sympathy except the bowler, Reg. Reg was a West Yorkshireman of late middle age who'd played for years in the unforgiving environment of the Bradford League. He had a jaw like a kerbstone, cheeks the colour of ox liver and lived his life in a mood of simmering resentment.

'Well, if you're from Yorkshire,' the captain had said breezily when I first joined the club, 'you'll have to meet Reg. You and Reg will get along like a house on fire. He's a proper Yorkshireman is Reg.'

I smiled and nodded politely. I thought it best to humour him. This was the second cricket club I had tried to join since moving to London. The first had asked me to leave before a ball had been bowled after an incident at the pre-season cheese-and-wine party involving the treasurer's trousers and a gallon of mulled vin de pays.

'He's a real Tyke, is Reg,' the skipper continued, adding by way of emphasis a series of 'Ey Ups', 'Ee by Gums' and assorted other nonsensical phrases in what appeared to be an Irish–Geordie accent. 'I look forward to meeting him then,' I said without much enthusiasm. I had grown to mistrust Southerners' views of what constituted a 'real Yorkshireman' for much the same reason I ignore betting tips from shirtless men.

Because to Southerners, and the world in general, 'real Yorkshire' is the West Riding: Bradford and Leeds, the dark satanic mills, the flat caps and the dark satanic faces that glower beneath them. It is Ilkley Moor bah't'at, brass bands playing Haydn, Nora Batty, Arthur Scargill and places with names like Abattoirwyke and Arsethwaite. That is part of Yorkshire, but it is not my part. I come from the North Riding. It is an altogether gentler place. Well, except for Middlesbrough, obviously.

The club captain knew nothing of such things. 'Aye up t'lad, thars nowt as queer as t'folk,' he jabbered pronouncing the Ts so it sounded like he was trying to get a hair off his tongue.

'Yes,' I said, 'I think I can see what you mean.'

I went home that evening and thought about Reg. I pictured a man in grey flannel trousers that were too tight round the backside and too short in the leg, a blue blazer with brass buttons, a pale yellow shirt and a maroon tie with a large knot in it. I imagined his age to be about thirty-seven, his height about five foot nine. His body stocky, his hands as big as pint pots, his feet pointing slightly outwards. I imagined a large face, thin lips, narrow eyes and dark hair swept back and lacquered with Brylcreem. I imagined him chewing gum with remorseless vigor and wearing wristbands.

So when a man answering that description walked into the clubhouse the following Saturday I had no doubt who it was.

'I bet that's Reg,' I said to the skipper. 'Well, that's uncanny,' he remarked and then, dropping into his Irish–Geordie accent, 'ee lard, it teks t'one to know t'one.' He looked over to the bar where Reg was standing, 'Reg!' he shouted in his normal voice. 'Reg, there's a new chap here I'd like you to meet.'

Reg turned slowly and scowled at us. 'Bugger off,' he growled and turned back to the bar. I looked at the skipper expecting him to remonstrate, to deliver a lecture on discipline, to punch the bloke. Instead he began to chuckle. 'You're a blunt and forthright lot, you Yorkshiremen,' he said.

I stared over at the broad emblazered back of Reg. I felt as a Frenchman might if he was confronted in a foreign land by a fellow countryman wearing a striped jersey and beret, twirling his moustache and singing 'Thank Heaven for Little Girls'. The fact that the locals were so delighted with the stereotype only made it more depressing. Though not as depressing as having to field when Reg bowled.

In *A Flame of Pure Fire*, Roger Kahn's entertaining biography of Jack Dempsey, there's a story about the husband of a Hollywood actress who, suspecting his wife is having an affair, comes home early from a business meeting with the intention of catching her in flagrante. Sure enough the wife is in bed and sensing that somebody is hiding in the en suite bathroom the husband flings open the door with a loud 'Aha!' And finds himself face to face with the heavyweight champion of the world.

Well, you can believe me that at the precise moment he stared into the cold dark eyes of the Manassa Mauler the husband's discomfiture and fear were as nothing compared to the cascade of humiliation and terror that engulfed a man in the seconds after he had dropped a catch off Reg's bowling.

'Next time you decide to grab one with your teeth, try opening your mouth a bit wider,' was all he said on that occasion, though from then on I got the feeling he was just waiting for the chance to push me under a bus. I left that club before he got the chance.

Carlisle's Edenside Park is on the north bank of the river, overlooked by big Georgian and early Victorian houses and a public school. There's a rhododendron-fringed bowling green on one side and a bank to the north that's sharp enough for a dry ski slope, possibly the only one in the world with a sightscreen at the bottom of it. Carlisle Cricket Club are sponsored by Carlisle Refrigeration which, given the temperature in late May, is highly appropriate.

The visitors, Vickerstown, are from a planned estate on Walney Island, the hinterland of Barrow. Vickerstown was built to house workers at the military shipyards and is probably best known to the world at large because it features – as Vicarstown – in the Thomas the Tank Engine stories. Vickerstown cricket club was founded in 1892.

Carlisle won the toss and decided to bat. Vickerstown have a good attack built around Gareth Benson and Colin Lucas, and a decent batting line-up in which the former Barrow rugby league player Geoff Luxon is the star, but Carlisle are the big boys in Division One. (As in professional football, league cricket has tried to broaden definitions of success – division one is hardly the top division anywhere any more. It's the sporting equivalent of that moment in a coffee bar when the assistant says smugly, 'Our large is our regular'.) Relegated last year and determined to get back into the top flight at the first attempt, they've invested heavily in a young professional, Saliya Saman, who has been imported from Ragama CC in Sri Lanka via Whitehaven.

Saman is twenty-three, played for his national under-19 side and so far in his first class career has taken fifty-three wickets

and hit two centuries. Backed up by a decent bunch of amateurs, Saman's performances with bat and ball have ensured
that so far this season the Borderers have taken maximum
points from every match they've played.

Marc Brown is a classy opening bat. Early in his innings
he signalled his intentions, taking a few paces up the wicket
and smashing a delivery straight down the ground for four.
A few balls later he leaned into a forward push and picked
up another, then forced the ball between mid-on and midwicket with a twitch of the wrist for a third. Carlisle raced to
fifty in fifteen overs, but then Brown was out, caught in the
deep for thirty-four from a big hoik that flew up off the
splice. As it dropped into the fielder's hands Brown let out a
roar of dissatisfaction and as if in answer a police siren
blared as squad cars raced across the nearby bridge and into
the city centre.

The pro came in to bat. Saman is tall and slim and glided
into his first few shots, directing all of them along the ground
through extra cover. The red-headed bowler who opened the
attack had just been set for a spell of rest at third man. After
watching the Sri Lankan slap his team mates around, he
turned to the spectators on the boundary, raised his eyebrows
and said, 'Quite glad I got took off, all round.'

The redhead's replacement was a tall young paceman, Lee
Hogg. He has a seventies haircut and strode back to his mark
with the angry briskness of Dennis the Menace's dad going off
to fetch his slipper. He beat the bat with his first delivery and
with his third had Brown's opening partner caught at the
wicket. 62–2.

Saman recognised this as an excuse to launch an assault on
the bowler from the Eden end. The first ball was driven
straight for four, the third went through the covers for another
boundary, the fifth was smacked straight over the sightscreen.

'You've got him in two minds now. He doesn't know whether to hit you for four or for six,' a wag in the crowd chortled, recycling a popular cricket joke originally made by the Yorkshire wicketkeeper Arthur Wood when the South African batsman Jock Cameron was badly mistreating the usually imperious Hedley Verity, a man almost as venerated in Yorkshire as Wilfred Rhodes.

In the next over the field was posted out when the Sri Lankan was on strike. If the plan was to frustrate him into a false shot, then it worked perfectly. After a couple of dot balls Saman banged the next straight at mid-on, but with such force it rebounded straight out of the man's hands with a noise like somebody slapping a halibut. Well, almost perfectly.

When Frank 'Typhoon' Tyson had begun his cricket career playing for Middleton in the Central Lancashire League he'd been hit on the glove by a short ball in one of his first matches, shook his hand in pain and was given out. When he returned to the pavilion one of the old men sitting on the steps called out, 'That'll teach you. Next time, rub your chest.' Saman offers a psychological variant of this theme after the near miss, staring at the toe-end of his bat as if the willow – rather than his timing – had malfunctioned.

With the next ball normal service was resumed. Saman cut between first and second slip for four. A few balls later he cuffed a good length delivery between midwicket and mid-on for another, then produced a wristy slap through point to bring up Carlisle's hundred.

Aggravated, Hogg fired one in short, striking the pro on the thigh, and then whizzed a bouncer over his head. The Sri Lankan responded aggressively, pulling another short one over square leg. The next ball was a good length. Saman heaved at it and missed. 'Get your bloody head down, pro,' one of the spectators bellowed crossly.

Briefly Carlisle's innings was becalmed. Vickerstown's field was spread, an accurate military medium bowler operated from one end, the red-headed pace bowler was back on at the other. Carlisle's number four was struck on the pad three times in a row, but the umpire turned them all down, as unwilling to listen to appeals as Judge Jeffreys.

Taking the law into his own hands, the redhead clean bowled the batsman with his next delivery. 121–3 in thirty overs. In the next over Saman played on. The Sri Lankan has made forty-five in the sort of maverick, big-hitting style expected of the professional, whose job is not only to help his team win but also to entertain the paying customers.

Saman's departure came as a huge relief to the Vickerstown team and they cavorted around slapping palms and whooping. In days of old, Northern cricketers got altogether less carried away. The redoubtable Yorkshire batsman Arthur Mitchell summed up the prevailing attitude of his era with his reaction when team mate Ellis Robinson took a diving catch off his own bowling. Far from racing across and leaping on top of his comrade, Mitchell simply looked down at him with mild contempt. 'Get up, Ellis,' he said, 'you're making a spectacle of yourself.'

Some people felt this sort of reaction showed a lack of passion. I wasn't so sure. I'd imagine Sir Winston Churchill was pretty chuffed when he received the news that the Nazis had surrendered, but I bet he didn't pump his fists in the air and simulate sexual intercourse with his drinks cabinet. It's a question of context. A handshake from some people means more than a bear hug from others.

The departure of Saman sent the game into a torpor. It reminded me of the feeling of anticlimax that came over a ground when Ian Botham was out. Everyone's concentration seemed to wander. Carlisle stepped on the gas and their number five, Jonathan Musgrave, rapped a swift fifty. Hogg returned to the attack and was thumped for fifteen in a single over before Musgrave fell to a well-judged boundary catch for sixty-one. Number seven attempted to make room on the leg side and got caught in the gully off a leading edge. The innings closed with a reverse sweep that flopped over first slip for a single. 231–6 in forty-six overs, that number cut from fifty because of the late start. On a slow outfield it seemed like a tall order for Vickerstown, especially against a side that the previous week had blasted out one of their main rivals, Appleby-Eden, for just eighty-seven.

The pavilion has half-timbered eaves, mullioned windows and a general air of the stockbroker belt about it. A sign on the gate that leads into the enclosure in front of it reads, 'No access to the ski slope', which must be unique. The pavilion was built in 1892, the year the field was bought by the club from the Duke of Devonshire. Cricket had been played in the Great Border City since the 1820s when the local paper was called the *Patriot*, just in case anybody thought Jacobitism might still be lurking in the city. Carlisle CC had begun life in the Border League, switching to the North Lancashire League in 1949.

In the clubhouse a big screen TV was showing *SpongeBob SquarePants*. There are rows of photos on the wall, including one of a game played at Edenside Park in 1926 between the touring Australians and G. Palmer's XI. It was the final match of what was something of a marathon visit for H. L. Collins's side. They arrived in Carlisle on 16 September, having played their opening game on 28 April. As well as playing five test matches and all of the first class counties they also took on: Minor Counties, the MCC, the South, the North, Cambridge University, Oxford University, Public Schools, an England XI (at Folkestone), the Civil Service, C. I. Thornton's XI and an England XI (Blackpool). If the Aussies were sick of cricket by this stage you could hardly blame them, but the public plainly couldn't get enough of it because five thousand tuned up to watch the game at Carlisle.

G. Palmer's XI included some of England's finest players – Percy Holmes, Herbert Sutcliffe, Patsy Hendren, Roy Kilner, George Gunn – and one local man, Cumberland wicket-keeper Roland Saint, but the visitors were too strong for them, winning a one-innings match by six wickets thanks mainly to a century from Charlie Macartney.

I have a particular fondness for teams like G. Palmer's XI because every August during my boyhood my father and I would go to Marine Road, Scarborough, to see T. N. Pearce's XI play the tourists. My father had been going to watch this highlight of the premier cricket festival in Yorkshire (and there-fore, by extension, clearly the entire world) since he was a youth. Back in those hazy days of ration books and the wire-less, however, the responsibility of selecting a side to play in what was dubbed by Yorkies 'the sixth test match' fell to H. D. G. Leveson-Gower (Leveson-Gower had himself taken on the mantle from the aforementioned C. I. Thornton). How the succession was arranged I am not certain, but a cursory inspec-tion of the respective careers of H. D. G. Leveson-Gower (known to his chums as 'Shrimp') and T. N. Pearce (perhaps best remembered for being the facing batsman when Jehangir Khan's delivery killed a sparrow) uncovers two things the pair had in common – neither of them played for Yorkshire and neither of them came from Yorkshire. (When asked why Leveson-Gower organised a team to play at Scarborough my father replied that he believed him to be 'some sort of a relation of the Duke of Sutherland' – the exact relevance of which to the matter at hand I am uncertain.)

Whatever his qualifications for picking a team to play at Scarborough, these days I find T. N. Pearce both a comfort and an inspiration. There are few cricket fans who have not spent idle moments selecting a World XI to take on and thrash visitors from some weird, alien civilisation (or Australia, as it is more commonly known). T. N. got to do it for real, though admittedly by the time I saw the results the pool of players available to him seemed to consist entirely of Yorkshire seconds, a couple of unknown Barbadians who happened to have a weekend off from playing in the leagues and Robin Hobbs of Essex, a leg-spinner whose appearance at Scarborough was compulsory under local by-laws.

T. N. was not the only one to get to make his mark in this way, of course. A. E. R. Gilligan, whose XI traditionally played the tourists at Hastings, was another. In fact, dozens of 'special selects' have been and gone, writing their names across Wisden for posterity and the puzzlement of future generations. What, for example, of Sir Julien Cahn's XI that played Glamorgan in 1936, or J. G. W. Davis's XI, which took on Cambridge University in the J. C. Stevens Memorial Match (not first class) at the Saffrons in 1969, or L. Robinson's XI that lined up at Attleborough to do battle with the Australian Imperial Forces in 1919? And then, of course there were the International Cavaliers, who mysteriously got to play a first class match against Barbados. At Scarborough.

D. H. Robins had a first class cricketing career that stretched from 1947, when he played two games for Warwickshire, to 1971 when, at the tender age of fifty-seven he turned out against the Indian tourists, and encompassed a grand total of five matches. For a decade he picked a team that played the tourists in a three-day game, took on various counties and universities and made sporadic forays to South Africa (Robins displayed a frankly international cavalier attitude to decent opinion. As well as offering succour to the apartheid regime he also, while chairman of Coventry City, appointed Jimmy Hill as manager.) The team were based at Eastbourne. I imagine their HQ was a stucco-and-glass penthouse apartment complete with tubular steel furniture, zebra-skin wall hangings and a Scandinavian PA played by Julie Ege in a terry-towelling bikini. Though no doubt the truth was far more glamorous than that.

Graham Gooch, David Gower, Mushtaq Mohammad, Tony Greig, Barry Richards, Gordon Greenidge and Clive Rice all turned out for D. H. Robins's XI over the years. Occasionally he captained the side, selflessly batting at number eleven and, with a restraint that is nothing short of saintly, steadfastly refusing to bring himself on to bowl even when conditions were entirely favourable.

In 1969 D. H. Robins's XI played Wilfred Isaac's South Africans shortly after that redoubtable team of visitors had thrashed Cambridge Quidnuncs at Chislehurst. In my view, this sentence alone entirely justifies the existence of humankind.

With the honourable exception of Lavinia, Duchess of Norfolk's XI, these days the select XI here in the UK appears to have passed into history. This is a great pity. For when a man reaches his late thirties he experiences a change. His whole perception of life is altered. He stops being able to fantasise about playing test cricket. Because even a daydream must have a tenuous thread attaching it to reality and, once you turn thirty-nine, the rattling-Marcus-North's-ribcage-with-a-vicious-delivery-rising-from-just-short-of-a-length thread has snapped with the kind of reverberating twang your waistband makes whenever you bend down to tie a shoelace.

It is at this point in your life that you come fully to appreciate T. N. Pearce and D. H. Robins. For if back spasms and an increasing sense that your feet are your body's answer to the Falkland Islands (you know they belong to you but you have no idea what is going on down there) preclude you from believing you are the new Shoaib Aktar you can at least still lie awake at night and imagine you are in charge of your own star-studded XI. It is not perhaps the same as uprooting Ricky Ponting's middle stump, but I think you'll agree that the chance to utter the words 'I'm going to have to take you off now, Warne, you're bowling utter crap' has its compensations.

G. Palmer's XI didn't have the longevity of D. H. Robins's teams but they paved the way to Edenside Park becoming a regular venue for tour matches throughout the thirties, forties and fifties. Large crowds came to see Cumberland and Westmorland take on the visitors, but then the tours were cut short and another of the game's traditions died. Australia's tour of 2009 would hardly merit the name. It was more of an excursion.

After the tea interval and fresh from his success with the bat, Musgrave opened the bowling for Carlisle from the ski slope end with his twirly leg-spinners. He whizzed the ball down at a steady clip and did that spin bowler thing of looking down the wicket after every ball, biting on his thumb as if trying to figure something out. After a moment he jumped out of his reverie and walked back to his mark with the jaunty stride of a man who'd just concocted a fiendishly brilliant plan. It is a psychological ploy that Shane Warne was the master of. He always looked at the batsman with a sly grin, as if everything his opponent did – whether he'd played and missed or swiped him for a six – was just what he'd been hoping would happen. In Accrington they'll tell you the Aussie picked up the trick

when he was pro-ing for the Lancashire League club back in
1991. Certainly there was a long tradition of cunning in the
Northern leagues. When Bill Alley had joined Colne he'd
been warned, 'They won't get you out. They'll diddle you
out.' To prove it in his first innings, away to Haslingden, he
was bowled around his legs by a ball that turned several feet
off a patch of mud apparently specially prepared for just such
a delivery.

At the opposite end from Musgrave Saman opens. The
wicketkeeper stands a very long way back and it is easy to see
why, as the ball fizzed through even off the docile Northern
turf, the wicketkeeper reaching up to take it in front of his
face. Saman has a quick, short run up and a high arm. In
many ways he's like a younger, springier version of Ranga
Godage. Between the two of them this opening pair throttled
the life out of Vickerstown using a mixture of hostility, accuracy and cunning. Carlisle were a team that wanted to win,
they fitted the Northern archetype perfectly.

In Musgrave's second over Vickerstown's burly opener
edged one into the slips. It went fast and about two feet off the
ground but Saman dived and took it two handed, hurling it
into the air with a roar of delight as he jumped to his feet.

I'm always impressed with the way top-class cricketers can
take a catch, throw the ball in the air and run off without concern for where it has gone. Those of us of lesser ability are not
so nonchalant. Personally, if I throw a cricket ball in the air I
always keep an eye on it, knowing that if I don't it is all too
likely to come straight down on my head.

While the Sri Lankan tied up one end with his pace, the
spinner ran through the Vickerstown batters at the other. In
his third over Musgrave took another wicket, clean bowled
with a full toss. Two balls later the reluctant umpire finally
raised his finger on an LB and Vickerstown were 8–3.

In Saman's next over he let out a mighty shout for leg-before and after considering for what seems like half an hour the second umpire decided to join in the fun. 9–4. Sitting back in the enclosure with a pint, I started to wonder if the visitors would make fifty, but gradually the pro tired. The ball flew more often down the legside. One such delivery is glanced for four, another goes the same way this time for byes. No more wickets fell, but after this flurry the total hardly advanced either.

Vickerstown limped onwards against Musgrave, wickets coming as often as boundaries, and eventually were all out for 65, giving Carlisle victory by 166 runs. The sky was beginning to darken as the players trooped off, their thoughts on Saturday night in the city, and the girlfriends in sequinned miniskirts who wobbled around the boundary on foxy heels.

The home side went on to win the first division title by a record margin and pick up the Sowerby Cup too. Marc Brown finished the season with 485 runs at 44.09. Saliya Saman scored 385 runs and took fifty-seven wickets, including six five-wicket hauls. Despite the crushing defeat at Edenside Park, Vickerstown went on to finish second. Their bowler Gareth Benson was voted the Division One player of the season.

Spilling Blood for Victory

Radcliffe

At the Racecourse Ground in Unsworth Road, Radcliffe, the sun was beating down so hard I could feel my skin crisping up like grilled bacon. On the field the home side were struggling badly against the visitors from Middleton. Middleton's pro Ken Skewes, a twenty-four-year-old South Australian who'd attended the singularly named Humpty Doo Primary School, was on top of things. Radcliffe's own professional Usman Tariq – who'd hit twelve first class hundreds in Pakistan – was bowling his leg breaks but it looked as if he'd have got more turn out of Margaret Thatcher than he could out of the wicket.

Radcliffe is near Bury. It had once been a centre of coal mining, cotton spinning, paper milling and bleachworks, but lately it had been engulfed by Greater Manchester. The great north-west metropolis seemed to spread further with each passing day like some sci-fi blob swallowing up previously independent towns and villages and littering them with DIY superstores and identikit sports centres – if it hadn't been for the road signs you could have been anywhere from Horwich to Hyde.

Radcliffe CC had once had ambitions to host Lancashire

second-XI matches and the wicket at the Racecourse was the sort of benign strip the counties demanded. In league matches batsmen might be expected to make runs on a strip where the ball threw up clods, but in the first class game that sort of thing got you a hefty fine and a warning about future conduct.

I wasn't paying that much attention to the cricket, to be honest. I was sitting on the boundary talking to Paul Rocca. Paul Rocca had been a top league cricketer during the sixties and seventies. He played as a professional all over Lancashire and whenever you picked up a record book you'd likely find his name in it somewhere. In 1972, for example, he'd hit 212 for Heyside against Droylsden in the Saddleworth and District League and 112 not out against Moorside. Before that he'd been at St Annes and Blackpool.

Nowadays Rocca was umpiring in the Central Lancashire League, which was where he'd started out as a schoolboy. 'When I was young I just wanted to play for Middleton, my local team,' he said. 'That was my ambition. I thought if I could get in the Middleton first team then that would be grand.' This may not seem like much of an aim for a cricketer of Rocca's talent but it should be said that Middleton weren't just any local team. Their list of former players was a roll call of giants of Britain and the Empire. Radcliffe didn't lag far behind them either. In terms of prestige and quality the CLL lagged behind only the Bradford League and the Lancashire League in the Northern cricket pantheon, though it was wise not to express that notion too loudly in the area around Rochdale and Bury.

Rocca is a smiley-faced man, with a chuckle in his voice. He exudes such warmth that talking to him is like sitting in front of a log stove in your slippers eating crumpets. When I was at school the English teachers always told us we shouldn't use the word 'nice'. But sometimes nice is the correct adjective.

Certainly that is the case with Paul Rocca. He is profoundly, movingly nice.

Rocca had made it into the Middleton first team when Eric Price was the professional at Glebe Road. Price was born in Middleton and played county cricket for Essex. He was a typical English medium pace bowler and he'd been on the receiving end of a famous hammering from Don Bradman's 1948 Australians. At Southend the tourists had posted two hundred before lunch on the first day, Bradman thrashing Price for five consecutive fours and reaching his century in seventy-four minutes.

'They scored 721 in a day and Eric finished with 0–156 off twenty overs. Though, of course, the way he told it if it hadn't been for a few poor LBW calls and a couple of spilled catches he'd have got five for twenty-seven and they'd have been all out for ninety-two,' Rocca said with what I'm pretty sure was a chortle.

Cricket in Lancashire had an edge to it, Rocca said. 'When I played cricket in the army during my national service people from down south were surprised by how competitive I was,' he said. 'But that was the way cricket in the leagues was always played. It was hardnosed, played to win. Mind you, there wasn't any of this sledging.'

Not even from Cec Pepper? I asked

Paul Rocca sucked in his cheeks and raised his eyebrows, 'Well,' he said, 'you know. Pepp was Pepp.'

Many people believe the Australians invented sledging. In fact, some even go so far as to lay the blame at the steel-toed boots of one bloke, Cecil George Pepper. Pepper was a man who lived up to his name. He was so fiery it's a wonder his cap never caught fire. Rocca had played with and against him on many occasions.

Pepper was regarded as one of the finest all-rounders of

the post-war years. But he never played test cricket for Australia. This was because he had roundly abused Don Bradman in a Sheffield Shield match at Adelaide in 1946. The exact wording of Pepper's verbal onslaught is not known, but since he taunted another batsman who had played and missed at his leg breaks throughout an eight-ball over with the words 'You can open your fucking eyes now, mate. I've finished,' reacted to a loud blazer worn by the Indian batsman Vijay Manjrekar by yelling 'Jeez, where'd you get that jacket, off the back of a bloody horse?' and responded to a spectator criticising his, to borrow a phrase from Brian Close, frequent invocations of the conjugative verb in a Central Lancashire League match by smacking him in the mouth, we can probably hazard a guess that it didn't include any quotations from Proust.

Cec Pepper was born in 1916 in Forbes, New South Wales. He was built like an Edwardian bobby, with a meaty face and even beefier forearms. He was a hard-hitting lower middle order bat and a dynamic bowler of leg spin. He made his name as a teenage prodigy in grade cricket with Parkes, hitting 2834 runs, and took 116 wickets in a single season

When the Australian Services team toured England in 1946 playing a series of 'Victory Tests', Pepper outshone even the brilliant Keith Miller. His amazing hitting in a game at Scarborough, in which he sent the ball sailing across the sky above the boarding houses and into Trafalgar Square, is the stuff of legend. 'Pepp could have been one of the all-time greats,' Paul Rocca said as Ken Skewes smacked the ball over the heads of the Radcliffe fielders and it bounced into the wall of the gents' toilet beneath the scoreboard.

Bradman, though, was known as 'The Don' and in the post-war years he ruled Australian cricket like the Boss of Bosses. After the Adelaide business word soon came down to

Pepper that he would never play for any Australian team Bradman was involved with. Pepper decided to come to England instead. Alley, a man very like Pepper in temperament, felt similarly wronged by The Don. Bradman had assured Alley he would be picked for a tour of New Zealand and the future Colne and Blackpool pro had gone out and ordered several fresh sets of whites for the tour, only to learn via the wireless that he hadn't actually been selected.

Keith Miller, or so it was rumoured, had been deprived of the Australian captaincy by Bradman. After The Don retired from playing and became a selector everyone expected the charismatic former fighter pilot eventually to take charge of the national side. He didn't. It was said that this was because in the game against Essex in which Eric Price had been so severely mauled, Miller – feeling that Australia were simply humiliating weaker opposition and having been commanded to bat by his captain – deliberately got out for a duck. Nobody defied Bradman and got away unpunished. He vetoed Miller's appointment as successor to Lindsay Hassett, insisting on Ian Johnson instead. When I asked a veteran of the leagues what he made of this suggestion he said it sounded highly plausible. 'I played with a lot of Australians,' he said, 'and the impression I formed was that, while they all agreed Bradman was a genius as a player, most of them regarded him as a right little prick.'

Miller almost went into the leagues himself. He signed a contract to play for Rawtenstall in the 1947 season, but, allegedly under pressure from Bradman, later reneged on the deal. The Lancashire League charged him with breach of contract and put him on the blacklist with 'Bagger' Barnes. Bradman, incidentally, had been offered a contract in the Lancashire League by Accrington during the winter of 1931–2. After some thought he turned it down because, 'The

Accrington offer would of course have involved me in becoming a professional cricketer, which I did not want to do.' Well, quite.

After his problems in Australia, Pepper, in his own words, buried himself in league cricket. He signed up for Rochdale in the Central Lancashire League in 1947 and did the first double of a thousand runs and a hundred wickets in CLL history. After two seasons he moved on to Burnley in the Lancashire League where he did the double again, one of only three men ever to do so (the others were Vijay Hazare and Colin Miller). Shortly after his arrival in Lancashire the veteran league professional George Pope had told the Australian that, 'The important thing as a pro is that when you are on the field you project your personality.' League crowds liked big characters and Pepper was about as wide as would fit.

'As a bowler I'd put Pepp on the same level as Shane Warne,' Paul Rocca said. As a batsman he was one of the biggest hitters around. During the 1946 Victory series he'd almost hit the clock at Lord's. He'd struck a six during the Commonwealth XI tour of India that sailed straight out of the massive Wankhede Stadium. At the SCG he smacked the ball from number two ground over the stand to number one ground, a distance estimated at 140 yards from strike to first bounce.

Pepper was a roaring success at Burnley. Unsurprisingly he also fell foul of the authorities and had to write a letter of apology to the League President after some of his more ribald remarks had carried through the walls of the dressing room and into a function suite where an awards dinner was being held. After five seasons at Turf Moor the Australian returned to the CLL, playing for Radcliffe, Oldham, Royton and Worton.

On the field Pepper bristled with purpose and aggression. Anybody who didn't match up was likely to feel the rough edge of his tongue. Despite the fact that he was a spinner, Pepper expected to open the bowling. On one occasion the skipper of the side decided to hold him back and bring him on first change. After a dozen overs the batting side were sixty for no wicket and the captain threw the ball to the Australian. 'You're on now, pro,' he said. Pepper shook his head and threw the ball back. 'You bowled them in. You can fucking bowl them out.'

The umpires in particular suffered. During one Central Lancashire League game he rapped one off the batsman's pad. 'How's that?'

The umpire shook his head. 'Not out.'

'Not out?' Pepper asked in an apparently calm tone.

'Yes,' the umpire replied, 'it would have missed leg stump.'

'You are quite right, umpire,' Pepper said genially. 'It *would* have missed leg stump. It would not have hit the off stump either.' He paused for a moment to fill his lungs with air and then bellowed at a volume that rattled the windows in the clubhouse 'IT WOULD HAVE HIT FUCKING MIDDLE STUMP.'

Not that Pepper got everything his own way. In a game umpired by Harry Wood, a rejected shout for caught behind saw Pepper give vent to various colourful expressions relating to Wood's eyesight and parentage. When the Australian took his sweater at the end of the over he apologised for his outburst. 'No need to worry,' Wood replied, 'in the heat of the moment we all say things we may later regret'. In the next over Pepper had a large shout for LBW. Wood stared at him. 'Not out, you fat, bald, Australian bastard,' he said. Pepper enjoyed that immensely and it was apparently Wood who persuaded him to take up umpiring when he retired from the game in 1964.

Pepper was on the first class umpires list until 1979, but though he was well respected in the county game he was never appointed to umpire a test match. It was said that this was because the authorities thought he was a racist.

Pepper was great friends with Frank Worrell and Colly 'Mighty Mouse' Smith, and he also reputedly helped Radcliffe pro Gary Sobers financially, but some of his reported remarks, particularly to Indian and Pakistani players, don't read too well.

Cec Wright, who'd come up against Pepper when pro-ing for Crompton, said that he had always got on with the Australian: 'In the clubhouse he was good company, very friendly. What he said on the field was a different thing. When he crossed the boundary ropes he did what he thought would help his side win. I took no notice of it myself. It was just non-sense, you know?' Like Paul Rocca, Cec Wright is a man of unimpeachable niceness. It's hard to imagine everybody would be quite so forgiving.

Pepper made his home in Lancashire and died in Littleborough in 1993. In old age he was as forthright as ever. When Ian Botham was destroying the Australian attack during the 1981 Ashes series Pepper was asked what he made of him. 'Ian Botham?' he said. 'I could have bowled him with a cabbage with the outside leaves still on it.'

Pepp's fellow countryman Paul Skewes eventually fell for a quick forty. Yet despite the loss of the pro and the vociferous intervention of a large group of women who had congregated to the left of the clubhouse making a noise like a flock of Vera Duckworths, Middleton's innings continued to skip pleasantly along.

Middleton had a reputation for nurturing great players. It was at Glebe Road that Hedley Verity had learned his trade

as a professional, arriving at the club after a difficult time at
Accrington where, he complained plaintively to his father,
the amateur fielders refused to stay where he placed them.
It was there, too, that Frank Tyson, possibly the fastest
English bowler of all time, had started a career that would
reach its peak when he terrorised the Australian top order
during the 1954–5 Ashes series. Middleton was also the
place where Basil D'Oliveira made his entry into English
cricket.

D'Oliveira had been a sensation in what was known as the
'non-European' cricket of Cape Town. He'd hit lightning
quick hundreds, huge sixes and bowled opponents out single-
handedly. Since apartheid prevented D'Oliveira from playing
cricket professionally in South Africa, in 1958 he wrote to
John Arlott asking for help finding work as a cricketer in
England.

The writer and broadcaster may have disliked certain
aspects of Northern league cricket but he saw that it offered
the most realistic employment opportunity for an unknown
cricketer, so he in turn contacted John Kay, a journalist with
the *Manchester Evening News*. Kay had played for Middleton
and had strong family ties with the club. Initially lukewarm to
the idea of offering a contract to a man they'd never heard of
and whose experience of cricket was limited to playing in
leagues few English people knew anything about, the committee finally agreed to give the South African a chance in
1960. By then D'Oliveira had played successfully, and more
publicly, on a tour of Kenya with a South African Non-
European XI, though the fact that he was cheap – his first
contract was worth four hundred and fifty pounds for the
season and the cricketer was expected to pay his own fare
from Cape Town out of that – may have been more of a
factor in the final decision.

D'Oliveira travelled to Lancashire in the spring and into a
very different world from the one he was used to. 'I remember when Basil first came to Middleton,' Paul Rocca said. 'It
would be April, pre-season nets. He came into the dressing
room and was introduced to us all. And after we'd all said
hello, he asked, "Where do I get changed?" We said, "Well, in
here with us, of course."'

In his first season in the Central Lancashire League
D'Oliveira struggled to come to terms with conditions both on
and off the field. Claremont and the other grounds on which
he'd played in Cape Town looked to the outsider like patches
of wasteland with a piece of matting flung down as the batting strip. He'd never played on grass wickets before, on
mowed outfields, or in the sort of damp conditions where the
ball swerved around in the air.

Socially he was disoriented. 'When we went out with Basil
we noticed how when we walked down the street he always
lagged behind us slightly,' Paul Rocca recalled. 'We had to
really persuade him to come into pubs or cafés with us. If you
went to the pictures he always wanted to leave before the
house lights went up.'

Cec Wright recalls meeting D'Oliveira in Manchester one
night. 'We got on the bus to go home and Baz said, "I think
we ought to go and sit upstairs." I said, "Listen Baz, man.
This is England. We can sit wherever we like."'

'It was very sad,' Paul Rocca said. 'He was such a decent,
polite, quiet man. You didn't hear so very much about
apartheid in those days. But being with Basil, it really made
you realise how badly people were treated over there.'

D'Oliveira, like Learie Constantine, was intelligent and
resourceful. He knew Middleton was his big chance and he
worked hard to make the best of it. Everyone at the club liked
him and they helped him adapt as best they could. D'Oliveira,

the old-timers noted, often made mistakes but he never made the same mistake twice. He learned as he went.

After a shaky start the new professional began to get the measure of the conditions. In his sixth game, against Werneth, he struck seventy-eight. 'No innings in my life, before or since, has given me so much joy or been as significant as that one,' D'Oliveira would recall. He finished the season second in the CLL batting averages behind Radcliffe's Gary Sobers and also took seventy-one wickets at eleven apiece. Impressed, Middleton offered him another contract on improved terms. When he returned in 1961 he had his wife and son with him. That year, Sobers finished behind *him*.

After three seasons at Middleton D'Oliveira went to play in the Birmingham League to gain the residential qualification he needed to join Worcestershire. His verdict on the game in the Midlands: 'The Birmingham League cricket left me profoundly uninterested. It was pleasant enough, much closer to the southern game than anything I had known up north . . . Missing was the cut-throat determination to win that made the Lancashire leagues so exhilarating. Up there you had to be prepared to spill blood – and you often did – for victory. The Birmingham League was less fanatical. It was also of a lower standard.'

D'Oliveira's success paved the way for other 'non-European' South Africans to come and make a living in Lancashire (Clive Rice, a white cricketer who'd protested so vehemently against apartheid that he'd effectively been banned from playing in his own country, followed them). Cec Abrahams came over from Cape Town in the mid-sixties, played for Milnrow initially and then moved to Radcliffe where his big-hitting and medium pace off-cutters were instrumental in winning them back-to-back titles. Later he played for Oldham and for Elland in the Huddersfield League.

Abrahams made his home in Lancashire and his son, John Abrahams, captained the county side and now coaches England age-group teams.

Sulaiman 'Dik' Abed was signed by Enfield of the Lancashire League in 1968. He stayed for ten years, taking 969 wickets with his Barnes-like cutters and scoring 5528 runs for the club. In a poll of members in Enfield's centenary year Abed was voted the club's best ever professional, ahead of Clyde Walcott, Conrad Hunte and Madan Lal.

Omar Henry came to play as a professional in Lancashire in the seventies. He broke all batting records at Mickelhurst in the Saddleworth and District League. After the release of Nelson Mandela, Henry became the first non-white player to play for South Africa in the modern era.

Intriguingly, the only non-white player to play for South Africa before the dismantling of apartheid had also played as a professional in the Lancashire Leagues. Charlie Llewellyn was the illegitimate son of a white Englishman and a black woman from the island of Saint Helena. He was born in Pietermaritzburg and raised in poverty. A hard hitting left-hand batsman and a bowler of conventional left-arm spin with the occasional 'chinaman' dropped in after the manner of Johnny Wardle, Llewellyn was good enough to overcome the already entrenched racial prejudices of the South African Cricket Board and earn a place in the 1896 test team when he was still a teenager. The need to earn money brought him to England and he played first class cricket for Hampshire as a professional, impressing enough to be selected for an England test squad (he didn't make the final XI). In 1910 he was one of *Wisden*'s five Cricketers of the Year. Twelve months later he signed to play for Accrington in the Lancashire League. His arrival created a real stir. Llewellyn was the first overseas star to play in the Northern leagues. Large crowds came to watch him. In his first season Accrington's gate receipts doubled. The spectators were not disappointed. After an early innings the *Northern Daily Telegraph* noted, 'Every stroke was made with the ease and confidence of an artist with the bat.'

Llewellyn stayed at Accrington for ten seasons, hitting 6276 runs including a league record 188 not out against Bacup, which would eventually be surpassed by Learie Constantine. He also took nearly a thousand wickets and fielded superbly. He carried on playing for South Africa too, appearing in the Triangular Tournament of 1912 and scoring seventy-five against England at Lord's. Llewellyn's racial background seems to have passed unmentioned. It is said that this was because of his pale complexion – Wilfred Rhodes commented that Llewellyn looked 'rather sunburned' – though in truth he was little different in that respect than D'Oliveira, Abed or a host of other players who were denied any opportunity for advancement under the mad schemes of Hendrik Verwoerd and his followers.

Middleton's innings closed on 186–6. Up in the clubhouse I asked for a pint of mild. 'Do you want dark mild, or light mild?' the barmaid asked. I'd guess this is the only area of the country where you'd get that question.

When D'Oliveira arrived at Middleton the first man to come and introduce himself and to try to help the new boy settle in was the West Indian Roy Gilchrist. Gilchrist had been Middleton's pro for the two previous seasons. His act of kindness, fondly recalled by D'Oliveira many years later when he was an England star, may come as a surprise to some people, because Gilchrist's reputation is more for ferocity than generosity.

Roy Gilchrist was born and raised on a Jamaican plantation. He was destined for a life cutting sugar cane and seems to have received little in the way of formal education. During the 1951 tour of England it was noted that he could barely sign his name. He made his first impact taking six wickets for a Jamaican side in a game against the Duke of Norfolk's XI, who were touring the Caribbean. The game also saw his first disagreement with Gerry Alexander, a Cambridge blue and future West Indies captain. According to Gilchrist, Alexander was a brave but limited wicketkeeper, far less talented than either Clairmonte Depeiza or the Leeward Islands' stumper John Reid. To hear Gilchrist tell it, Alexander only made the test side because of class prejudice, the continuance of which would sour relations between the two men. 'Gilly from the plantation could never be on the same level as Gerry from the varsity,' he wrote in his 1963 autobiography *Hit Me for Six*. 'While fellows knew me as Roy Gilchrist, everyone seemed to regard him as Mr F. C. M. Alexander of Cambridge University.' It was the sort of chippy sentiment Northerners could identify with.

Gilchrist was selected for the 1957 tour of England. In the two previous tours the England batsmen had been bamboozled by those two little pals of mine, Ramadhin and Valentine, while the Three Ws – Weekes, Worrell and Walcott – battered the bowlers. This time around things did not go so well. In the first test at Edgbaston Peter May and Colin Cowdrey played Ramadhin with such determination and eventually ease that in a single innings they more or less destroyed his international career. Ramadhin bowled ninety-eight overs and took two wickets for 179 runs. Observers said the spring went out of Ramadhin's step and the sparkle out of his eyes long before England declared on 583 for four with May 285 not out.

At Lord's Gilchrist took four England wickets, but indications of what was to come occurred when wicketkeeper Godfrey Evans hit a streaky half century featuring numerous thick edges and lucky snicks. This, he later wrote, 'angered [Gilchrist] greatly . . . His eyes bulged ominously, and the next one he sent down would be a bouncer, even a head beamer. I'd lash out at him and get a tickle and run a single.'

At the other end Colin Cowdrey was not amused by Evans' antics. 'If you're going to keep doing that don't let's run any singles,' he shouted, 'I'm getting bouncers that are meant for you and they are very dangerous indeed.' Gilchrist was working himself into such a fury that even the fielders were alarmed. According to Evans, Frank Worrell called out from slip, 'Stop slashing at Gilly. I'm frightened to death standing here.'

If Gilchrist could terrorise Cowdrey and Worrell with his speed and ferocity there's little wonder he scared amateurs in the Lancashire leagues. And Gilly did scare people. When he was annoyed and bowling with the accelerator pressed to the floor it was said brave men would often walk even when they knew they hadn't hit the ball. 'As soon as that delivery thumped into the wicky's gloves they'd be off without even waiting for an appeal,' Paul Rocca said with a chuckle.

Dr Don Longbottom, the captain of Royton, had a plan to deal with Gilchrist. He decided that the thing to do was to keep on the Jamaican's good side. When Middleton batted Longbottom took up a position at slip. 'Oh good shot, Roy' he called whenever the Jamaican put bat to ball. 'Well played. Lovely drive, Gilly.'

'The Doc's idea was to mollify him,' John Cleary, who'd played in that game, told me. John had been a headmaster and was now President of the Central Lancashire League, though locally he was best known for running the Slipperama slipper stall in Congleton Market. 'We all had to try and prevent Gilly getting upset or excited,' he said, 'that was the plan.'

Did it work? I asked. Did Gilchrist bowl any slower?

'Absolutely not,' Cleary said. 'The first ball I faced was so quick I couldn't even see it.'

Cec Wright was a big friend of Gilchrist's. They'd known each other in Jamaica. It was on the quick bowler's recommendation that Cec had been offered a contract to play for Crompton. I asked Wright if his friendship had made any difference when he'd faced 'The Black Flash'. 'No it did not,' Cec said. Then a few seconds later he said, 'Well no, there was one time. I come in to bat against Gilly. The wicket was a fast one. First delivery I played forward and the ball jumped up and – bang – into my thigh.' Cec winced at the memory and rubbed the top of his leg reflexively. 'No thigh pads in those days. It hurt. Next ball I go forward again. Same thing. Bang! And the next one too. At the end of the over Gilly come down to me. He had his cap in his hand. He give it to me and says, "Put that in your front pocket, Cec. Next time I hit you on the thigh it will cushion the blow."'

No thigh pads, and no arm guards or chest protectors, or helmets either. Facing Gilchrist in fading light on a rough pitch was the stuff of nightmares. Unlike some later West Indian pace bowlers who'd play league cricket – Griffith, Garner, Walsh, Bishop, Wes Hall, Michael Holding, Franklyn Stephenson, Wayne Daniels et al – Gilchrist wasn't a tall or a powerful looking man. He was short and slim, with narrow shoulders. In photographs of Gilchrist when he's not bowling he doesn't look like a paceman at all. The photos of him when he is bowling are a different matter. The sort of mighty leap associated with the heroes in radio serials preceded Gilchrist's delivery stride. His arm, sleeves buttoned down, is high and straight, his wrist cocked. Even in two-dimensional black and white stills you get a genuine impression of speed and motion. In full colour, 3D and coming straight at you it must have been genuinely hair-raising.

Like Pepper and D'Oliveira, Gilchrist's career in the leagues was a kind of exile. During the winter of 1957–8 Gilchrist had blasted his way through the Pakistani batting line-up. In 1958 he was doing something similar on the West Indies tour of India. In boiling temperatures and on feather-bed tracks he took six wickets in Bombay, nine in Calcutta, five in Madras and six more in Delhi. Things off the field went less smoothly. There was a row with Basil Butcher at fielding practice that ended with Gilchrist hurling a ball at his legs, a reprimand from Alexander for shouting too much in the pavilion, and then there was the beamer problem. Head-high full tosses had always been part of Gilchrist's arsenal but in India Alexander banned them. 'They are too dangerous,' he told the West Indies pace trio of Gilchrist, Wes Hall and Jaswick Taylor.

Gilchrist disagreed. The crisis came during a game against North Zone whose skipper, Swaranjit Singh, was an old Cambridge buddy of Gerry Alexander. The patrician Singh (who also played for Warwickshire and the MCC) aggravated Gilchrist by smacking him for four and then remarking, 'A beautiful shot, was it not?'

Gilchrist's answer was to whizz a beamer at him. Next ball he dug one in short, the batsman popped it up to short leg where Alexander dropped a simple chance. By now apoplectic with rage at what he probably viewed as an old school tie conspiracy, Gilchrist flung down two beamers in a row, both of which flashed past Singh's chin. At the end of the over the West Indian's captain told Gilchrist to go immediately to the dressing room, he wouldn't bowl again in the match and a substitute would replace him in the field. The following day Gilly was sent home in disgrace.

By now home meant Lancashire. Gilchrist had been signed up by Middleton during the 1957 tour of England. In 1958 he'd taken 137 wickets for the Central Lancashire League club, ninety-seven of them clean bowled. His tally included five hat-tricks, and Middleton won the title for the first time in decades. 'In most games,' Paul Rocca said, 'I was the only fielder in front of the wicket. Gilly always had four slips and two gulleys.'

The 1959 season was equally productive. The Jamaican picked up 145 wickets and Middleton were champions again. The season however was not a happy one for Gilchrist. His expulsion from the West Indies tour had brought negative headlines, doubts had been raised about his action and the fear his hostility had raised in opponents had now turned to resentment. In away fixtures the Middleton pro was baited by spectators. At Oldham a group of women sitting on the boundary yelled 'Killer!' at him. In the final game of the season, the return fixture against Oldham, a Gilchrist beamer struck a young batsman on the thigh, causing him to collapse in agony. Bill Lawton. the captain of the Oldham team (and husband of comedy actor Dora Bryan), was so upset he called his team off the field and refused to play on. 'He was trying to kill our players,' Lawton said. The incident made national headlines, though Paul Rocca now feels that Lawton's actions were pre-planned. 'It was a bit of a publicity stunt,' he told me.

Feeling that umpires and opponents were persecuting him, Gilchrist left Globe Street and signed to play for Bacup in the 1960 season. Once again his pace was brutally effective. He took 126 wickets and the Lanehead club carried off the championship. The West Indian had signed a four-year deal but asked to be freed from his contract when a better offer came along from Great Chell of the North Staffordshire League. Sensing perhaps that forcing Gilchrist to stay wouldn't be the wisest course, Bacup agreed.

The 1961 season was to be even more tumultuous than those that had gone before. In Staffordshire Gilchrist was no-balled for throwing, staged a go-slow on the pitch and, after suffering racial abuse at various grounds, finally cracked at Stone and attacked a spectator who called him a 'black bastard'. The League Committee phoned him a few days later and told him that he had been banned from ever playing in the League again. His contract was terminated with immediate effect.

While all this was going on Gilchrist had received a letter from the West Indies Cricket Board inviting him to travel to British Guiana for a test trial, and asking about his availability for future West Indies tours. Out of work and broke, Gilchrist took the boat from Liverpool to Georgetown. Unfortunately by the time he arrived news had reached the West Indies of his North Staffordshire League ban. His journey had been in vain. The authorities in the Caribbean told him that in light of his behaviour in England they could no longer consider him for selection. His test career had effectively ended when he was just twenty-four. He'd played thirteen games for the West Indies and taken fifty-seven wickets.

Gilchrist went back to Lancashire and signed on for Bacup again. Off the field he worked on the buses, driving with the same passion for speed he showed when bowling. He had two more seasons at Lanehead, then returned to the Central Lancashire League with Crompton, who promptly won the league title. His next stop was the Saddleworth and District, then he crossed the Pennines and played for East Bierley in the Bradford League. Then he returned once again to the CLL, this time with Castleton Moor. By now Gilchrist's action was constantly questioned and he became so paranoid about it that he almost had a fight with Johnny Wardle when the

Yorkshireman turned up with a new cine-camera and started filming the game.

The rage that filled Gilchrist seemed to increase rather than diminish as he got older. 'Whatever the opposite of mellowing is, that's what Gilly did,' people said. Part of his problem was that he was no good with money. 'He was well paid but whatever he got he always spent more,' they said. 'The minute Gilly had money he bought a car, or a new suit. He never saved anything. He was always in debt.'

In 1967 Gilchrist was sentenced to three months' probation after burning his wife Lynn's face with a hot iron. 'I hate to think that English sport has sunk so low that brutes will be tolerated because they are good at games,' the judge said.

Despite his problems Gilchrist went on playing league cricket until 1979 and took over a hundred wickets every season. He returned to Jamaica in the nineties and died there of Parkinson's disease aged sixty-seven.

Gilchrist was certainly one of the greatest bowlers of his generation. Paul Rocca, who'd faced all the famous pace men who'd come to pro in the north during the sixties and seventies, rated him as 'the fastest bowler of all time'. So did John Cleary. When I asked Cec Wright if Gilchrist was the quickest bowler he'd ever played against he thought for a moment, 'One of the two,' he said. I asked him who the other one was. 'Patrick Patterson,' Cec replied.

Patterson (whose other given name was Balfour) was a raw, ungainly-looking Jamaican who'd ripped through the English batting like a buzzsaw in the 1985–6 tour of the Caribbean. Cec had encountered Patterson when he'd pro-ed for Austerland in the Saddleworth and District League and he winced slightly at the memory of it.

Graham Gooch rated Patterson as the scariest bowler he'd

ever come up against. Gooch had played against all the West
Indian greats, against Dennis Lillee and Jeff Thomson, Imran
Khan and Allan Donald. If he said Patterson was the fastest,
then it's hard to argue. And Cec Wright said Gilchrist was as
quick as Patterson. You can draw your own conclusions from
that.

There was no one of Gilchrist's pace bowling for Middleton at The Racecourse, but the attack they did have rattled
through Radcliffe, who limped to ninety-eight all out, Saiyed
picking up 4–72. Middleton won by eighty-eight runs.

In the pub where I worked with Mrs Jessup there was a
regular who drank on his own at the bar every pay night. He
batted at number five for Redcar in the North Yorkshire South
Durham, but he'd been born and brought up in Lowerhouse
and had played for his hometown club as a teenager when
Gilchrist was pro-ing for Bacup. Recalling it, sitting at the bar
with a pint of Cameron's Strongarm between his fists, he said,
'Put it this way, it's an experience I'm glad I've *had*.'

Middleton finished in fourth place. Ken Skewes scored 782
runs at 60.15 before a blow in the face during the warm up for
a Twenty20 match put a premature end to his season. Usman
Tariq hit a thousand runs and took forty-four wickets for
Radcliffe. Despite his efforts, the team ended the season
second from bottom.

Pot Pie and Savage Ignorance

Bacup

It was pouring down in Haslingden. The dark stone houses clutched close together and interspersed with three-storey sixties maisonettes, were the architectural equivalent of a hooded mob. Everybody you saw seemed to have at least one limb in plaster or be walking with a mechanical aid. 'Cars Attacked Here This Week' read a police notice in the car park off the main street. 'Put A Burglar Away Today' urged another hanging from a lamp-post round the corner, near a shop advertising cheap booze and low tar king size. In the window of one of the houses a sign with a picture of a Rottweiler on it bore the legend 'Go ahead, break in, make my day!' In the rain the town looked resolutely grim and so did the prospect of watching cricket.

Cissy Green's pieshop in Deardengate was a haven in the gloom. 'Fantastic pot pie with peas £1.25' it said in the window. The pie was indeed fantastic, the first genuinely made-on-site baking I'd had all summer. The cheese and onion version had real Lancashire cheese, white, acidic and crumbly, in it. The pastry was hand crimped and encouragingly misshapen. The marrowfat peas were the grey-green of iguana skin. The jam turnover was filled with red conserve as

vivid as a party balloon. The Chorley cake was a proletarian
Eccles, with thicker, less buttery pastry and fewer currants.
This – for better or worse – was really authentic British food.
The gastronomy of cold, wet days, poverty, and pits and fac-
tories. It was so high in cholesterol, eating it was practically an
extreme sport. 'If you lived on this you'd soon have a heart
attack,' Catherine said. I looked outside at the charcoal sky
and the woman in the Adidas shellsuit bottoms slapping her
little girl on the legs, 'Maybe that's the idea,' I said.

The pie was hearty and we'd got good chips too, from the
Big Lamp Chippy, served by cheery Chinese ladies, in a place
with net curtains and condensation running down the windows. There's a café out the back and I noticed that when the
staff put the battered cod on to the plate they punched a hole
in the middle of it and poured in a colourless liquor. I had no
idea what it was. To me, East Lancs is as exotic as Ulan Bator.

After we'd finished our meal we drove around trying to
identify the Woolpack pub, which is the landmark for
Haslingden's Bentgate ground. But by the time we found it,
the water was running down the gutterings with a big gurgling
noise that sounded like the death rattle of today's proposed
Lancashire League game between Haslingden and local arch-
rivals Rawtenstall.

Convinced that any thought of play was the distant dream
of a madman, we headed instead up Rossendale, past a factory that billed itself as the manufacturer of Venor Tufting
Machines, with a plan to call in at Bacup, and then go off up
towards Clitheroe and Settle in the hope that the weather
might clear, or we'd find a pub that didn't look like strangers
would be chased out of it by an angry mob throwing alcopop
bottles.

We drove through Rawtenstall with its civic gardens and
domed public library and other sturdy monuments to heavy-

handed Victorian philanthropy. Rawtenstall's apparent respectability made it appear the polar opposite of neighbouring Haslingden. It's like they are two brothers from an Alger Hiss story, one of whom has chosen the path of rectitude and the other who hasn't.

Mind you, by all accounts Bacup makes Haslingden look like St Moritz. In the 1840s a visitor to the town, the Reverend J. W. Kennedy, had noted that 'a savage ignorance seems to reside in the place' and claimed that the only civilised persons he came across there were the schoolmistress and the policemen. Government sanitary inspectors meanwhile discovered quarters where 'men, women and frequently dogs form a promiscuous herd, all sleeping in the same close confined room'.

Things improved dramatically in the years following the end of the American Civil War when the sudden influx of cotton created a gold-rush atmosphere in East Lancashire. Suddenly Haslingden, Rawtenstall and Bacup had become boomtowns. The populations of the three boroughs doubled in thirty years. By the twenties, when Learie Constantine arrived in Nelson, however, those days had passed. The first trade depression had occurred in the 1890s and recoveries since had been fitful at best.

These days Bacup has an air of *The League of Gentlemen* about it, which is maybe not so surprising as parts of the BBC comedy series were filmed there. Narrow streets of terraced houses lead up to the Lanehead Ground. They are the same terraces that feature in Tony Ray Jones's evocative sixties photographs of the Britannia Coconut Dancers, a local clog-dance troupe who performed with blacked-up faces.

We passed Bacup Borough FC's ramshackle stadium, turned down a road called Cowtoot Lane and drove into the cricket ground through the Howard Gates, past a little sentry box embossed with a frieze of a stag's head. It was a quarter past two. The rain had slackened slightly and some old geezers were standing around outside the clubhouse smoking amid the puddles. 'Any chance of play?' I asked. I expected a gale of derisive laughter in response. Not a bit of it. 'We've phoned Blackburn and they say the weather's fine and coming this way,' one of the men said. 'It drains well, this field. Once rain stops we'll be on in twenty minutes.'

Lancastrians take cricket seriously. A bit of weather doesn't put them off. When the Antiguan Andy Roberts signed to play for Haslingden in 1981 he'd spent his first Saturday night in the clubhouse watching a blizzard swirl around the town. The next morning the captain picked him up in the car and they followed a snowplough through to East Lancashire's ground at Alexandra Meadows. Roberts couldn't see the point of the journey, but the game was played even though there was still ice on the outfield. The West Indian bowled seventeen overs and took 1–50. It's fair to say the conditions were not what he was used to.

Bacup Cricket Club was founded in 1860 and promptly lost a two innings match to Rossendale rivals Haslingden by four wickets. When the two met again at Lanehead in 1865 things turned distinctly nasty, the game played out in a 'torrent of hisses, hoots, curses and ungentlemanly conduct'. Little wonder that when the Lancashire League was founded in 1892 one of the first things the ruling committee ordered was that posters commanding the crowd to respect umpiring decisions be posted in all the grounds.

Lanehead is much calmer these days. The ground is high up above the town, perched on a hillside and overlooking the valley. It's a neat, well-kept patch of vivid green in the middle of the dark industrial landscape. It's hardly surprising that local people would choose to spend time here. There's a lovely old pale and dark green wooden pavilion-cum-café with decorative lattice panels on the outer walls, a glass-windowed scorebox and a solid one-storey brick clubhouse that stretches practically the length of the square boundary and includes what may well be the best tea hutch in the sporting world. There are no notices telling spectators not to hiss or hoot any more, but on the brick groundsman's shed near the entrance a sign does advise that stray dogs will be handed over to 'the local dog warden' 'by order of the committee'.

The players' pavilion is a modern red brick building with a balcony the teams can sit out on whenever the weather allows. It's set well away from everything and given that it includes the changing rooms I think that's a wise idea. Sports club dressing rooms are not generally places for those of sensitivity. And you certainly wouldn't want them near a food preparation area. Put a dozen men in an enclosed space, especially on a Sunday morning, and you are likely to end up with a scent so rich and complex even Jilly Goolden would struggle to pick out its myriad pungent strands. Though one thing is for certain – after a spell of trying she'd certainly reconsider using the phrase 'a really strong whiff of farmyard' about a glass of vin de pays.

One Sunday cricket team I played for took less than ten minutes to fill the changing area with a stink so thick it hung in the air like ectoplasm. Athlete's foot, mouldering socks, cheap deodorant and the collateral damage of a Saturday night of beer and curry produced something less like a hum than a full production of Wagner. It was just as well most pavilions are securely pinioned to the ground otherwise there'd have been a severe danger of us floating away like a hot air balloon. You know the opening sequence of John Carpenter's film *The Fog*, when all the shelves in the mini-mart start vibrating? Well, that's pretty much what it was like around that team.

One of our number, Demon Bob the wicketkeeper, had guts that hissed and gurgled like a Gaggia coffee machine. He was given to such savage and unholy eruptions that at one point a visiting umpire threatened to call a priest and have him exorcised. To this day, whenever I hear the phrase 'you could cut the atmosphere with a knife' I think of Demon Bob. Though in his case you'd have needed a two-handed saw and a squad of lumberjacks at the very least.

The combination of Demon Bob's explosive intestines and the crouching position of the wicketkeeper was not a happy one. If he'd had a curry the night before he was quite capable of blowing fine leg's cap off.

When the rain stopped at Bacup there was the usual palaver of removing the covers, players and groundsman sponging the moisture off them with what looked like giant paint rollers. The big sheets of polythene that had been covering the rest of the square were so vast it took ten men to carry each of them to the boundary as they flapped in the breeze like mainsails.

As they warm up, the Ramsbottom coach hit catches with a fluorescent orange bat, while a black pace bowler, Toby McClean, thick set and square-shouldered like Wayne Daniels, went through a series of stretches so vigorous that at times it looked like he was trying to flick his head over the clubhouse. Ramsbottom Cricket Club was established in 1845. They play at Acre Bottom. The club badge is a ram's head, which seems a missed opportunity, all in all.

Like Bacup, Ramsbottom were founder members of the Lancashire League, which grew out of the earlier North West Cricket League. The North West Cricket League had begun in 1890, inspired by the formation of the Football League, itself a Lancashire invention, one that, right up until the arrival of the new millennium, would maintain its head-quarters on the coast in Lytham St Annes.

The Lancashire League has barely altered since its foundation. The only major changes it has undergone were that in 1899 the rule allowing two professionals was amended to allow just one, and that one of the founder members, Bury, had quit after two seasons and been replaced by Todmorden which, controversially, was just across the county boundary in Yorkshire. The League's line-up of teams has not altered since. The fourteen clubs, all from a thirty-mile-wide belt of land to the west of the Pennines, have been playing each other twice a season every season since.

The Lancashire League was stoutly independent and right from the start has pursued a policy of robust egalitarianism that stood in marked contrast to what went on in the South. Here no distinction was made between players of different backgrounds. There were no separate dressing rooms, entrances or gates for gentlemen.

In county cricket a clear demarcation was made between the professionals and the amateurs. On the scorecard only the surnames of the professionals were printed while the amateurs' initials were recorded in full. Later this system was refined, the amateurs' initials being placed before their surnames and the professionals' after it. This lead to the now infamous Lord's PA announcement: 'On today's scorecard F. J. Titmus should read Titmus, F. J.'. There was nothing like that in Accrington or Church, Burnley or Nelson. Here the only distinction between the players was their ability.

I should say that in many ways I deplore the move away from players' initials. The players' initials were once a source of fascination to juvenile cricket fans of all ages. During my teenage years I wasted many hours that might more profitably have been spent vandalising phoneboxes, poring over the

Playfair Cricket Annual. I have forgotten much that I learned during my adolescence – how to calculate velocity, the names of the bones in the ear, where I put the keys to my grandfather's shed – but I will go to my grave knowing that the T in J. R. T. Barclay (Sussex) stood for Troutbeck, and that had Gordon Greenidge opted to be called by his first given name rather than his second we'd have known him as Cuthbert.

Wind snapped the black and white Bacup CC flags as the sun briefly appeared and spectators, apparently alerted that a start was about to be made, began to arrive by car and on foot. 'Play will commence at three-fifteen,' a passer-by bellowed as the umpires disappeared into the little room reserved for their use under the scoreboard. (It's quite palatial compared to what they have at some grounds. At one place I visited in West Yorkshire the umpires huddled in what looked like an open-plan coal bunker.)

People stroll around the ground talking in their soft Lancashire accents. 'Well, I would of got it, but Laura got to the front before us,' one woman said to her husband. 'How'd anybody as big as that run faster than you?' he asked. 'Did you have a fridge on your back?'

An old man, asked how he's getting on, replied, 'Not great. To be honest, it's only thought of getting the free TV licence that's keeping us going.'

Bacup is rough and ready, but Ramsbottom has high-class restaurants and an award-winning farmers market. It's much nearer to Manchester than Rossendale and I suspect a bit more in footballers' wives territory. Their captain won the toss and elected to field.

The opening bowler, from the Howard Gate end, is McLean. He has a sparkling ear stud and a general air of cosmopolitan swagger about him. He once took seven wickets, all clean bowled, in a second-XI game and it was easy to see how, as he worked up a fair head of steam in the blustery conditions. In his second over a snorting delivery knocked back the Bacup number one's off stump; unfortunately it was a no-ball. At the other end Michael Haslam, a left-arm pace man of more homespun style, ran in against the backdrop of a primary school. Haslam produced one of the best spells of fast bowling I'd see all summer, right up there with Ranga Godage's display at Lascelles Hall. He bowled quick and slightly short of a length, smacking the batters about the knuckles as frequently and brutally as an old-fashioned schoolmaster.

The wicket played its part, too. It was damp and the ball broke the surface. At least one delivery an over popped up unexpectedly. You needed stout gloves. Anybody playing forward could do with a gum shield. I once played in a match for my father's works team and saw a bloke get his front teeth knocked out through his top lip going forward to a good length ball. In the same match I was caught at gully the fielder diving to grab the ball one-handed. It was a good catch, but what really stuck in my mind was the fact that the bloke that caught it had a fag in his mouth at the time and it didn't even fall out.

Bacup has its own Barmy Army. There is only one of them, but he made up in volume what he lacked in numbers. Sitting behind the bowler's arm, just beyond the boundary fence, nursing a carrier bag filled with superlager and a natural sense of injustice he kept up a constant stream of hooting and hissing. 'Run 'em up, move 'em out,' he yelled. 'That's his only shot, is that. He's Backfoot Bertha, this boy. Get it up his nose.'

The quality of professionals playing in the Northern leagues is certainly not as high as it had been in the fifties and sixties. Even the seventies and eighties seem like a faded and glorious era. A steady lowering of quality had begun in the mid-nineties. The problems were the proliferation of international cricket, with its endless cycle of tours and limited-over competitions, the tighter work permit restrictions that had done for Simon Beare at Workington, and falling attendances (the latter was not a new problem – between 1950 and 1959 Lancashire League gates had dropped by 40 per cent). Yet despite these obstacles the bigger leagues continued to attract high-class cricketers, and there were none bigger than the Lancashire League. While nobody could claim that the overall standard was as high as it had been in, say, 1962 when Wes Hall, Roy Gilchrist, Chester Watson, Conrad Hunte, Basil Butcher, Johnny Wardle, Seymour Nurse, Chandu Borde and Peter Philpott had all been playing, the fact was that of Australia's first choice starting eleven for the test series with England, three – Michael Clarke, Marcus North and Nathan Hauritz – had played here. For the 2009 season West Indies regular Brendon Nash was at East Lancashire, New Zealand test players Ian Butler and Robin Peterson at Lowerhouse and Nelson. Colne pro Anwar Ali, meanwhile, had played Twenty20 matches for Pakistan.

Not that all the big-name pros were a rip-roaring success, it should be said. Huw 'Toey' Tayfield, a South African off-spinner who'd tormented England's batsmen in the mid-fifties, had a very thin time of it at East Lancashire in 1956, while the great Ray Lindwall, whom Nelson paid a massive £1300 for the 1953 season, hardly proved a good return on investment. When the Australian made some mild remarks about the quality of the slip fielding not being quite of the standard he was used to, the response from beyond the boundary was swift and brutal: 'You should try bowling at the bloody stumps, then, shouldn't you?' Many rate Ray Lindwall as the greatest fast bowler of all time, but in East Lancashire the feeling persists that he was over-rated.

And then there was Fred Trueman. The great Yorkshireman had been brought in as a stand-in pro for Bill Alley at Colne for a match with Burnley and travelled over the Pennines convinced that a huge collection was his for the taking. He returned home having bagged three wickets for ninety-seven runs and been clean bowled for a duck. The fact that Trueman took over three hundred test wickets only added to the local view that international cricket wasn't all it was cracked up to be.

Ramsbottom's pro for 2009 was Brenton Parchment, a Jamaican who had captained the West Indies under-19 team and played a couple of tests as opening bat in the 2008 series in South Africa. He'd now turned twenty-seven and, having been a teenage wonderboy, seemed to have shown little indication of developing into a top-class player. He'd been picked up by Ramsbottom after three good seasons in the Bolton League with Farnworth. He'd also had a spell at Middlesbrough in the North Yorkshire South Durham League. He's tall and loose-limbed and when called on to bowl at Bacup jogged easily to the wicket before delivering the ball with a whippy arm action that generated surprising pace and hop. His use of the bouncer provokes the Barmy Army to bellow, 'Come on, umpire! Intimidation!'

The ease with which Parchment produced this venom seems to me the measure of the professional sportsman. What the rest of us would have to risk a strangulated hernia to achieve he can do with the languid nonchalance of James Bond lighting a black Sobranie at the conclusion of a fine dinner at Maxim's.

With Haswell and then Parchment in full flow Bacup struggle. A man walking by shook his head as he watched one of Bacup's middle order struggling to cope. 'He's all bottom hand. He's a right ruddy shoveller, this lad,' he complained. Parchment took four wickets and Haslam got five as Bacup were bowled out for 131, Kiwi professional Nathan McCullum top scoring with twenty-nine. McCullum is from Otago, and knocking on thirty. He's played a couple of one-day internationals for New Zealand, but is only in the Bacup side because of an injury to the appointed pro, Ryan Broad, a beefy Aussie who opens the batting for Queensland.

During the interval Catherine and I added to our calorie count by buying big mugs of steaming tea and delicious slices of moist Bakewell tart from the tea bar. The latter was easily the best thing I'd eat at cricket all summer. Others punters are queuing up for pie-and-peas, coating the pastry with the pickled red cabbage that sits on the bar top with the salt and the vinegar.

In the clubhouse, between the ladies' and gents' toilet doors, there's a big picture of the great West Indian batsman Everton Weekes, side parting, pearly-toothed grin, standing in front of the old pavilion at Lanehead.

Weekes spent seven seasons at Bacup in the fifties, scoring 9069 runs for them at an average of 91.61, and including twenty-five centuries. He wore an Army and Navy greatcoat even on what the locals considered the hottest summer days and lodged in Gordon Street, where the landlady, Mrs Sharrold, fed him up on meat-and-potato pies. Weekes got his Christian name because his father supported Everton. When the West Indian told Shipley-born Jim Laker this, the off-spinner replied that it was just as well his dad hadn't been a fan of West Bromwich Albion.

The Barbadian was a brilliant batsman who could produce his effervescent best on any surface. His style was so special, precise yet exuberant, that dozens of cricket lovers turned up at Lanehead on weekday nights just to watch him in the nets. Like Constantine, Weekes knew the value of a bit of showmanship. One day when a young medium pacer was bowling to him, the Bajan waited until the ball had left the bowler's hand, dropped his bat, reached back, uprooted the middle stump and cover drove the delivery perfectly with that instead. The applause from the spectators went on for several minutes. This might be apocryphal, but it has become part of history.

Weekes, along with Frank Worrell and Clyde Walcott, was part of the famous trio of West Indian middle order batsmen nicknamed the Three Ws. Frank Worrell was the professional at Radcliffe. An elegant stroke-maker, the Jamaican was a man of quiet dignity who studied for an economics degree at Manchester University during the week and impressed everyone who met him. At Radcliffe there was a bronze sculpture of Worrell in the bar and a plaque on the terraced house where he and his family had lived. The old fellow who as a boy had watched George Francis bowl at The Racecourse had lived next door. 'Our daughters were born at the same time,' he recalled, 'and every afternoon when it was coming up to visiting time Frank would knock and we'd get the bus to the maternity hospital. I can still picture the two of us sitting together on that bus, him with a little jar of homemade jam in his hand as a gift for his wife. He was a great cricketer, a smashing fellow, and everyone in Radcliffe loved him.'

While Weekes was at Bacup and Worrel at Radcliffe, Clyde Walcott was playing for Enfield, where he became the first batsman in league history to finish the season with an average of over one hundred (Weekes shattered the record the following year, averaging a staggering 158.25). On Saturday nights the three of them would meet up at a chip shop in Clayton-le-Moors, which belonged to Lancashire stalwart Jack

Simmons's Aunty Bertha, for a fish supper. It's the sort of scene, combining the fabulous with the homespun, that was the hallmark of league cricket in the North.

As Catherine and I ate our Bakewell tart and wondered about having a scone or two, a couple of old men standing nearby started talking.

'Are you going to Rammy tomorrow?'

'I am.'

'Have you got a lift?'

'I have.'

'Who's taking you?'

'Me.'

There's a similar comical air to nearly everything we overheard. It's something about the Lancashire accent. Although Bacup doubled for Royston Vasey, the style of humour is less grim, more gentle. At one point a ball crossed the boundary and a man standing nearby made a fumbling attempt to pick it up, mis-fielding the ball several times and then chasing after it trying to pick it up. Watching the display his mate yelled, 'He's not practised, you know. It's pure reflex, is that.'

Bacup's 131 didn't seem like much of a total, but it was hard to tell given the way the ball jumped about when Ramsbottom bowled. In the field, Bacup wore white fleece jumpers with numbers and names on the back and a sponsor's logo on the front. The bowler from the school end was Spencer, nicknamed Dingus. Short, stocky and balding, he bowled at a lively clip with a vigorous action. My impression is of him red-cheeked with effort, though I may be projecting.

At the Howard Gate end McCullum bowled tight off-spinners round the wicket. He didn't seem to turn the ball much but he was accurate and niggled away. He took the wicket of Wood with the score on three and Parchment strode to the wicket, windmilling his arms. Without bothering to play himself in he straight drove a four, pulled another delivery so heartily the ball raced out through the gate and down the hill as if it had had enough and was making a getaway. As if to chastise it for its escape the Jamaican then smashed it into the radiator grille of a Land Rover Discovery parked at long on.

For about fifteen minutes it looked as if the professional would win the game for his team single-handed and inside the hour, but then he essayed a mighty head-in-the-air swish at a shortish ball from Spencer that didn't bounce much and was clean bowled. The one-man Barmy Army is exultant: 'You are out!' he bellowed, adding, 'I could have played a better shot than that at the seaside.'

The Ramsbottom coach walked past shaking his head in disgust. 'How much are you paying that one, then?' a man leaning on a Ford Focus shouted at him. 'Too bloody much,' the Barmy Army crowed in response as the coach stomped silently on his way.

Another Ramsbottom wicket went down to an excellent overhead catch on the square leg boundary, and the visitors were reduced to 40–4 after a run out from a good throw by cover. Frustrated, Ramsbottom's opener Webb slogged across the line and was caught at mid-on for ten. Bacup's fielding is sharp as a tack. Little doubt the pre-season kickboxing they'd done at Alf's Black Belt Academy in Stacksteads had paid off.

When Brown was trapped LBW by McCullum with the score on sixty-six it looked all over for the visitors, but they recovered thanks to the late middle order. Mark Dentith hit mightily. One huge six sailed over the wall and into a garden, fours thump into the whitewashed boundary walls. Jack Walmsley played equally ambitiously at the other end and the pair added forty for the seventh wicket. Suddenly Rammy needed just twenty-five to win. On the field and round the boundary the atmosphere intensified. The joking stopped. This was what writer John Kay called 'the raw meat of league cricket'.

In response to the crisis Bacup brought back Dingus Spencer. He hurtled to the wicket, puffing with strain and clean bowled two batsmen in a single over. The last man spooned up a simple catch and Ramsbottom were all out for 117.

As the players trooped back to the pavilion the Bacup Barmy Army marched off, carrier bag in hand, his triumphant muttering accompanied by the rhythmic clacking of empty lager cans.

Ramsbottom finished the season in ninth place. Brenton Parchment scored nine hundred runs and took sixty-four wickets. His contract was not renewed, however, and in the autumn the club announced that he would be replaced by the former Indian test player Aakash Chopra. Bacup finished second bottom, just above Rawtenstall. Ryan Broad will not be returning in 2010 because he 'is getting married'. Accrington won the title on the final day. The winning runs were scored by sixty-two-year-old David Lloyd.

Stroking it like a Kitten

Ashington

Some years ago I met a famous retired sportsman. The famous retired sportsman had once been one of the most feared bowlers on the planet. When he was in what sportswriters like to call 'his pomp' he ran in whirling, knees and elbows pumping. It was not elegant. The only thing that was coordinated about him was that he was wearing the same coloured shirt and trousers.

When I met him, though he had aged. His back was bowed and his hair had taken on a greyish hue.

A small and slightly nervous audience had gathered round the great man. No one quite knew how to proceed. There was a series of silences punctuated by foot shuffling and coughs. Then one among us ventured to remark that Viv Richards looked set to miss an upcoming test match because of haemorrhoids. 'Wonder if that's a common complaint among international cricketers?' someone else speculated jokily.

'Oh yes,' he said. 'Very common. I mean, old Bob . . . had 'em terrible. Gary . . . had to stop fielding at slip on account of he couldn't bend down. Then there was Tony . . . the guys on the State circuit didn't call him "Grapes" for nothing. Alan . . . he used to have to sit on an inflatable cushion when he was waiting to go in to bat. Jack . . . ate his tea standing up. Made you fair wince to watch him put his jock-strap on . . .'

On and on and on he went ('Dave . . . had to have his trousers made with extra gusseting. You should have heard Frank squeal that time he mistook the Deep Heat for the Anusol . . .') while we nodded and exclaimed, 'Really?', 'You don't say' and 'You'd never have thought it when you watched him bat at Bramall Lane' whenever we thought fit. Because, surprising though it may seem, English etiquette does not advise on the correct response when one of the world's leading test wicket takers begins discussing the rectal problems of men you hero-worshipped as a boy.

After half an hour the famous retired sportsman finally shut up. Whether he had run out of proctologic information, or simply been sent into a coma by the sound of his own voice we were unable to determine, such was the speed of our exit.

The X32 bus heading north out of Newcastle rambled in much the same manner, though it didn't tell me anything about cricketers' bottoms, obviously. In Bedlington the shutters were down at the Open Learning Centre and in front of me on the bus a twelve-year-old girl read a magazine article with the headline 'His Out-of-Control Demands for Sex' while her mother stared at her mobile phone like somebody awaiting a sign from God.

Northwards and eastwards we went, through Bomarsund where the local cricket club Bomarsund Welfare had once been star performers in the Haig National Village Cup. In 1975 they'd won the trophy at Lord's, swatting aside the challenge of Collingham (Nottinghamshire). When people in the pavilions of the south country thought of village cricket, however, it was hard to imagine Bomarsund was the sort of village they had in mind. Like Horden, it's a coalfield settlement. In Bomarsund lads in Henleys hoodies with peroxide marine crewcuts, weight-machine chests and Polynesian-tattooed biceps drink Irish cider outside a pub that offers a weekly five-hundred-pound cash draw. There are front-room beauty salons and Union flags pasted in the upstairs windows of terraced houses. If there's a village smithy, a spreading chestnut tree or a district nurse on a bicycle round here they are tucked away behind the lock-ups, the pigeon lofts and the allotments sheds.

It had been baking hot all week, but by Friday rain clouds had started to appear like vultures circling the dying oxen of the weekend. A strange misty rain swirled around the Tyne Valley for twenty-four hours until all the plants were sodden and drooping forlornly. But it had stopped by nightfall and as the bus chugged into Ashington the day had turned fair and men in their shirtsleeves were smoking in the car park of the Elephant pub.

I got off at the bus station and walked up the street past the Rohan Kanhai public house. Kanhai was a silver-haired Guyanese of East Indian extraction. The fact there is a pub named after him in Ashington was another example of Northern league cricket's ability to make unlikely but successful matches. Kanhai had played test cricket for the West Indies for seventeen years, and for three of those he'd coupled batting in one of the world's outstanding test sides with the job of professional in Ashington, a Northumberland town that back then was often described as the World's Biggest Coal Mine.

Kanhai had been the pro at Langwell Crescent in 1964, 1965 and 1967. At that time he was widely regarded as one of the half-dozen best batsmen on the planet. Kanhai was praised by Learie Constantine's old friend, the writer and historian C. L. R. James (who'd squeezed in a couple of games for Nelson Seconds during a visit with his chum), for his 'adventuresome attitude' and the unorthodox brilliance of his stroke play. One of Kanhai's former team mates, the wild and crazy Roy Gilchrist put it more poetically. Kanhai, he wrote, eschewed power, preferring to 'stroke the ball as gently as if it were a kitten sitting on a hearth rug'.

The ball presumably purring contentedly all the while, Kanhai hit fifteen test centuries, captained the West Indies at the start of their rise to eighties dominance and played in the team that won the inaugural World Cup. Sunil Gavaskar, captain of India, was so impressed by seeing Kanhai play in Bombay he named his first son after him.

Kanhai's trademark shot was the falling-over hook, which culminated in him lying flat on his back. He always hit his on-drive off one leg, and generally drove the purists mad with his improvisational style. Like Constantine he was a showman. Kanhai played league cricket for much of his early career. He started out with Aberdeenshire on the east coast of Scotland, where he'd struck four thousand runs in three seasons, and turned out for Milnrow in the Central Lancashire League before following Bill Alley as pro at Blackpool. In cricket terms, arriving after Alley was a bit like going on stage after Elvis. But Kanhai carried it off, batting superbly and coming within a whisker of breaking the big Australian's club record tally of 1345 runs in a season.

My old next-door neighbour had been a policeman in Ashington during Kanhai's time. The police station was practically next door to the cricket club and he'd spent many happy evenings with the great West Indian. 'Canny lad. Liked a rum and a game of dominoes,' he said. Whatever your cultural or ethnic background, a liking for rum and dominoes would always serve you well in the North-East.

Ashington's other cricket legend was England pace bowler

Steve Harmison, who'd begun his career as a junior at the club. He'd also played for Ashington AFC. Harmison had frequently complained of homesickness when he'd been on tour with England. I asked the secretary of Ashington Football Club if he'd ever had similar problems with the big paceman when he'd been their centre half. 'I didn't notice any,' he said, 'but then we never travelled any further than Northallerton.'

For a while Harmison was rated as the world's best bowler. I didn't see it, though. Harmison was always caught on camera fielding at fine leg with a finger up his nostril. He was hostile on his day, but to me he just seemed, well, too lugubrious to be a great fast bowler. There was no natural ferocity to the man. Top fast bowlers were often filled with barely suppressed rage. Sylvester Clarke, Roy Gilchrist, Dennis Lillee, Rodney Hogg, all seemed perpetually at boiling point. Harmison looked more like he'd been defrosted under the hot tap.

Harmy wasn't the only first class opening bowler Ashington had produced. John Inchmore, the medium pacer I'd watched under the influence of cider at New Road, was also from the town. J. D. Inchmore had taken over five hundred first class wickets and, thanks to my misspent youth, I knew without having to look it up that the D stood for Darling.

I turned left at the Kanhai pub and walked down Station Road, past the greengrocers yelling 'Cheap raspberries, girls. Melons two for a pound.' At a bus stop near the police station I asked an old man for directions to the cricket field. 'It's off,' he said gloomily. I must have look puzzled because he added, 'I've just come from there and it's off.' I looked up at the sky. There was no rain. The pavements weren't even wet. 'I've no idea why, but it's off,' the man said with a shake of his head for emphasis. 'I come down special. On the bus, like. They say it's waterlogged but . . .' his voice trailed off and he shrugged in disbelief.

It wasn't that I didn't believe him, but I wandered round the corner to the ground anyway. The wickets weren't even pitched. Yet the outfield looked about as dry as Salt Lake City on the Sabbath.

When I was a small boy there was a roped-off stretch of grass in a field near my house that had strange and mystical properties. If ever my friends and I wandered within twenty yards of it the old man who apparently lived behind the peculiar red-brick bungalow in the corner of the field would come running out and yell at us.

The old man had been a gunnery sergeant in the Desert Rats. He had the puffed-out chest of a pouter pigeon and a face so creased and lined by exposure to the elements he made later-period W. H. Auden appear a candidate to become the new face of Revlon. Whatever the season he dressed in a long and formless gabardine mackintosh and as he ran towards us it whirred about him like the leathery wings of some prehistoric flying beast. 'Geee-yat horf may-ah squee-ah!' the old man shrieked as he flapped towards us, 'Gee-yan, bugg-ah horf!' And we would scamper away, concealing our terror with laughter.

For many years I thought the former NCO was protecting something military: a minefield, an unexploded Luftwaffe bomb, a top-secret gadget the boffins at HQ had dreamed up to foil the Russkis. Later, of course, I discovered that it was actually something far more sensitive and important than that – a cricket square.

The old sergeant was a groundsman, and in the cricket heartlands of Yorkshire a groundsman guarded his square day and night with the ruthless determination of a gamekeeper protecting pheasant chicks. Indeed, had the law allowed it I'm sure many groundsmen in the White Rose county would have adopted the gamekeeper's singular habit of displaying all the vermin he had executed on a convenient fence, and we would have been treated to the disturbing sight of barbed wire decorated with decomposing moles, terriers, bicycles, footballers and girls in high heels.

Only three categories of people were authorised to go on the cricket squares: groundsmen, umpires and cricketers. And the cricketers were pretty fortunate to be allowed, frankly. In fact, if it had been down to the groundsman they'd have stayed on the outfield for the entire summer.

Mind you, they really should have considered themselves lucky to get that. At my primary school the groundsman guarded the entire playing field with the tenacity of Horatio defending the bridge. Sir Bobby Robson's first volume of autobiography was entitled *Time on the Grass*. If he'd been at my primary school it would have been two sentences long. We were not allowed on the field because it was too wet, too dry, or had just had fertilizer spread on it, or weedkiller, or new seed.

The playing field, to us, was like some unrealisable dream, for ever within our grasp and yet strangely unreachable. If a ball should bounce on to it from the playground we had to get permission from a teacher to retrieve it, tiptoeing across the turf as if it concealed venomous serpents. On the very few occasions when the headmaster announced that 'the school field will be in-bounds this playtime', we were so excited that when we got on it all we did was run around in circles squealing. No wonder we lost every inter-school football match we ever played.

When I started playing cricket I realised that while the old groundsman disliked children and dog-walkers, he reserved

the full fury of his hatred for cricketers. He hated us because
we wilfully damaged his beloved square. He had nurtured
that square. He had protected it, fed it and watered it, and
tucked it under the covers on cold nights. And now here we
came, all leery and disrespectful, and stamped on it, and
smacked it, and gouged and prodded it. Watching a batsman
scratching his guard into the wicket with his foot made the
groundsman wince as if the spiked boots were digging into his
own flesh. That is why there was nothing that brightened the
groundsman's weekend more than telling the teams: 'The
game is off.'

Like the traditional English publican pointing out to the
tourist that 'we stop serving food at 2 p.m. prompt' at one
minute past two, or the old-fashioned shopkeeper informing
a potential customer that 'the item you require is out of
stock', the groundsman never announced that conditions
were unplayable without an ill-concealed note of triumph in
his voice. It was the victory of the putative servant over his
would-be masters.

'The game is off,' he'd say as he stood with arms folded, his
head tilted slightly to one side, a stubby Woodbine clamped
in his jaw and a look in his eye that said, 'I defied the Afrika
Korps, sunshine.'

'Maybe it will dry out later?' the captains would suggest
plaintively, and the groundsman would look at them as if
they'd asked to poke his daughter.

The old groundsman died many years ago, but his spirit
clearly lived on in Ashington.

Disgusted, I went and found a café and had some banana
milk and a toasted teacake. When I'd said I was writing
this book, a friend of mine from up near Alnwick had
sighed and said, 'I always get the feeling that, though they
play cricket round here, the game never really took hold in

Northumberland.' For the first time I started to feel the same way.

Certainly you couldn't have imagined them calling the game off so early in Lancashire or West Yorkshire. At Bacup they'd put the game on in conditions that looked hopeless.

'They don't take cricket seriously up here,' a mate of mine who'd played his early cricket in the Bradford League and the Yorkshire Conference said. When he'd first moved to Northumberland he said he was amazed. 'The players took their bloody holidays during the season. To me that was unbelievable, a total lack of commitment.'

At Lascelles Hall back in the Edwardian era the rules stated that any player not giving written notice of an absence a week in advance would be fined. If you didn't take cricket seriously round Huddersfield you could bugger off and play tennis instead.

Despite what appeared to be a laissez-faire attitude, the Northumberland and Tyneside Senior League had produced its fair share of tough competitors. One of them was Harmison's Durham and England team mate Paul Collingwood. He'd turned out for Shotley Bridge, just north of Consett.

Whenever Paul Collingwood gets a big score my father phones up. 'See that Collingwood did well again,' he'd say. My father likes Collingwood. He thinks the Durham all-rounder is 'a proper sort of a cricketer'. He has 'a bit about him'.

My dad approves of Collingwood's sensible haircut and the fact he has no visible tattoos or piercings. He likes him because he is strong off the back foot. Being strong off the back foot suggests a man who has not been mollycoddled in his youth. Batsmen who have spent their formative years playing on good, true wickets get on the front foot at every opportunity. Those who have been brought up playing on nasty, deceitful wickets prefer to wait and see what happens. They don't take things for granted. They know that every once in a while the ball will jump up unexpectedly and slap them in the chops. Just like life.

My dad had learned to bat on treacherous tracks around Teesside. Even in the back garden playing with a tennis ball he watched each delivery suspiciously as if it were an armed intruder. If you play on good wickets you can get your head over the ball. If you try it on a bad wicket the ball is likely to pop off a bump and bury itself up your nostrils. In days gone by coaches used to instruct their pupils to 'sniff the leather', but you can take things too far.

Collingwood got a fair amount of criticism in the press because of his lack of elegance. He was a grafter, a sticker. He was resourceful and eked out every ounce he could from the talent he'd been given. He was not David Gower. And that, of course, was why northerners liked him.

I munched the last of my teacake and caught the bus back into town. The sun was glinting off the River Wansbeck, there was a smell of barbecue charcoal in the air and kids in face paint were bouncing on trampolines in the gardens of Gosforth.

Though Asif Masood and Wasim Raja had both played for Jesmond, it's fair to say that Kanhai was the biggest star Northumberland cricket had ever attracted. The clubs in the region simply didn't have the financial clout of those to the south and west. The Indian test cricketer Chandu Borde had been the professional at South Northumberland in 1955 and performed brilliantly, but the club couldn't afford to keep him and he went to the Lancashire League instead.

Kanhai wasn't the only West Indian star to play in the Northumberland Senior League, however. I've already mentioned that Ian Bishop played for Tynedale. So did the great Courtney Walsh, though at the time he was an unknown toothpick-thin teenager. One of the most popular pros at the Hexham club was a Trinidadian, Kelvin Williams. My friend said that Williams was so laid back he'd often nod off in the pavilion when he was waiting to bat. 'They'd have to wake him up,' he said, 'and he'd come out to the wicket yawning and rubbing his eyes. And the first ball he faced, bam! Straight back over the bowler's head. It was bloody irritating, really. He was better half asleep than I was wide awake.'

Williams had scored 5370 runs and taken 378 wickets for Tynedale before moving on to play for Middleton. At the Central Lancashire League club the all-rounder had suffered the sort of fate that had been visited on many a pro. He'd not had the best of seasons and at a committee meeting in September it was agreed not to renew his contract. The committee decided the wisest course would be to tell him after the next game, so as to continue to get value. In that game Williams batted superbly and hit a League record score of 223.

'Afterwards he was sitting in the bar with the rest of the team, having a drink and celebrating,' a club official told me. 'And I had to go over and say, "Well done, Kelvin. Congratulations. Oh and by the way, you're fired." I felt terrible. He was such a lovely fella.' Williams is now head coach of Trinidad and Tobago.

Another West Indian who played for Tynedale was a Barbadian I'd never heard of before the season began, but with whom I was now becoming increasingly familiar. It started during a rain break at Horden Welfare Park. I took shelter in the clubhouse and found myself looking at a framed photo of a successful Horden team of the early seventies.

Standing in the back row was a middle-aged West Indian wearing wire-framed spectacles and a benign expression. I read the caption and made a note of his pleasingly poetic name, Clairmonte Depeiza.

A couple of weeks later, when I was down at the Fountains Garth to watch Guisborough play Blackhall, I wandered into the members lounge and the first photo I looked at was of the team that had won the 1970 Kerridge Cup, and who should be there among them but Clairmonte Depeiza.

Before I went to Haslingden I was checking in David Edmundson's centenary history of the Lancashire League to see who had played at Bentgate. And there, in a great and illustrious list that included George Headley, Dennis Lillee and Phil Simmons, sandwiched somewhere between Vinoo Mankad and Clive Lloyd, was the name C. C. Depeiza.

I looked through the cricket books on my shelf. The only pre-seventies *Wisden* I own is the 1955 edition, inherited from a work colleague of my father's. I flicked through it and, sure enough, there on page 874 was Clairmonte Depeiza scoring 122 against Australia in the fourth test at Bridgetown. 'Another Australian victory appeared in prospect when six West Indies batsmen were dismissed for 146,' read the report, 'but Atkinson and Depeiza came to the rescue, defying the attack for more than a day.' Depeiza played in five tests in total, that record-breaking stand with Denis Atkinson against Lindwall, Miller and Benaud a memorable high point.

Depeiza had played as wicketkeeper batsman for Barbados. You can gauge how good he must have been by the men around him in the island top order – Conrad Hunte, Colly Smith, Everton Weekes and Gary Sobers. You didn't get into that line-up just because you'd captained your university.

After his success against Australia, Depeiza was selected for the West Indies tour to New Zealand. It doesn't seem to have been a particularly happy trip, though admittedly my sole reason for thinking that is because on the way to the Land of the Long White Cloud, Windies somehow contrived to lose to Fiji.

C. C. Depeiza was one of many West Indians who have come to play league cricket in the north of England. Quite a few, like Bishop and Walsh, were pace bowlers of a type you wouldn't ordinarily expect to face on a Saturday afternoon. There was Gilchrist, of course, but also Charlie Griffith, who during a single season at Burnley picked up 144 wickets at 5.20 apiece and hospitalised his West Indian team mate Basil Butcher (playing for Bacup at the time) into the bargain. When he was at Littleborough in the mid-seventies Joel 'Big Bird' Garner so terrorised opposition batsmen that one of them, Les Whittle of Crompton, came in to face him wearing a yellow fireman's helmet. The mighty fast bowler burst out laughing when he saw him, but the league committee weren't in the least amused and handed Whittle a three-month ban.

Depeiza wasn't as dramatic as Gilchrist, Griffiths or Garner. He'd ditched wicketkeeping and turned his hand to medium pace bowling. He could generate a fair bit of nip off the right surface. At Tynedale he took 241 wickets at 13.17 apiece. Not bad for a stumper.

Depeiza was no Rohan Kanhai or Learie Constantine, but he was a highly skilled, popular, a good coach, particularly of younger players, and did his job well enough to find his way into the reckoning whenever veteran cricket fans in what were once the cotton towns start discussing an all-time Lancashire League West Indian XI.

He settled eventually in Manchester and died in 1996. As well as Horden, Guisborough, Tynedale and Haslingden, Clairmonte Depeiza also did his job for Heywood and

Crompton in the Central Lancashire League, Greenfield in the Saddleworth and District League, and Ashton-on-Mersey in the Manchester Association. He began his life in Britain as a professional at Forfarshire CC just outside Dundee, where elderly cricketers still recall the helping hand he gave them when they were starting out. Depeiza wasn't one of the greats, but he was a good professional and everybody liked him.

B. R. Findlay's Casebook

Settle

All week long the humidity had been building. Taking the dog for a walk was like having a sauna. An old man I met along the river bank said, 'It's like Sumatra, is this,' adding, 'not that I've ever been to Sumatra, mind. But if I had, I imagine this is what it would have been like.' In the heat and damp the grass grew madly, the courgettes engorged and the potato patch looked like a jungle. Gun dogs leapt into rivers, sausages sizzled on outdoor grills. The atmosphere was unnervingly still.

I had an hour to wait for the train to Settle, so I went into a department store in Carlisle and asked for some aftershave. The lady behind the counter told me she no longer carried aftershave as there wasn't a demand for it. 'Most men these days want more bouquet,' she said. 'They want something longer lasting. And they find that aftershave stings too much.'

I told my friend Tony this later in the week, as we were getting changed after five-a-side. 'Imagine,' I said, 'it stings too much. Ooh! Ooh! It's *soooo* astringent! Good God, is that how we won the war?'

'I'm not sure aftershave was high on the Nazis' list of weaponry,' Tony replied. 'Though if it had been, clearly the outcome might have been different. Hitler would have waited until the British Tommies had freshly razored chins, got the Luftwaffe to drop a load of Old Spice on them and then attacked while they were all running up and down shrieking.

'But to be honest,' he continued, 'I haven't used aftershave myself for a number of years. I prefer an emollient cream'. Another bloke came into the dressing room at this point. 'We're just talking about aftershave,' Tony said. 'Do you use it?'

'No, no,' the man replied, 'I switched to balm ages back. I did use moisturiser for a while, but I found a lot of the proprietary brands to be very greasy.'

And so I sat in a football changing room in County Durham listening to two middle-aged men talking about the relative merits of various skin conditioners. I can't recall what the conclusion was, but the very fact there was a debate convinced me that the world had moved on much further than I'd imagined.

I'd bailed out on Settle previously, put off by the prospect of rain, and gone to Edenside Park instead. In fact, they'd played a full match that day, easily disposing of Blackburn Northern. The visitors today were Clitheroe. It seemed that just about everywhere in Lancashire shared its name with a cake (Eccles, Chorley), a famous cricketer (Atherton, Leyland) or a comedian (Formby, Crompton – Colin in the latter case, MC at the Wheeltapppers and Shunters Club). When I was a boy I'd loved Jimmy Clitheroe. The sound of the opening music and the cry of 'It's the Clitheroe Kid!' would send me into paroxysms of excitement that I now realised were totally disproportionate for the chance to watch an elderly man pretending to be a cheeky schoolboy.

The train to Leeds via Settle was jam-packed with OAPs on an organised trip, firmly marshalled by badge-wearing officials with brisk manners and knitted brows. The journey took us through a whole variety of places that sound like characters out of a Mrs Gaskell novel. The hay had already been cut and baled in the fields around Langwathby. Fat lambs lazed under ash trees at Armathwaite, crimson willow herb shivered in the breeze at Kirkby Stephen, and at Kirkoswald a herd of grey horses cantered through thigh-high grass. All along the route down the Eden Valley there were drystone walls and dog daisies, bracken and birch, and the sort of small, settled old-fashioned villages where children play with sticks and old spaniels saunter across the streets and lie down on warm paving slabs.

Past Kirkby Stephen we entered the high moorland of Ribblesdale, where a farmer keeps a herd of water buffalo and turns the milk into cheese, and rattled on over vertiginous viaducts into Garsdale and Dent. The journey from Carlisle to Settle is so lovely and so celebrated you can buy DVDs of it from the refreshments trolley.

As we pulled into Settle I could see the panama-hatted umpires striding out to put the bails on at Marshfield. Clitheroe were batting and by the time I'd walked from the station to the entrance one of their openers was already back in the pavilion.

A six-foot high drystone wall painted white from ground to copingstones surrounds the Marshfield. Beyond the boundary at one side is a council estate of semis rendered sludge grey, at the other a Booths supermarket. There's an old wooden pavilion with a corrugated-iron roof unused in one corner – I read somewhere it used to be a kindergarten – next to the green and white scorebox, some white-painted sheds covered in ivy and, at the entrance, a swanky modern clubhouse in stone, polished wood and slate. Inside two men were sitting, their backs turned resolutely to the cricket, waiting for the

Lions *v* South Africa rugby union test to start on Sky Sports.
I bought a pint and wandered up to sit under the huge ash
tree opposite the clubhouse.

Settle's pro in 2009 was a New Zealander, Brent Findlay
from Canterbury. He was bowling from the supermarket end
at a fastish pace, though accuracy was arguably probably his
strongest suit. Like most of the pros he seemed able to bowl
quicker than the amateurs without wasting much effort and
drop the ball on a length more or less from force of habit.

At the other end a silver-haired pace man, John Tarbox,
whirled to the wicket and bowled off his wrong foot, like Mike
Proctor of Gloucestershire and South Africa. Proctor was
quick and devastating, but it's a method of bowling that
always looks uncomfortably like a recipe for a dislocated knee.
The wicketkeeper, Airey, stood up at stumps for Tarbox,
which when you're an opening bowler has the vague feeling
of an insult about it.

Findlay got a second Clitheroe wicket, Peter Dibb caught
behind. McDowell, the new batter, was a left-hander and
clubbed the pro for three runs over point. Inspired, Dewhurst
at the other end eyed up a short one before hooking it first
bounce into the boundary where it scattered a group of pensioners who'd arranged themselves neatly under green
umbrellas. 27–2 in ten overs.

Dewhurst hit Tarbox for four through the covers. He was
a businesslike fellow with a wide-footed stance, the bat
between his feet. It's a position I used myself until my school
games teacher told me to stand properly, the bat behind my
back foot. 'You'll never get any runs if you stand that ridicu-
lous way,' he said. I didn't tell him I'd copied my silly stance
from photos I'd seen of somebody called Don Bradman.

Dewhurst seemed to be getting on top of the bowling when
he hooked another short one from Findlay. The ball looked

like it was heading out of the ground but suddenly plummeted like a shot pigeon and was brilliantly caught by Tarbox, two handed and diving forward at fine leg. 34–3 and all the wickets to the professional.

'Tighten the screw, Settle,' yelled the skipper as the new batsman, Bolton, walked to the wicket.

The Ribblesdale League was founded in 1893. It covers a widely scattered area of East Lancashire and the Pennines that includes two Yorkshire teams. Earby are the other one. It had once stretched even further, but in 1951 the more western and northerly of the League's clubs, including Blackpool, St Annes and Leyland, had split and formed the Northern League. It was the cross-Pennine nature of the fixture between Settle and Clitheroe that had drawn me to the Marshfield today. It was a smaller version of the traditional Yorkshire versus Lancashire rivalry, a dwarf roses match.

Despite the departure of some of the larger and wealthier clubs, over the years the Ribblesdale League has continued to provide a leg up, or a last staging post, for a lot of doughty Lancashire pros: Jack Simmons, Bernard Reidy (whose frizzy hairstyle John Arlott once dubbed an 'Afro-Accrington'), Paul Allott, Glen Chapple and Ian Folley have all played in it, and Ian Austin is currently captaining Baxenden. It also produced two of the county's greatest batsmen. Cyril Washbrook and Eddie Paynter both started their careers at Barrow, a village just outside Blackburn. For England Washbrook formed an imperious opening partnership with Bradford League old boy Len Hutton. Paynter played for England twenty times and finished his test career with a batting average of 59.23, higher than that of any other Englishman with the exception of another Bradford League man, Herbert Sutcliffe.

Paynter had the lean face and twinkly eyes of a music hall turn. In David Foot's brilliant biography of Walter Hammond there's a great story about Paynter. When the great batsman was asked by a journalist for his recollections of Hammond he thought for a moment (at this point I like to think of the interviewer sitting back in his chair and anticipating the description of an elegant cover drive or balletic slip catch) and then said, 'Wally liked a shag.'

Frank Keating told me he had once interviewed Paynter and his Lancashire and England team mate George Duckworth and asked them if they could spot Australian leg spinner Bill O'Reilly's googly. 'You couldn't pick it out of his hand,' Paynter said, 'but you knew it was coming because he signalled to the wickie by scratching his arse.'

'He didn't scratch his arse,' Duckworth interrupted, 'he scratched his bollocks.'

'He scratched his arse,' Paynter insisted.

'It was his bollocks,' Duckworth retorted.

And Frank Keating said he sat there while two of the finest players of their generation yelled Arse! Bollocks! Arse! Bollocks! at one another like two characters from *The Fast Show*.

Settle, who'd taken up residence at the Marshfield in 1885, had been founder members of the Ribblesdale League. In 1903 they'd taken part in one of the League's most memorable matches, dismissing fellow Yorkshiremen Earby for just three runs, with Charlie Swale and Jack Guisedale both taking five for one.

Despite early success Settle had briefly joined the Yorkshire Cricket Council (Bradford Division) largely because of the difficulties and expense involved in travelling across the Pennines to play teams in Lancashire (up until the thirties Clitheroe's trips to the Marshfield had involved a long haul on a horse-drawn wagonette and an overnight stay) and even flirted with the Craven and District League before returning to their original home in 1946.

Bob Ratcliffe of Lancashire and the South African test player Rudi Steyn had both turned out for Settle, but the club's most famous former player was probably Don Wilson. Wilson, born in Settle, was a slow left-armer and hard-hitting late order batsman who'd been burdened with having to follow the likes of Wilfred Rhodes and Hedley Verity into the Yorkshire side. Despite the fact that he played for seventeen seasons, took 1189 wickets and appeared in six test matches, a sense of disappointment always seemed to hang over him. To be picked for Yorkshire was not only to battle your opponents but also history. All players were measured against the past, and when the past includes Rhodes and Verity any slow bowler is more or less knackered before he's started. Wilson went on to become one of the most influential coaches in the country, though it's worth noting that he worked his magic at Lord's cricket school not Headingley.

At Marshfield Tarbox was replaced by a younger bowler, Will Davidson, who – in the tradition of the thing – got lots of advice from the professional. Davidson bowled medium pace. 'You're getting it wobbling,' slip yelled in encouragement to him, but McDowell the Clitheroe batter was unimpressed and walked into a cover drive that skimmed over the ground to the boundary. The shot was greeted with a series of impassioned yells and whoops, but they turned out to be in response to something the Lions were doing in Johannesburg.

Findlay earned his money, bowling flat out and undertaking a series of elaborate field adjustments. For the left-handed McDowell he deployed a gully and two points. The batsman responded by planting his foot down the wicket and straight driving for four, then flicking neatly off his legs to fine leg for another. He has narrow, square shoulders, buttoned down sleeves and a fidgety manner. He stands upright to receive the bowling 'like a guardsman', as the veteran commentators would have said. The pro went round the wicket to him, trying to force him back on to the back foot and shake him up with a series of short deliveries that whizzed past his chest. After each delivery the Kiwi strode back to his mark with the stiff-legged strut of an angry terrier.

Will Davidson, the young medium pacer, was replaced by a veteran off-spinner, Andrew Davidson, whose thinning grey hair and ample waistline reminded me of Hampshire's Peter Sainsbury, whom John Arlott always liked to describe as 'the wily old fox' even when he was being battered all over the ground during a John Player League match by somebody like Keith Boyce. Davidson played for Settle for a couple of decades, and had been picked for the Ribblesdale League Representative XI a few times back in the early nineties. He's a shrewd operator and set his field with a short mid-off and nobody out at midwicket, inviting the batsmen to hit against the spin.

That being said, I have to admit that the sight of Davidson calling for long off to move slightly round to the right filled me with a strange sense of dread. Andrew Davidson has two sons playing for Settle.

A few seasons back a friend of mine was very excited because *his* son had just been picked to play in the same cricket team as him. His son was thirteen and had the pale skin, gangling limbs and tiny body of an exotic nocturnal insect. He batted at number six and bowled medium pace. His run up was like an emu in a tumble dryer, but his father saw Allan Donald.

'It's a dream come true,' my friend said when he brought

me the glad news. A dream come true for him maybe, but a nightmare for his team mates. Because there can be few things in sport as stressful as playing in a cricket team with a father and son.

I remember a father and son, years ago. They were both nice enough, but once they got on the field the dad was instantly transformed. He became so pushy on his kid's behalf he made Geoff Boycott look like a man in need of assertiveness training.

'Time to bring the lad on, Skip, wouldn't you say? Shouldn't someone as quick over the ground as the lad be in the covers, Captain? I think the lad would fancy turning his arm over on this strip, Skipper. A dry surface is ideal for the lad. The lad's itching to have a crack at 'em on this greentop, Skip. Wouldn't a natural athlete like the lad be better at first slip? On this wicket the lad would relish batting at three. If you need an end blocking you can rely on the lad, Skipper. When it's quick runs you're wanting the lad's your man, Captain.'

On and on he went, game after game. The lad meanwhile said nothing. He was as silent as a sloth. And had much the same cricketing ability.

The worst moment of any game was when the captain finally bowed to the pressure and brought the lad on to bowl. When the captain signalled for him to take off his sweater the air was suddenly filled with a discordant sound such as you might imagine an elephant would produce if it sat on a harpsichord. It was the twanging of the fielders' nerves. Because it was well known to all of us that on the scale of human sin, just below mass murder and slightly above being Kevin Pietersen's hair stylist, was the heinous crime of Dropping a Catch off the Lad's Bowling.

The repercussions of such an act of vile and total wickedness were so horrendous that any one of us would rather have been trapped in a lift with John Motson than stuck under a skier struck off one of the lad's gentle long hops. Pressure is a terrible thing. It twists the minds of men.

If you did have the misfortune to find yourself watching a mis-hit pull sailing in your direction while Dad yelled, 'Catch! Catch!' strange things happened. As the ball fell out of the heavens you were gripped by cold fear. The ball was suddenly transformed. It was no longer an ordinary cricket ball, it was now a great greasy meteorite thundering towards you at the speed of sound, swerving from side to side like Freddie Flintoff chasing the last bus home. It was as slippery as an eel, as hard as steel and heavy as the heaviest thing you can think of, doubled.

And when this frankly uncatchable object slid, inevitably, from your grasp and fell on to the grass at your feet you could be certain of one thing: in whatever direction you looked, towards whatever point of the compass you turned, the first thing you would see would be Dad staring straight at you with that look on his face. I still wake up at night screaming.

Andrew Davidson is surely more reasonable than that bloke, but I kept a wary eye on him just in case. Meanwhile Findlay clipped one off the outside edge of the left-hander's bat. It flew low and fast to second slip's right hand side. He dived, grasped and then dropped it. Afterwards he lay on his back, shielding his eyes from the sun, a picture of despair.

The score has crept up to 77–4 and the missed chance felt like a turning point, especially when a couple of overs later another snick evaded the wicketkeeper and flies down to the third man boundary. The pro is in his thirteenth over, still bowling at a rapid clip, too fast perhaps for the Settle fieldsmen. He says nothing when the catches go down, just wipes the sweat off his forehead with the right sleeve of his shirt before turning and going back to his mark.

Not all league professionals have been so circumspect. The standard of catching in league cricket was the thing the pros moaned about most. Lindwall had been upset by the quality of slip fielding in the Lancashire league, Cec Pepper had delivered some particularly salty outbursts on the topic and Johnny Wardle – never the easiest man – was often withering in his contempt. On one occasion a youngster at Rishton spilled a simple chance at mid-off from the Yorkshireman's bowling. When he apologised Wardle shook his head. 'Don't worry,' he said, 'it was my only bloody fault for putting you there.'

The point for the pros was that dropped catches cost them money. A five-wicket hall brought in a collection. There were other bonuses too, sometimes for the number of wickets taken in the season. There was a story about a Yorkshire pro, Horace Fisher, who played for Middleton, that summed it up nicely. Fisher, a Yorkie so hardcore he made Arthur Mitchell look like Dame Margot Fonteyn, had been offered a bonus of one pound for every wicket he took over a hundred. By the second weekend in August he'd passed the three-figure mark, which was good for him but murder on the fielders. When one missed a catch and said sorry Fisher turned to him and snapped, 'Never mind that, just give us ten bob and we'll call it quits.'

In Settle an ice-cream van went by playing 'O Sole Mio'. Shotguns sounded in the distant wooded hillsides of the Forest of Bowland. It's a lovely setting, Marshfield, the wooden pavil-ion backed by the arches of the railway viaduct and a backdrop of the fells. The town itself is lovely too. It's hardly more than a village really, with a population that doesn't quite reach 2500. Settle was once a Yorkshire cotton town, with five mills employing nearly the entire workforce, but the last of them shut down decades ago and now the local economy is driven by walkers, cyclists and potholers attracted by the local limestone caves. On summer weekends it's the sort of place where you feel under-dressed if you're not wearing wool knee socks and a lanyard with an Ordnance Survey Pathfinder map on the end of it.

A couple of overs passed uneventfully, then the Wily Old Fox lured Bolton into a false shot and had him caught at mid-on. 80–5. Three balls later a mix-up over calls saw both batsmen trapped at the same end, the run out so easy it hardly seemed worth taking the bails off. 91–6 and with his next delivery Findlay trapped the new batsman, Turner, LBW. The batsman left reluctantly, walking back to the pavilion like a schoolboy going to the dentist. It was Findlay's fifth wicket and the hat duly came round. Though it wasn't literally a hat. In fact, it looked like the bottom half of a salad spinner. I noticed that there was a fiver in it, though.

McDowell was still battling away and he got decent support from Farook Butt at the other end. However, after cutting Davidson for four to bring up the hundred, McDowell succumbed next ball, bowled off his pads one short of his half century. 103–8. Five runs later Findlay clean bowled the number ten.

As had been the case during Ramsbottom's innings at Bacup and Blackhall's at Fountains Garth, it's the tail that seemed to enjoy batting most. The last pair for Clitheroe, Butt and Marquet, had a really merry time. There was a big straight six off the professional and a couple of straight fours off Wily Old Fox, who was then deposited into cow corner for another six. 'Shit!' he exclaimed loudly as the ball was lobbed back over the wall from a neighbouring garden.

By now Findlay was into his nineteenth over and clearly wilting. He was tonked for another six over mid-on by Butt and crouched down afterwards, wiping sweat from his brow like a man exhausted. At the other end Andrew Davidson was taken off and replaced by a stocky blond-haired lad with the general air of Matthew Hoggard about him, he was the third Davidson to bowl so far, Tom in his case. He got the number eleven caught behind off his fifth delivery. The last pair had put on thirty-four in thirty balls helping Clitheroe to 142 all out. Findlay who had bowled excellently throughout finished with 6–58 off twenty overs.

Was it a good total? In club cricket it's often very hard to tell. Though Findlay had fizzed the ball through, the wicket seemed a good deal more benign than the one at Bacup. 'It'll all depend, won't it?' the man sitting on the next bench along from me says when I ask him what he thinks. It's not much of an answer but it's hard to fault it for accuracy.

Clitheroe CC was formed in 1862 after an amalgamation for the cricket teams of the local rifle corps and Clitheroe Alhambra, the latter named after a travelling circus. Clitheroe's greatest player was George Hudson, a locally born man who, as pro in 1949, set a league record by taking 124 wickets at just over seven apiece. In a twelve-over spell against Settle he took 9–10. They won the title in 2006 thanks largely to the exploits of pro Shaid Nawaz, who topped the League batting averages for three seasons on the trot.

By the time the teams returned from tea the sun was going full throttle. Clitheroe's opening bowler, from what I had come to think of as the Booth's End, was Marquet, a massive bloke, hefty and huge. He is genuinely hostile and slightly wild, grunting with each delivery and then trudging back to his mark afterwards as if the effort is killing him. He is quick, no doubt about it, and as the slips exhortations of 'Bowled Big Red' echoed around the ground he trapped the Settle number one, Wildman LBW. Findlay came to the wicket. His second ball from Marquet pinged off his helmet with what must – for the bowler at least – have been a satisfying *kerplunk*, but the Kiwi simply shook his head in response, eased a bit of tension out of his neck, looked around the field and settled back into his stance. Like a good boxer, a batsman should never let a bowler know he's rattled.

At the other end Ben Dowling, a young paceman with a crew cut bowled quick and cut the ball around off the wicket. When the Settle opener Verden shouldered arms to his third ball it jagged back sufficiently to whack him on the buttock. The bowler responded to this encouragement by zipping one past the batter's nose. But when he tried another short one next ball Verden slapped him, flat-batted, over long on for six.

The next ball struck the front pad. There was a big leg-before shout, but the umpire shook his head sadly in response. Unsettled by these misfortunes Dowling tried for extra speed and ended up whipping one down the leg side for four byes. As the over ends he gets involved in a frank exchange of views with the batsman and has to be ushered away by a team mate.

The next over, after much advice to 'Channel the aggression, Benny Boy' from the designated talkers in the field, Dowling clean bowled Verden. Settle are 14–2 and a lot is resting on Findlay, who having bowled unchanged throughout the Clitheroe innings is clearly going to have to earn his money today.

At the Booth's End Big Red hammered the ball into the wicket as if he was aiming for the earth's core. The pro, though, is unfussed by the short stuff and calmly leaves five balls well alone, before nudging the sixth for a single to square leg. There's a lack of hurry about him that gave a clear impression of control. I'd enjoyed watching Findlay bowl and his batting is impressive too in its no-nonsense way. He's a fine example of what John Kay once called the leagues' 'bread-and-butter professionals', the sort of man who fortifies his side. His is the kind of plain, craftsman-like approach that exemplifies the Northern attitude to the game. Leave the expansive stroke play to the posh boys in the fancy caps – we'll get 'em in singles.

The other batsman, Settle wicketkeeper Shaun Airey, was altogether more fidgety. Dowling rapped him on the pads twice and tucked him up with a short one. In some sort of symbolic gesture the sky overhead began to darken. The gunfire became more frenetic. Rain fell. Then stopped.

On the midwicket boundary a Clitheroe fan of ancient vintage, with a mass of shaggy white hair, mahogany tan and white vest that gives the impression of Old Father Time on a gap year bellows, 'Git them outta thur' every few overs for no apparent reason.

After five overs Marquet had worn himself out and was replaced by another paceman Jack Dewhurst. The pro gave the new boy short shrift, pulling him for four with a satisfying crack and then driving him to the cover boundary. The score galloped up to 38–2 as a stiff wind started to whip across the ground, bringing more rain. Findlay, perhaps sensing a coming stoppage and resultant overs reduction, became more adventurous, cracking a straight drive off the youngster and then slapping an intended bouncer between midwicket and mid-on. At the end of the over, frustrated by his treatment, Dewhurst took his cap from the umpire and threw it to the ground with a big shout. It was a bit petulant, but I could understand his feelings. Against Findlay he was totally overmatched. It reminded me of the times when I was a kid and my granddad would put his hand on top of my head and, holding me at arms length, invite me to hit him. I'd swing impotently away, unable to get within six inches of connecting.

Farook Butt, who bowls at a pace so military it should have epaulettes on, replaced Dowling next over. His first six balls cost ten runs, the score leapt up to 61–2 and Settle were coasting.

News came in via mobile phones that Jake Brown, the newly arrived Australian pro at Ribblesdale Wanderers, had just set a new League batting record, hitting 238 not out against Blackburn Northern, including eighteen sixes and twenty fours. Northern won the title in 2007 and once featured India's Chetan Sharma in their line-up, but they were having a poor season and were rooted to the bottom of the table.

Bolton, a spinner, came on for the frustrated young Dewhurst, but the runs kept flowing. The pro drove ferociously at Butt and inside edged to fine leg for four and then clipped the next two deliveries away off his legs. Settle had raced to 77–2 after just fifteen overs.

One of Geoffrey Boycott's favourite maxims is that if you want to know the state of the innings you should look at the score and add two wickets. It's a grand piece of wisdom and it applied at Marshfield where Butt produced a good one to clean bowl Airey, and then two balls later trapped new man Tom Davidson LBW.

The rain started to fall in earnest. The covers came on. When the teams returned two overs had been lost and the victory target adjusted to 135. Four ducks flew past and a blackbird began to sing in the garden of a council house as the fielders took up their positions, but before a ball had been bowled the rain began again, heavier this time, and the players fled.

Inside the clubhouse they were setting up a disco and women were bringing plates of sandwiches and catering boxes of corn-based snacks through from the back seats of Nissan Micras. When the players came back for the second time the target had been reduced to 114. Findlay helped himself to a fifty – his second collection of the day – as Settle nudged towards victory.

At six-thirty I walked back up to the station to catch the last train to Carlisle. As I stood on the platform I could hear shouts from the field and the occasional ripple of applause. When the train passed the ground the players were leaving the field, the umpires following them with the stumps under their arms. Settle had won by six wickets.

Brent Findlay finished the season with 861 runs at 33.21 and sixty-four wickets at 19.13. His contract was renewed for 2010. Settle finished in eighth place. Clitheroe were second from bottom. Blackburn Northern's fortunes went from bad to worse. They faced disciplinary action after refusing to play on a damp wicket that the umpires had passed as fit and were booted out of the league at the end of the season.

Shabash Khanie, Lad

Windhill

At seven in the morning it was baking hot in Tynedale and a film of dew lay on the stubbly grass like sweat on Richard Nixon's top lip. The train south from Newcastle was once again packed with crowds going to York races. I squeezed into a seat next to a bearded American. 'So, d'you think England can win the Ashes?' he asked when he saw me reading the cricket reports. 'I don't know much about the game, but I've read a few books. I mean to say, I don't know what silly mid-off is, but I'm a history nut and sport is part of the social fabric of a nation,' he added wisely.

The American was also interested by the York races crowd, the eclectic mix of people. 'Seems you gotta either have a top hat and tailcoat, or a tattoo and a beer belly to get in,' he said.

At Shipley in West Yorkshire I left the station and walked past the Drovers pub where two smokers chatted to a woman so heavily pregnant it looked like her legs might snap under the strain. Windhill seemed in the grip of economic collapse. Elaborate Victorian buildings built of golden stone – the Liberal Club, the Carnegie Library – were boarded up, the For Sale signs sticking out from them tattered and forlorn. In the window of a terraced house a home-printed poster

showed a picture of a little blonde girl in a red raincoat splash-
ing in a puddle under the legend, 'Today take pleasure in little
things'.

The road from the station rose up and after a few hundred
yards the countryside opened out. There was a sudden scent
of gardens and a view across the narrow valley. Down below,
a red longboat sidled up the Leeds–Liverpool canal. A train
on the MetroLine to Bradford rattled past allotments and
dahlia beds as a cockerel sounded off, its haughty call echoing
through the still summer air.

Two mothers with a herd of small children in tow trudged
up the road ahead of me, past a fenced-off play area where
chubby teenage girls in replica Serie A shirts sat on the swings,
listlessly smoking and texting. The women leaned into their
pushchairs for leverage and balance. One told her kids, 'You
won't want the paddling pool out when you get home. You're
hot now. But you'll be cold when you stand still,' desperately
trying to head off the inevitable bucket parade and wet foot-
prints over the clean kitchen floor.

I was too early for the start of play so I went off in search
of local delicacies. I didn't hold out much hope. The only
shops I'd seen so far were a junk shop with a sign that read
'We buy ANYTHING!' and a front-room beauty parlour
promising 'optimum solutions, nail bar technology, hair exten-
sions and spray tanning'. There was a bit of a Barry
Hines/Ken Loach feel about Windhill. It didn't look so much
a place where people eat as where they are eaten.

Eventually I found a sandwich bar. A van driver was standing at the counter waiting. 'Eee sorry, lads,' a middle-aged
woman said, coming in through the back door, wiping her
hand on her pinny. 'I didn't realise you were there. I was out
back watching the bin men.'

The van driver asked for a cajun chicken bap and a bottle

of chocolate milk. 'Chocolate milk's on offer because it's almost past its sell-by date. Is that all right for you, luv?' the woman asked. I opted for a tinned Canadian salmon and salad cream roll and a custard tart. 'My husband will be right mad when he sees that's gone,' the lady behind the counter said as she bagged up the tart, 'He's had his eye on it all week.'

At Windhill Cricket Ground in Busy Lane all was quiet. Grey-rendered council houses surround three sides of the ground. A row of new three-storey houses – The Stumps – with Toyota sports cars parked in the drives has been flung up behind the bowler's arm at one end. Whoever the builder was clearly didn't know much about cricket otherwise he'd have put fewer windows overlooking the ground. A cricket ball can do a lot of damage.

On the street outside cars *ka-bumped* over the traffic-calming hummocks as Windhill's players went through their catching drills. I wandered round the ground and looked for some-where to sit down. None of the benches on the boundary had backs on them. It used to be the same on the Western terrace at Headingley, as if everybody involved with Yorkshire cricket was trying to stamp out slouching.

The Windhill Clubhouse is a squat brick building with an aspect that seems designed to warn off potential intruders. The Cross of St George, the Union Flag and the Yorkshire Rose banner flapped from the flagpoles. A large scoreboard stands at square leg, the scorers' heads visible through a slit to one side. The umpires' room is a small larch-lap shed of a type in which you'd normally expect to find a Flymo, a paraf-fin heater and some bags of potting compost.

It wasn't particularly pretty, but I didn't find that at all surprising. When it comes to playing cricket most people tend to come over all misty-eyed and start burbling fondly of tree-fringed parks, long shadows on the greensward and strawberries and cream for tea. The reality though is that most club cricket – in the North and the South – is actually played on council pitches in grim suburbs where the sound of willow on leather is drowned out by the overflying 747s and the barking of gigantic dogs, and third slip is what happens when you step in yet another Rottweiler turd. The teas are nothing to write home about either, unless your parents happen to be health inspectors.

Windhill played in the second division of the Bradford League. Despite its august history I have to admit to a slight prejudice against this league. It was just a bit too West Riding for me. It had that I've-done-very-well-for-myself Masonic regalia and golf club ties aura about it. If it had spoken it would have sounded like a radio broadcast by J. B. Priestley in which he quoted himself and chuckled. A friend of mine who also came from the North Riding called this self-congratulatory attitude Duxburyness. 'I'm not fond of Betty's Tea Rooms,' he'd say. 'There's a bit too much Duxburyness about them'.

My friend had coined this expression in honour of Councillor Duxbury, the pompous, self-made West Yorkshireman from Keith Waterhouse's novel *Billy Liar*. He felt that the Bradford League was rank with Duxburyness, and he didn't like it. Where we come from in the North Riding, the worst thing you could be accused of was showing off, of having ideas above your station. 'I've took again him,' people would say. 'He's a bit over proud of himself.'

The Bradford League is very proud of itself. Not, I hasten to add, that it doesn't have plenty to be proud about. The Bradford League is the beating heart of Yorkshire cricket, make no mistake about that. It was founded in 1903. Every club that plays in it is located with a ten-mile radius of Bradford town hall, and just about every great player the

county has ever produced was either raised in it or played in it
at some point. Len Hutton started out as a schoolboy at Pudsey
St Lawrence, so did Herbert Sutcliffe. Percy Holmes had played
at Great Horton, Jim Laker at Saltaire, Ray Illingworth at
Farsley, the undemonstrative Arthur Mitchell at Baildon. As its
reputation grew nationally, the Bradford League had sucked
in other greats from all over the place. Jack Hobbs played for
Idle, S. F. Barnes for Saltaire, Charlie Llewellyn and George
Gunn at Undercliffe, Frank Woolley and Bill Hearne at
Keighley. Windhill had Les Ames, mainstay of a legendary
Kent batting order that tripped off the tongue like the ship-
ping forecast: Todd, Fagg, Crapp and Ames. And, as it
happens, Jack Crapp played at Eccleshill and Arthur Fagg at
Saltaire.

Part of the reason I'd chosen to come to Windhill was
because Learie Constantine had captained the side in the
1940s. The Trinidadian had left Nelson as a player in 1937 –
he continued to live in the town for another twelve years – and
gone to play for Rochdale in the Central Lancashire League.
He spent the 1939 season with the West Indian team that was
touring England and during that summer signed to play at
Windhill the following year. The contract was by all accounts
the largest of his career, though in typically canny West
Riding style it included various clauses that reduced its value
in the event of war. Still, it was worth twenty-five pounds a
game – three times what first-division footballers were earning in 1939.

His old West Indies bowling partner and fellow Lancashire
League stalwart Manny Martindale joined Constantine at
Windhill. A fearsome five foot eight Barbadian paceman,
Martindale had split Walter Hammond's chin open with a
bouncer at Old Trafford in 1933, a ball that was said to have
finally convinced the MCC to outlaw leg theory. He played all

over the north, settled in Lancashire and was still turning out in the Bolton Association when well into his sixties. Such longevity was not unusual. S. F. Barnes was still formidable in his seventh decade and Sonny Ramadhin, who like Martindale had made his home in Lancashire, was still twirling his spinners well enough aged fifty-six to take 9–12 playing for Delph and Dobcross in a Saddleworth and District match in 1985.

When I met up with Cec Wright he'd just celebrated his seventy-fourth birthday but that hadn't stopped him bowling twelve overs for Uppermill seconds. I asked Cec if he ever considered retirement, 'At the end of every season,' he said, 'but then the spring comes and I think, well maybe one more.' Cec had come over to England from Jamaica to play as a professional for Crompton in 1959 and stayed, turning out for Colne, Walsden, Astley Bridge and a handful of other teams. 'Everything I have,' he said, 'my house, my wife, everything, is because of cricket.'

Constantine led Windhill to the title in his first season. Selected for a Bradford League XI to play Yorkshire he entertained a crowd of seven thousand by striking a century in under an hour. Not that those who paid to watch seemed much to mind what Constantine did, so great was his legend. When he played in charity matches in the North to raise money for the war effort and was out for a duck the crowd would still give him a standing ovation, delighted simply to be in his presence.

I took a seat on what looked a slightly more comfortable bench over by the scoreboard. Windhill were batting. Bowling Old Lane's side is entirely Asian. The club was one of the first in the Bradford League to make an effort to strike up a relationship with the new immigrant community back in the

sixties. This was largely thanks to a club stalwart, former captain
Jack Hill, who'd served in the army in India during the Second
World War.

Unlike the sons of West Indian immigrants who seem more
or less to have given up on cricket altogether, the sons of Asian
immigrants are as keen on the game as their fathers. It was as
much a part of the culture of Pakistan, India and Sri Lanka
as it was of Yorkshire and Lancashire. At a time when more
and more white players seemed to be drifting away from the
game, leaving clubs in Durham and Northumberland, for
example, struggling to put teams out, the influx of Asian players has reinvigorated the game in the areas of the north where
it had traditionally been strongest.

Not that everyone viewed it that way, of course. In the
leagues on both sides of the Pennines you heard mutterings
around the boundary about the number of 'coloured lads' in
the teams. Some of these were casual observations of fact,
others certainly racist in tone and intention. At one game in
Lancashire a man told me that he didn't think Adil Rashid
should 'be playing for England with a name like that'. I make
no pretence to bravery of any kind, moral or physical, but I
am quite bad tempered. I said to the man, 'Listen, I'm a
Yorkshireman. When I was growing up you could only play
for Yorkshire if you were born in Yorkshire. Adil Rashid was
born in Yorkshire. So, as far as me, Yorkshire County Cricket
Club and the ghost of Lord bloody Hawke are concerned he
is a Yorkshireman. And,' I said, 'if you look, I think you'll find
more Yorkshiremen have played for England than players
from any other county, including Lancashire.'

'Aye well,' the man said, 'at least he's not a South African,'
which was a small victory for the forces of liberalism, I suppose.

*

Bowling's bowler from the Stumps end of the ground was nicknamed Billy Boy. He struggled to find his line against the home side's tall left-handed opener and was flicked away down the leg side for a couple of fours.

At the Leeds Road end an old-fashioned looking chap named Zubair with bushy hair, baggy trousers, a sleeveless wool sweater and a neat officer-class moustache ran in with a rolling motion, and a slight list as if his hip was giving him gyp. His line was accurate and niggardly. His appeals – right arm outstretched, left tucked in to his side – had a loud yet judicial quality to them. The umpire was unmoved.

Amjid Khan, the bearded captain of Bowling Old Lane, soon brought himself on in place of Billy Boy. His second ball was over-pitched and slapped to the boundary. 'Keep going, Khany. Keep going, boys,' the wicketkeeper called out and slapped his gloves together.

Khan was a good cricketer, but seeing a skipper bring himself on to bowl so early brought back unhappy memories for me. Anyone who has ever played club cricket will know that in a substantial minority of cases captaincy brings with it certain privileges, not the least of which is selfishness.

I once played under a captain – now dead – known to one and all as The Wangler. When it came to dedication to his own cause, The Wangler made Kevin Pietersen seem like Mother Theresa. The Wangler batted at number four, fielded at first slip and, like a cricket version of John Lewis, was never knowingly under-bowled.

Like all skippers, The Wangler was sensitive to accusations that he abused his power by bowling himself too much. So he claimed he only delivered long spells when 'the situation demanded it'. Strangely, the situation demanded it more or less every Saturday and Sunday throughout the summer. In fact, I am sure that at times a combination of a sudden frost,

the falling value of sterling and Lord Howe leaving the foreign
office saw The Wangler bowling from both ends on some
midweek afternoons during February too.

The Wangler had been captain of the club since before
records began and nobody ever challenged his authority. This
was partly in acknowledgement of his experience and dedication, but mainly because he drove an eight-seater Peugeot
estate and had somehow persuaded his wife that making tea
for two dozen blokes and that odd lad with the specs held
together with Elastoplast who did the scoring was a stimulat-
ing and creative hobby. As anyone who has played club cricket
will know, when it comes to selecting a leader, a man's ability
to transport and feed a team far outranks his playing, tactical
or motivational skills. Most club sides would pick the owner of
a burger van over Ricky Ponting any day. Mind you, these
days so would a lot of Australians.

Occasionally, after a twenty-seven-over spell, a team mate
might venture to ask The Wangler if he had ever considered
retirement from the game. 'Retire, me?' he would chortle.
'Absolutely not. You know, nothing would suit me better than
to die on the cricket field.'

'If you did,' somebody asked, 'and play was abandoned as
a result, would we get our match fees back?'

By all accounts The Wangler had once been a pace bowler
of primal menace. But by the time I first encountered him
the only frightening thing about him was his appeal, a blood-
curdling yell delivered from a bow-legged squat that gave the
impression of a man with piles sitting down on the wrong end
of an invisible shooting stick.

Where once The Wangler's bouncer had jumped and spat
like a cobra, now it rose with the relaxed and cheery hum of
a post-coital bumblebee. Batsmen watched its stately progress,
adjusted their headgear, surveyed the leg side field and

whistled a few bars of the theme from Rocky before swatting it to the boundary with a merry chuckle.

In response to the debilitating effects of time, The Wangler abandoned pace and took to bowling tweakers, a polite version of the off break that is as unlikely to deviate from the straight and narrow as Ann Widdecombe during Lent. The gentle curve of his arm ball was directly related to the rotation of the earth. According to The Wangler, he 'winkled batsmen out' using a mix of guile, flight and variation of pace and line. This, of course, is the internationally approved club cricket code for bowled really slow crap in the vague expectation of eventually getting somebody caught at deep midwicket.

As an opening bowler I suffered more than most from The Wangler's determination to bring himself on at the earliest opportunity. I make no great claims for my bowling, I should say. Once I had believed myself to be a more stylish version of Michael Holding, purring to the wicket with loose-limbed elegance. Then a team mate bought one of those early video cameras that were the size of a small bungalow and got his son to film a match. To paraphrase Byron, no man is a hero to the camcorder. I looked like a squid fired from a catapult. It was clear I took my wickets, not through speed or swing but as a result of the sheer astonishment of the batsmen that anything so gangling and unruly as my action could actually propel the ball at all, never mind in his direction. But even so . . .

If I didn't take any wickets in my first four overs The Wangler removed me because 'the conditions aren't right for you today', and if I did take wickets in my first four overs he gave me a pat on the shoulder and whispered that, 'You're in danger of making them go into their shells, old man. I think we need to tempt them a bit, bait the trap, so to speak . . .'

'We'd scored two hundred and thirty-two,' The Wangler

would explain in the clubhouse afterwards. 'After seven overs the opposition were eighteen for three. It was obvious to me that if I continued with the opening bowlers the opposition batsmen would just shut up shop and play for a draw. So I brought myself on to buy a few wickets.' When it came to buying wickets The Wangler rarely haggled or shopped around. When he turned his arm over holed-out-to-long-on went hyper-inflationary. He regarded 2–127 as a real bargain.

Apart from myself, only about six other people had turned up at Windhill to watch the game. The outfield was bumpy but the wicket seemed decent enough. Khan took a sharp return catch to dismiss the right-handed opener and Windhill were 35–1 off ten overs. At the other end Zubair laboured without much luck. 'Well bowled, Zub. Shabash,' his team mates yelled in their chunky West Riding accents, 'you've got it going, lad.'

Windhill became frustrated as Khan and Zubair pinned them down. The new batter, a beefy chap after the style of the late David Shepherd, was struck on the hand by Khan and next ball tried to withdraw his bat with an upward flourish, got an edge and was pouched by first slip. 38–2.

The new batsman, another left-hander, had a wide-footed stance and a high back lift. His name is Farakh Hussain and he has a high local reputation. He exuded the air of a man with no time for poncing around, smacking the ball hard into the area between point and cover.

Zubair had begun to tire and was replaced by a bespectacled off-spinner. He was unsettled bowling to the two left-handers and the ball fizzed down the leg side repeatedly for deflected singles, or byes. When he did pitch it outside off stump Hussain smashed him for a couple of boundaries. The spinner was withdrawn and replaced with a tall medium pacer nicknamed Cammy.

At the other end Khan continued, grunting and grimacing with effort and continually getting the ball to rise unexpectedly off a length. An edge from opener Neil Johnson flew between third slip and gully. Another cannoned off the splice and was spilled by the fielder at point. It was a simple chance – not the first I had seen go down this season – and after it hit the deck Khan squatted down in the middle of the strip and stared at the grass, breathing heavily.

Though it took him quite a while to rally, he came back with renewed effort, letting out a bull-like roar as a mis-timed pull looped just over the head of midwicket. The errant point fielder tried to catch his eye at the end of the over in the hope of some forgiveness, but Khan studiously ignored him and the fielder moped off looking disconsolate.

The left-handed Johnson had been becalmed for some while, when Khan eventually got him caught at the wicket. The next man in was solidly built and a big hitter. He slapped Cammy over mid-on for four and then over cover for another boundary. Khan was pulled through square leg, and Cammy hooked for a huge six that flew over the boundary wall and into a neighbouring garden.

Billy Boy was brought back at the Leeds Road end in an attempt to restore order. The new man flat batted him for four, but was then clean bowled advancing down the wicket. Whatever control Bowling Old Lane had been exercising had been broken by this wild flurry, however. Windhill had reached 102–4 in just twenty-five overs.

Bowling had one last chance to find a way back into the game when the dashing Hussain hit the ball high into the air off Khan. At mid-off Cammy called for the catch, positioned himself perfectly to take it and then inexplicably allowed the ball to bounce up and out of his hands.

Hussain didn't offer another chance. Spurred on by his

lucky break he launched a determined assault on the houses of the Stumps. Sixes crashed into balconies and rebounded off walls. One smashed straight through a roof tile and disappeared into the attic. The scoreboard flicked round so fast it sounded like an angry rattlesnake. The left-hander reached his hundred and his partner, the all-rounder Sadaqat Zaman slashed his way to a rapid fifty as Bowling Old Lane's fielding disintegrated. Windhill finished on 259–5, the hard-working Khan taking 3–46. He looked totally exhausted as he walked off for his tea.

As the carnage unfolded I chatted to a nice old fellow in a fawn mac who'd played at Windhill in the fifties and before that at Idle. 'Don't get crowds like we used to,' he said. 'Maybe at Pudsey and them.' He said that back in the fifties the standard was very high. 'Real class players. I like to see it when a batsman just rocks back and eases the ball off the back foot through the covers. He can do that I say, "That's a good player."'

The Bradford League still featured a high number of top class cricketers, yet there was a feeling among old-timers that things were in decline. It was something you heard a lot in the leagues. The bowling in particular was criticised. 'They don't know a good line from a washing line,' blokes said. To my mind, though, it was the batting that appeared to have deteriorated. Ranga Godage, Brent Findlay and Jonathan Musgrave had all impressed with the ball, but even the centuries I'd seen had such an air of the rustic about them they might have had a straw between their teeth. Certainly I'd seen no one to compare with the style of Clayton Lambert or Desmond Haynes, or the raw power of Lance Cairns. At Guisborough I'd had a definite feeling that the cricket wasn't quite up to the standard I recalled, but I was reluctant to voice that sentiment too loudly.

*

Sport has a habit of making competitors grow old before our eyes. It can have the same effect on fans too, though the effects on us are more psychological that physical. Quicker than anything else apart from pop music, sport turns us into our parents.

It starts when you turn forty. At thirty-five you are still full of *joie de vivre*, but at forty doubts start to set in. You become jaded. You start to realise that you ask 'What was the score at Lord's?' less and 'Whatever happened to Fred Swarbrook?' more. 'Whatever happened to Fred Swarbrook?' you say, 'The balding spinner from Derby with the rock-the-baby action, whose cunning wiles belied the ancient adage "Derbyshire born, Derbyshire bred; strong in arm and thick in head"? Whatever happened to Fred Swarbrook of Derbyshire and Griqualand West? Come to think of it, whatever happened to Griqualand West?'

When Father Time's deliveries have started to land worryingly close to the corridor of uncertainty that lies just outside the off stump of forty you seek security in the past. Soon 'Where are they now?' is the second most common thing you say. The first is, 'What, are you all going home so soon?'

Like alcoholism, nostalgia takes hold slowly. You begin with a few low strength remarks about how England have never really replaced dear old Jack Russell and end in dark basements on sunny afternoons grunting 'hear, hear' whenever a caller to the Test Match Special edition of 6-0-6 decries the effect Twenty20 cricket is having on the England batsmen's shot selection. Without realising it, you have become your father.

The expression 'five-for', as in 'He's taken several five-fors this season' was the thing that did it for me. To start off with, it seemed only to be used by fictional first class numpty-journeyman Dave Podmore, but this summer five-for has gained such acceptance that the *Guardian* newspaper's style guide has formalised the hyphen and even Christopher Martin-Jenkins is saying it (though in fairness to CMJ he does pronounce it so that you can clearly hear the inverted commas).

All in all, I don't suppose there's anything really wrong with five-for beyond a Phillip Hughes-like inelegance. For starters it saves the bother of typing the word 'wickets', or remembering how many runs the bowler conceded. I'm not sure if the full implications of its use have yet been worked out, however. Saying somebody took a five-for doesn't tell the full story. At Kingston in 1930 West Indies spinner Tommy Scott took a five-for against England. Unfortunately for him, England scored 849 and 266 of them came off his bowling. Five-for – every time I hear it I feel a letter to the *Daily Telegraph* coming on.

'No. Not what it were,' the old chap at Windhill said. 'Still, that left-hander's kept us entertained. Hussain. He's not bad.'

I asked what he thought of the Ashes series. 'I think the Aussies are a busted flush,' he said. 'They've gone on and on about that Mitchell Johnson. Well, he doesn't even look like a bowler.' It was true: Johnson had hardly lived up to his reputation as a fearsome paceman. The Australians had called him their 'gun bowler', but on the evidence of the summer when it came to settling arguments he was less like a pistol than a stiff letter to the local paper.

Bowling Old Lane's innings began disastrously. The opening bowler, Craig Wiseman from the Leeds End, was left arm over. His first ball was banged in short. The opener went to pull but succeeded only in spooning the ball to midwicket. The batsmen had crossed, which brought the roughly treated off-spinner onto strike. He wears his spectacles to bat in, but they don't help him much with the first delivery. It smacked into his thigh and trickled narrowly wide of the stumps. The next struck him high on the pad, the one after that flashed past the outside edge. 'Has he brung his bat, this fella?' cover shouted to the wicketkeeper.

The bowler from the Stumps End was Iqbal Khan. Like Wiseman he beat the bat repeatedly, groaning as he watched the ball whistle into the keeper's gloves.

A couple of overs passed. Bowling's left-handed number three slashed Wiseman over third man for an improbable six but it was a brief respite. The bespectacled opener continued to prod and miss, and was eventually caught at mid-on from a half-arsed pull shot.

Bowling Old Lane battled back via the left-hander, a neat compact player who seemed unperturbed by the hostility of Windhill's opening attack. He unfurled a cover drive and cross batted a boundary as Wiseman, pawing the turf at the injustice of it all, began to run out of steam. At the other end the number four despatched Iqbal for four through mid-on and then cut for another boundary between second slip and gully.

Wiseman began his next over with a bouncer the umpire called a wide. The bowler was incredulous, 'It were past his ear. It weren't over his head,' he rumbled. He carried on chuntering throughout the rest of the over, his ill temper exacerbated by the umpire's decision to follow up the wide signal by warning him about running on the wicket. Happily there was no repeat of the Lascelles Hall-type confrontation.

The boundaries continued to come, but then Iqbal finally located an edge to have the number four caught at the wicket and Bowling Old Lane are 43–3 after eleven overs.

Wiseman, still grumbling to anyone who will listen and some who won't, was replaced by Drake, a big bloke with out-turned feet, a smiley face and the vague look of the late John Candy. I left as he took the fourth Bowling wicket.

*

At York the stragglers from the race meeting are stumbling about the platforms in great red-faced mobs. Geordie geezers, landed gentry, corporate freeloaders, accounts executives, scrap dealers, the old, the young, the rich, the poor, the beautiful and the damned, top hats and tattoos all united in egalitarian stupefaction. One fifty-year-old woman holds the hand of her mortally pissed husband and he staggers along behind her, a confused grin on his mush and dribble on his chin, looking like the world's largest toddler.

Learie Constantine stayed one more season at Windhill, helping them to win the title again. After that he played cricket solely as an amateur to help boost wartime morale. During the week he worked for the Ministry of Labour, helping organise the immigrant workforce that was flooding in from the Caribbean. 'We found time to play cricket,' he wrote later, 'and beat the Nazis too.'

In 1946 Constantine returned to Busy Lane. He played three more seasons in the Bradford League. He took a wicket with his final delivery and his last action with the bat was to strike the ball to the boundary for the winning runs. 'Who writes your scripts?' Graham Gooch famously remarked to Ian Botham. Whoever it was had clearly been plagiarising.

Iqbal Khan took 5–58 as Bowling Old Lane struggled to 192 all out. Windhill finished the season in third place narrowly missing out on promotion. Bowling were sixth.

Unhook the Elephant

Stockton

On Friday I'd had quite an exciting moment. I'd bumped into Jonny Wilkinson in the garage. Not my garage, obviously. That would have been more surprising than exciting. I mean it's not often you go into an outbuilding and encounter a sporting superstar, is it? 'I popped in the shed to get some creosote this afternoon and guess who was in there leaning against the wheelbarrow? Clive Hubert Lloyd.' These are words you seldom hear.

Anyway, I was in the petrol station when I bumped into Jonny Wilkinson. I had already been alerted to his presence by the fact that one of the two women behind the counter was fanning the other with a copy of *Farmer's Weekly* while simultaneously pouring a bottle of mineral water over her own head. Because, it has to be said, Jonny is extremely dashing and handsome. He appears literally to glow. It's as if he is perpetually bathed in the golden light of a late summer afternoon. I don't know why this is, whether it's natural charisma, the sheen of his achievements or simply the result of eating huge quantities of Ready Brek when he was a child, but the fact is that when you look at him it's like you are gazing through a thermal imaging device.

So I faced the glimmering Jonny down the aisle between the racks of cough sweets and the shelf of two-stroke motor-mower oil and found myself in a quandary. Normally I would say hello to anyone I met in my village, whether I knew them or not. However, I didn't want Jonny thinking I was just saying hello to him because of who he was. After some thought I decided that the best course was to greet him in a manner that was nonchalant but in no way off-hand, which suggested recognition without impertinence. And by the time I had settled on the exact tone and timbre needed to convey all this in a single word – 'Morning' – Jonny had walked past me, got in his car and was several miles down the road.

It took some while for the women behind the counter to regain sufficient control of their faculties to sell me my newspaper. When they did I was dismayed to see the news that Freddie Flintoff had announced that, because of persistent injuries, he would be retiring from test cricket at the conclusion of the Ashes. And I couldn't help feeling that there was an unhappy link between the man I had just encountered and the fellow I was reading about – the greatest English cricketer and the greatest English rugby player of their generation, both blessed with the gifts of gods and the bodies of matchstick models.

This may sound a little harsh. It is not intended to be. Both men are as tough as teak, but they do seem beset by more than their share of misfortune. You feel you could have dropped a rhinoceros on Ian Bell's head and he'd simply have bounced to his feet with a jaunty cry of 'Unhook the elephant!', while poor Freddie only had to sneeze to dislocate a knee.

Opinion on Freddie is that he is a large man whose mighty frame has simply buckled under the strain. Maybe that is right. Then again, West Indies paceman Joel Garner was like a family-sized version of Freddie and his mighty frame seemed to stand up pretty well. I don't have the stats to hand but I'm willing to bet that if you asked any batsman who played during the late seventies and early eighties how often Big Bird was injured the answer would be 'Nowhere near often enough, mate.'

It isn't just Freddie and Jonny who have been afflicted in this way. In fact it has been something of a theme in English sport over the past twenty-five years. When you think of all the England midfielders who could have been injury prone – Steve McMahon, Carlton Palmer, Ray bloody Wilkins – you have to wonder why it was Bryan Robson and Paul Gascoigne who ended up getting crocked all the time.

Admittedly Freddie, Jonny and Bryan Robson are men who played with reckless disregard for their own well-being, while Gazza was just, well, Gazza – the sort of bloke who if faced with a choice between having a lukewarm milky drink and sticking his genitals in a hornets' nest inevitably headed straight towards the sound of buzzing, unbuckling his belt. Yet even so it seems an unholy coincidence (or indeed a holy one, if you happen to be from one of the several thousand countries across the universe that takes gleeful delight in watching England lose). Bryan Robson managed the World Cup in 1982 and the 1988 European Championship; Gazza the 1990 World Cup and the 1996 Euros; Jonny was fit for a pair of World Cups; Freddie for one Ashes summer series and one winter. How come every very vital-spark team-playing male we have produced since 1980 seems to come with a tape-recorded message that says, 'This sportsman will self-destruct after two tournaments'?

Is it simply ill fortune, or is there something more to it than that? Are we willing it in some way? Perhaps as a nation we are temperamentally unsuited for the sort of long-term relationship with success enjoyed by Australia or Germany. Maybe all we want from sport is a brief and memorable interlude. So that in later years we can stare into a night sky, a glass of whisky in hand and a piano playing in the background, and say, 'Whatever happens, we'll always have Sydney,' while dreaming of what might have been.

That's one idea. I had another. People will say the string of injuries suffered by England's top cricketers – think of Michael Vaughan with his knee, Ashley Giles with his hip, Kevin Pietersen and his persistently swollen head – is just plain bad luck. Maybe so, though it is increasingly clear to me that in this case the harder you train the unluckier you get. Put simply, England's cricketers are too fit to play the game. Over the past few years they have worked on their athleticism remorselessly. They have abandoned the traditional training regimen of short shuttle runs between the pub and the baker that served titans of yesteryear such as Ken Higgs, Ken Shuttleworth and Mike Hendrick. The only thing that was likely to be ripped to the max on a cricket field in those days was the seat of Phil Sharpe's trousers if he bent down too far at slip. Not any more. The result is that England players' muscles have been gradually ratcheted tighter and tighter until all it takes is one ab crunch too many and in a glissando of twangs the body explodes like an over-wound clock. Many doctors believe that it is only a matter of time before a cricketer becomes so taut he actually turns himself inside out.

In my view this quest for super-fitness is counter-productive. The more exercise you do the greater your chances of doing yourself harm. That is not conjecture, or speculation. That is maths. We are told the cricketers are fitter than ever before. Well, they say the same thing about professional footballers too. Yet what do we hear, week in, week out, from Premiership managers? 'I haven't been able to get my first choice team out

on the park since August', 'Things will improve when we get
a few players back from injury' and 'I'm not making excuses,
but . . .' The players may have less body fat than a carpet tile
and be so tightly muscled that if you banged them against a
hard surface they'd hum like a tuning fork. But frankly my
idea of a fit person is not somebody lying in a hospital bed
with his leg in traction, eating grapes.

Aston Villa won the League Championship in 1981–2
using just ten players, Dennis Mortimer playing the entire
season in two positions and, on one memorable afternoon at
Anfield, even coming on as a substitute to replace Peter Withe
for the last ten minutes as well. The players were not as fit in
those days, yet they played more games. If I knew for certain
what a paradox is, I'd be tempted to say that is one.

And then there is the psychological effect of too much physical training. Because it is well known that the fitter someone
is the more they whinge. Ask the average slob with his stom-
ach hanging over the top of his comfort-fit slacks like a
knapsack filled with porridge how he is and the chances are
he will respond 'Not bad, thanks.' Ask the same question of
greyhound-thin fellow in Lycra running kit and you'd better
pull up a chair because what you will likely get is the full low-
down on every minor ache, niggle, twinge, tweak and jarp,
plus a long explanation of the peculiar burning sensation he
gets in the tendon of his left triceratops whenever he spends
time on the StairMaster. It is a fundamental rule of human
nature that as soon as you can name a muscle it starts hurting.

When I first started going to watch Yorkshire one of the star
turns was the medium pacer Tony Nicholson. Tony Nicholson
had pompadour hair and ruddy cheeks (come to think of it,
he could have been Steve McClaren's dad). His physique was
finely sculpted, though only if the sculpture you had in mind
was something by Henry Moore. Nics's strict daily work out

of two squat thrusts, a sit up and a pork pie may not have given him toned pecs and rock-solid glutes, but believe me he could run about the outfield quicker than a modern cricketer on crutches.

On the day I'd seen Jonny it had poured down. On Saturday, though the rain had ceased the air still felt damp. The train into Newcastle was packed with kids eager to see the latest Harry Potter movie. Just outside Dunston, in what must have been a spontaneous tribute to the recently departed Michael Jackson, a group of them suddenly burst into a chorus of 'Thriller'. Though their voices were marginally less high-pitched than Jacko's, obviously.

I changed trains at Newcastle and took the branch line that runs down the Durham coast. At Seaham – where George Francis had once drawn the crowds, and Peter Willey had started a cricket career that would reach its pinacle when Brian Johnston uttered his famous line of commentary, 'The bowler's Holding, the batsman's Willey' – the outfield of the cricket ground was covered in standing water. At Hartlepool Golf Club the bunkers looked like carp ponds. At Seaton Carew the road was flooded.

It didn't look too hopeful when I alighted at Stockton-on-Tees either. In more ways than one. When I was a child, Stockton was considered a bit upmarket, a place you came to get your school uniform, or see the film *The Battle of Britain* on a really big screen. But the town suffered some sort of physical collapse in the eighties and is now a gibbering ruin. Practically everybody you see has the look of someone who's fleeing a crime scene, or on the verge of creating one. There are blokes dealing drugs just off the high street, in front of rows of houses with steel shutters over the windows. Roving gangs of kids in track pants, whose sole form of entertainment seems to be spitting, stalk around in front of boarded-up pizzerias and bust kebab shops. Older people catch your eye and smile ruefully as if they know just what you are thinking and don't blame you one bit.

I'd come to Stockton partly for nostalgia. The Grangefield Ground is the only first class venue at which I've played (though it didn't actually become a first class venue until about two decades after this momentous event). It was also the first proper cricket match I'd ever played in. I batted at number four and was given out LBW to a ball that hit me on the toe of my boot, despite the fact I was playing forward to a right-arm outswing bowler (not that I'm bitter). I can still recall the seam marks in the leather. They were old-fashioned boots, ankle high and with steel toecaps and the signature of some veteran cricketer I'd never heard of (Alf Gover, Peter Loader, someone like that) squiggled on the side in red. My trousers were from Ken Barrington's sportswear company and had pegged fronts, a French fly and turn-ups. This was 1975, when everybody else was wearing Oxford bags and loon pants. Cricket, however, remained unmoved by fashion. As far as I can recall, Asif Iqbal's bell-bottoms were as near as the game came to embracing rock 'n' roll.

My own situation as a teenage cricketer was made worse by the heightist attitudes of sportswear manufacturers. The perils of ordinary life are bad enough for those of us who suffer under the certain knowledge that our nasal hair will never sprout unnoticed. We have to cram ourselves under desks, bend double to reach work-surfaces and face the danger of losing an eye to the spokes of someone's umbrella whenever we venture out in the rain. When it comes to sport, however, things are far, far worse. The tall person is the constant victim of athletic sizeual stereotyping, forced to deny his or her true nature and always play at centre-half. While the short or the medium are allowed to jink and shimmy, those who can dust the top of the wardrobe without standing on a chair must content themselves with being solid or towering. They will never know the freedom that results from being mercurial. Worst of all, they will find themselves frequently approached by grinning evangelical poltroons who ask, 'Have you ever thought of taking up basketball?'

There are no greater exponents of this casual sizeism than the manufacturers of sports clothing and equipment. The people who made cricket whites, for example, laboured under the illusion that the human shape is essentially cuboid. According to their philosophy, if you have a thirty-eight-inch inside leg measurement you must also have a thirty-eight-inch waist. This is by no means true. As a consequence I, and no doubt hundreds of others like me, including Curtly Ambrose, spent my teenage years torn between trousers that reached the top of my boots but had to be held up with braces and those that, while they didn't ever threaten to fall down around my ankles, didn't reach them either. Eventually I settled on the latter as marginally less embarrassing.

The shirt was another matter. In order to get one that was long enough to tuck into trousers I had to opt for a collar size that would have made a respectable batting average. The chest was similarly capacious. Indeed anyone who could have filled that garment would have made Matthew Hayden look like Mr Puniverse. When I put on the shirt and sat on the floor I was often mistaken for a half-erected marquee.

The shirt billowed, the trousers flapped at half mast. As a result, I invariably took the field looking as if I was making a bold but ill-advised bid to popularise cullottes and the poncho as suitable garments for our summer game. When play commenced things deteriorated still further, especially if it was windy. In even the slightest breeze my shirt became a sail.

Bowling was almost impossible. With the wind in my favour I sped to the wicket at such velocity I had often arrived before my arm was even raised.

If the breeze was against me I executed a kind of cricketing moonwalk, apparently advancing to the crease while actually travelling backwards until my progress was arrested by the sightscreen. Of batting I will say nothing save that the average pad provided ample protection for my shin while exposing a yard or so of sensitive, bony thigh and that even using the longest bat available left me with a batting stance that was once likened, unfavourably, to the crouch of a constipated toad.

Stockton were due to play Sunderland at the Grangefield Ground in a North-East Premier League fixture. The North-East Premier League is the invention of the ECB. A few years ago the ECB decided that English club cricket needed organising to serve the needs of the test and county teams. The boffins at Lord's had clearly been inspired by the Football Association's famous League Pyramid. Two decades before, the men from Lancaster Gate had reorganised all league football in England into a new triangular structure, at the top of which sat the national team. The initiative was introduced in 1980. Before it was put into place, the England team had won just one major international honour. Since it has been in place, however, they have won no international honours whatsoever.

The ECB did not allow themselves to be deterred by this sort of facile argument. Leagues such as the North-East Premier were introduced to prepare young cricketers for the demands of the county and international game. Matches started at eleven o'clock and were played in sixty-over innings. The North-East Premier had dragged teams out of all the

traditional leagues in the region. As a result, the Northumberland and Tyneside leagues, which had split apart in 1934, had
rejoined each other. It was noticeable though, that despite the
ECBs initiatives the most famous leagues in the country
remained aloof and independent, preferring to structure their
cricket to local rather than national demands.

Sunderland had originally played in the Durham Senior
League while Stockton had joined the North Yorkshire South
Durham League in 1895. The club had been founded in 1816
and in 1847 had played an All England XI, losing by forty-
four runs in front of a large crowd which had paid 'one
shilling for gentleman and sixpence for working men', with
ladies admitted free.

The club had moved to the Grangefield Ground in 1891,
raising the money for the pavilion with a series of bazaars. In
the thirties Learie Constantine had played in an annual exhi-
bition match at the ground as a favour to the local GP, who
was a friend of his. The Trinidadian got into hot water after
one of them when he gave an interview to the *Northern Echo*
and criticised the sort of cricket that was played in the Roses
matches. It was, he said, 'a wash out' and operated under an
unwritten law of 'no boundaries before lunch'. The affair
blew over quite quickly, but the comments were not forgotten
at Old Trafford. When it was suggested to Lancashire that
Constantine might make a valuable addition to the county
side, they cited his comments as one of the reasons for reject-
ing the idea, though race may have been a factor too. The
great West Indian would never play county cricket.

When I arrived at the Grangefield Ground there was
nobody around. I stuck my head in the clubhouse and a man
standing at the bar said that, though the ground staff had
spent the early hours of the morning pumping water off the
outfield, the umpires judged the wicket unfit for play. 'It was

called off at ten-thirty,' he said. 'It's the early start, isn't it? If we'd been pitching wickets at one-thirty we might have got it on.'

I walked back into the town centre. An Asian mother in a sari and anorak broke into a high-keening song, possibly it was a lullaby for the child who was nodding in the buggy she was pushing though it sounded like a heartfelt protest against whatever combination of events had brought her here. I got a bus to Thornaby in the hope that some sort of microclimate might exist there, but as soon as I got off at the stop near Mandale Bottoms I was soaked to the skin in a heavy shower. So I got on the train and came home again.

The Greatest Player We Never Saw

Blackpool

Years ago I worked with a man from the West Midlands who at the onset of August invariably regaled me with his fond childhood memories of holidays in Blackpool in the fifties. 'Bingo on the Golden Mile,' he'd say, rubbing his hands together with glee at the thought of it. 'Haddock and chips from Fleetwood, Stanley Matthews running down the wing at Bloomfield Road and Bill Alley bashing the bowling around at Stanley Park. They had a song, you know, "Glory, Glory Alley-lujah".'

By the time I first visited Blackpool, Stanley Matthews had been back in the Potteries for a decade and Billy Alley was batting for Somerset but, as our family's Riley drove slowly along beneath the glittering lights of the Illuminations it still felt as if you might catch a glimpse of them both galloping along the seafront.

Nostalgia is an integral part of the British seaside. Even now there seems to be a whiff of Brylcreem and No.55 cologne mixed with the scent of the sea and the vinegar and boiling beef fat. You could never go to a cricket match at Scarborough without somebody telling you of the time Cec Pepper had hit his mighty sixes into the boarding houses, and the game was punctuated by the pop-pop of gunfire from the model battleships on the lake in Peasholm Park that fought the Battle of the River Plate several times a day. Across the way Barbara Windsor topped the bill at the Floral Hall and the backlit Perspex mosaic at the Harbour Bar offered ice cream served in wafers shaped like clam shells. There was cinnamon toast inside when it turned nippy, or a bacon bun (banjos, the North Riding boys called them) eaten standing outside the Teapot caravan watching the waves rolling in from Norway and crashing against the sea wall.

Scarborough hasn't changed much since then, either. The Harbour Bar is as bright as ever (though the Knickerbocker Glories somehow don't seem as tall) and the battleships still blast away. Undoubtedly that's all to the good. The seaside resorts that have survived best are the ones that didn't try and adapt to modern trends, that kept the boating lakes, the crazy golf and the shops selling sunhats, saucy postcards ('He wants a stick of rock like that monkey's holding!') and models of lighthouses perched on promontories of cockle shells. Stasis, as Florence, Venice and Bruges have proved in an altogether grander manner, is a cornerstone of tourism.

A few years ago when we were staying on the coast in Devon we spent one rainy afternoon merrily watching *Shrek* in a cinema that still had usherettes who showed you to your seat by torchlight and emerged during the interval with trays of choc ices. In the café round the corner there was only Veronique on the 'evening dinner' menu and two old ladies talking about their ballroom dancing class, 'He's such a lovely man,' one was saying of the instructor, 'wonderful manners. Always smart. Immaculate fingernails. I'm surprised no young woman's snapped him up.' It was like parachuting back into my childhood.

It was like that when I got off the train in Blackpool too. We used to go to Blackpool Illuminations every year. We stayed in a B&B in Fleetwood that seemed to have been invented to provide material for Les Dawson – the landlady kicked everybody out at half-past nine in the morning and you were not allowed back in until five, even if it poured down every minute in between. In the evening we would drive up and down the Golden Mile admiring the lights. My parents showed a marked reluctance to get out of the car, however. This baffled me as on the one occasion we had, a jolly red-faced man who walked – as many of the people did – in an odd, staggery sort of way came up, patted me on the head and gave me a fifty-pence piece.

Blackpool is a bastion against modernity, still so becalmed it fails to attract the attention of the sort of global brands that have swamped high streets all over the country. There's even a branch of the Private Shop. With its blacked-out windows and furtive promise of marital aids, the Private Shop, which first appeared in the seventies, sums up the British attitude to sex in those days. People were struggling to come to grips with the new age. They wanted to be all free and Scandinavian, but they didn't have the background for it. At school we had sex education classes. The teacher told us that there was nothing dirty or rude about sex, that in fact it was natural and healthy. And then delivered a stern warning that if we revealed anything, anything whatsoever, of what we were about to hear to the younger children we would be soundly and robustly thrashed. Sex was nothing to be ashamed of, but you mustn't talk about it – that was the message.

I waited at the bus stop opposite the train station among pensioners in shirtsleeves, cavalry twill trousers held up with braces, and women in macs and gaudy holiday headscarves.

The bus to Stanley Park wound past theatres boasting outrageous comedians and transvestite dance troupes. It was a hot, sunny afternoon and on the walk to the ground builders were out laying 'Indian flooring' in the driveways of pre-war semis.

Blackpool's ground is on the western edge of Stanley Park. The playing area is sunk in a bowl. Concrete seats are set into the grass banking. Stanley Park used to host county fixtures and tour matches and it still has all the trappings of big time cricket, though things are looking a bit dilapidated these days. The ladies' pavilion hosts a kindergarten and advertises pilates classes, there's a smell of drains in the big stand at square leg and the boundary terracing looks in need of a coat of paint and a tidy up. Adverts for funeral homes and knee clinics dot the boundary.

The main clubhouse is smart enough, a two-tiered pavilion with half-timbered eaves and decking and an award from CAMRA for its real ale. Pink azaleas grow round the front and sides, giving it the air of a successful stockbroker's holiday house. There was a crowd of around three hundred, many of them holidaymakers who appeared to have little interest in which side was batting.

As it happens it was Blackpool, and one man who did care was the obligatory Lancastrian one-man Barmy Army, a skinny, elderly fellow in a Lancs Twenty20 top and an England baseball cap. He was knowledgeable and madly enthusiastic. 'A little cracker, this boy,' he said. 'Super bowler. I'm not kiddin' you, he's got all the talent to be the next Ian Foley.'

The player in question was St Annes slow left-armer Mike Baer, currently a university student but on Lancashire's books. Inevitably nicknamed Yogi, he bowled in tandem with Dinuka Hettiarachchi, who got a single test cap for Sri Lanka and has been bamboozling batsman in the Northern Premier League

since he arrived from Keswick in the North Lancashire and
Cumbria League back in April.

Blackpool had lost their own pro, another Sri Lankan,
Sajeera Weerakoon, who had been called up for a tour by the
national A side. Today his replacement was François du
Plessis, a twenty-five-year-old from Pretoria who had recently
won a contract with Lancashire. Du Plessis has played for the
South African A team but he also has league experience. A
few years back he was turning out in the Nottinghamshire
League for Mansfield Hosiery Mills. He had a spell with
Todmorden in the Lancashire League too.

Lancashire's county side don't have a game, so du Plessis
was joined by his county colleague Steve Croft, a Blackpool
native and former Stanley Park regular. Croft has had five seasons of first class cricket and was Lancs's player of the season
last year. He opened Blackpool's innings and hit a neat if
unexciting forty-eight.

Croft was helped by the fact that Hettiarachchi was totally
luckless early on, finding the edge repeatedly but never the
hands of a fielder. The Sri Lankan tied the Blackpool batters
down, though. His length was immaculate. It reminded me of
the stories I heard as a boy, of how the young Wilfred Rhodes
practised during the winter in a barn near Kirkheaton (where
else?), bowling the ball on a spot marked by a pocket handkerchief, hour after hour, until he could hit it every time. As a
result of his winter days in the barn Rhodes became famous
for his accuracy. He didn't charge at batsmen, he besieged
them, wearing away at their defences, waging a war of mental
and physical attrition. After a long afternoon session facing
Rhodes, the great Australian batsman Victor Trumper called
out plaintively, 'Oh come on, Wilfred, will you not give me a
rest?'

Du Plessis is built like a middleweight and punched the ball around, but thanks to the tightness of the St Annes attack and the enthusiasm of the fielders, runs come slowly and it takes Blackpool thirty overs to reach a hundred, by which time the excellent Baer had grabbed a couple of wickets.

I wandered off to square leg and took a seat in the stand by the ladies' pavilion. In front of me a group of shaven-headed Mancunians in town for a stag weekend drank Magners cider and passed around a spliff. Two blokes carrying cameras with huge telephoto lenses stood at the back of the stand snapping the action. At Lord's the world's most earnestly draconian stewards would have hunted them down like pack dogs.

The Blackpool team captain Paul Danson came round collecting the two-pound entrance fee as Hettiarachchi finally got through, clean bowling Smith for a score of nine. A few balls later he had Croft caught by Steve Twist and Blackpool were 129–4 with thirty-seven overs gone. Hettiarachchi then deceived Darlington with a flighted one, trapping him LBW on the back foot.

The new man Andrew Hogarth was out first ball, caught at midwicket hitting against the spin. 'I think I'm going to have to start trimming my armpit hair,' one of the Manc lads said. The Sri Lankan spinner had picked up four quick wickets. He was the shortest man on the field, balding and slightly pot bellied. Only in cricket could he be a sports star.

One of the pros who'd played for Blackpool was Jack Simmons, the man whose aunt's fish shop had been so popular with the Three Ws. Simmons had grown up in Enfield, and Clyde Walcott had lodged with his family. In fact Simmons later blamed the West Indian for giving him his notorious appetite for pie and chips, a diet that was responsible for the Lancastrian's unchiselled physique. When people described Simmons as an all-rounder, they meant it literally. He looked the sort of fellow whose appearance at an

all-you-can-eat restaurant buffet would shortly be followed
by the arrival of the official receiver.

The fact that somebody like Simmons could make a living
from the professional game while never looking much like an
athlete was one of cricket's appeals. Down the years many
men have risen to the top rank without regarding a six-pack
as anything other than a useful way of washing down a
double order of chicken biryani. As the late Colin Milburn
was fond of remarking, 'Touch my toes? I'm lucky if I can see
them.'

Certainly it was hard to imagine any other team sport that
would have found room for Pakistan's Inzamam-ul-Haq
(dubbed The Potato), India's Ramesh Powar, Mark 'Baby
Boof' Cosgrove of Australia or Bermuda's Dwayne Leverock.
The nineteen-stone Caribbean spinner was easily the biggest
presence on a cricket field since the retirement of the late,
lamented Indian test umpire Swaroop Kishen, himself a man
so wide he could easily have doubled as a sightscreen.
Leverock works as a policeman and you can't help feeling that
so long as he does the Bermudan constabulary will never want
for a roadblock.

Leverock was part of a tradition of greatness in cricket that
struggles to encompass everyone from W. G. Grace, through
Warwick 'The Big Ship' Armstrong to Arjuna Ranatunga, the
feisty Sri Lankan skipper whom many opponents referred to
by a name that sounded a bit like Big Ship. It was the roly poly
Ranatunga whose appearance at the crease provoked perhaps
the best bit of sledging of all time: Australian wicketkeeper
Ian Healy's instruction to the bowler, 'Put a Mars bar on a
good length, that should do it.' (The best heckle from the
crowd also concerned waistlines. When the silver-haired,
family-sized Mike Gatting arrived in Australia with the
England team in the late eighties one wag in the stands yelled,

'Strewth, what happened to you, Fatty? Did you blow all your pension at the pie stall?')

Years ago I went to Headingley for a Yorkshire *v* Lancashire Gillette Cup quarter-final. It was an exciting match, apparently. I base this view on the accounts in the following day's newspapers because I didn't actually get to see much of the action. This was entirely the fault of that man Jack Simmons. The off-spinner was a fine cricketer, a loyal club servant and a good egg in every respect, but he wasn't a man you'd choose to have fielding right in front of you.

Simmons was nicknamed 'Flat Jack' though when you watched him rumbling to the wicket in profile you couldn't help feeling an extra consonant had wandered in by mistake.

When Yorkshire batted that day Simmons came and fielded in front of us at fine leg. About twenty fans were enveloped by his huge shadow, though that number dwindled to sixteen shortly afterwards, four people having collapsed with seasonal affective disorder. At the end of the over, just when we thought we might get a glimpse of the wicket again, the Lancashire captain, David Lloyd, signalled for Jack to stay where he was, and so he fielded at deep mid-off instead. Wickets fell, glorious strokes were played, miraculous slip catches were trousered, LBW appeals were waved aside but neither I nor the people sitting around me saw any of it. Eventually one man became so exasperated he called over a steward. 'When I bought this ticket,' he growled, 'they never said owt about it being restricted view'.

Blackpool and St Annes were founder members of the Northern League (the Premier bit had been added recently, part of the ECB's rebranding programme), which had begun as a breakaway from the Ribblesdale League by West

Lancashire clubs grown tired of horse-drawn journeys to Settle.

Blackpool had fielded a lot of top class cricketers down the years. Harold Larwood finished his career as pro at Stanley Park while running a sweetshop in the town. Rohan Kanhai was here too, of course, and so were other top West Indians such as Collis King and Richie Richardson. Bill Alley had arguably been the most successful and exciting. He'd set a series of batting records in the fifties that are unlikely ever to be surpassed.

Like Cec Pepper, Alley conformed almost totally to the English cricket fan's image of an Australian: tough, fearless and filled with foul-mouthed bravado. During his early years he'd worked as a miner, a boxer, a blacksmith and a night-club bouncer, fighting brawls in back alleys including one with a red-haired Scotsman that turned into a long-running series. Alley liked a drink and he liked a joke. During a Commonwealth XI tour of India (the team included nine players from the Lancashire leagues, among them Pepper, Worrell, George Tribe and Winston Place) Big Bill had finished a lengthy session in the bar and got into bed only to find himself being attacked by a large green parrot, which according to his own account, almost severed his penis with a series of savage pecks. On another drunken night on the same tour he and Pepper almost asphyxiated when their roommate Jack Pettiford's bed caught fire in the early hours.

Alley bowled niggling right-arm medium pacers and batted left-handed. As in life, his style at the crease was pugnacious and uncompromising. In a famous innings against W. Green's XI he whacked half a dozen deliveries straight out of Stanley Park and on to the adjacent putting green. On another occasion, against Chorley, he smashed ninety-eight in a Blackpool total of 114–8. In four seasons with the Seasiders, Alley hit fourteen league centuries and finished with a career average at the club of over a hundred. While he was playing, crowds at Stanley Park regularly topped five thousand.

Alley married a Lancastrian woman and left Blackpool only because, at the remarkable age of thirty-eight, Somerset finally offered him the chance to play first class cricket again. Despite his advancing years he played four hundred county matches, scoring 19,612 runs and taking 768 wickets. Like Pepper, he became an unlikely but popular umpire.

Bill Alley was often described as the greatest cricketer who never played a test match. A man who also laid claim to that title was said to have played for Blackpool too. I'd first come across the name of Donald Rudolph Weekes when I was fourteen and *The Cricketer* magazine carried an article about him under the arresting headline 'The best batsman never to have played test cricket?' Weekes was a Barbadian, and a possible distant relative of Everton Weekes. He'd played most of his cricket in California and captained the USA in the annual match against Canada on three occasions in the late sixties and early seventies. He'd scored a century in one of those games and also hit double hundreds in various other matches across North America. All that was undoubtedly true. What was harder to verify were Weekes's stories of hitting seven hundred not out in a club match in India, sparring with Muhammad Ali in Tokyo and appearing as Othello in a Moscow theatre. Weekes did play for the Barbados B team and seems to have spent some time in England where he turned out in a single first class match, for Sussex. He also claimed that during his time over here he scored 2879 runs in a single season when playing as a professional at Blackpool. Certainly there was no mention of this feat in the records of the Northern Premier League and since it was more than double the tally Bill Alley had set in 1953 there really ought to have been. I haven't come across mention of Don Weekes in any of the literature I've read about cricket in the northern leagues. It's a pity, really, as with his big hitting and tall tales he'd undoubtedly have been highly popular up here.

At Stanley Park, skipper Danson was next man in for Blackpool. He walked out to some rather over-exuberant cheers from a gang of blokes on the opposite terrace, narrowly avoided playing on to the hat-trick ball and gloved the next one just short of mid-on. If Danson was riding his luck he soon crashed it into a ditch, holing out to mid-on after a few overs. Through all this du Plessis had moved seamlessly past the fifty mark.

At the other end the carnage continued. Harrison Clark was smartly stumped off Hettiarachchi and Gleeson caught at midwicket a few balls later. With the home side at 147–9 du Plessis danced down the wicket to the Sri Lankan and was beaten by a quicker ball and clean bowled. Hettiarachchi finished with 7–51 off nineteen overs.

I nipped out to Haywards ('So fresh we're famous!') down the road to get some lunch. I bought a creamy vegetable pasty and a Danish pastry. When I asked for them the woman behind the counter said 'Okey dokey!' with such Lancastrian jauntiness I half expected her to whip out a ukelele and start singing 'With My Little Stick of Blackpool Rock'.

Richard Gleeson opened the bowling for Blackpool. He is young, with a cock-wristed action, and worked up quite a pace. His fourth ball clean bowled Atiq Uz-Zaman for a duck. At the south end of the ground Andrew Hogarth got things underway. He is burly, short and accelerates nicely into his delivery stride. He trapped the other opener, St Annes' skipper Andy Kellet, LBW. Kellet trudged back to the pavilion shaking his head. Sawn off? He clearly believed so. In his next over Gleeson had Stephen Twist caught behind. Hogarth chipped in with a fourth wicket and suddenly St Annes were in all kinds of bother.

There might have been bother of another kind too as David Bartholomew, a middle-aged West Indian with grey tinges in his hair, walked around the boundary in his sandals and made it plain to everybody that he thought Gleeson was throwing.

It's a hard thing to judge, throwing. Accusations of it seem to run in cycles. There was a big spate of throwing scandals in the nineties – mainly surrounding Pakistani pace bowlers – and there'd been even more in the late fifties and early sixties. Gilchrist was no-balled for chucking, and so was Charlie Griffith. One of the worst offenders was said to be the Australian Ian Meckiff. Meckiff bowled (or hurled) Australia to an unlikely victory over Peter May's England team in 1958–9. May made no bones about the fact he thought Meckiff was cheating. Brian Close was similarly blunt about Griffith. Bill Alley, however, always maintained that English criticism of his compatriot Meckiff was motivated solely by envy. And that's what the man sitting next to me said about Bartholomew's allegations: 'It's just sour grapes, is that.'

At the other end Hogarth limped off clutching his calf and was replaced by Croft. The Lancashire player bowls right arm fast medium. He knocked back Bradley's off stump in his second over and quickly dismissed the Sri Lanka pro and Michael Baer to leave St Annes struggling badly at 35–7.

Whaley and Jones began a slow recovery for the visitors, egged on by some away fans who line up on the boundary bearing letters that spell out 'WANKER D', for reasons that remain opaque. The score rose gradually and the chances stopped coming. 'It's not a silent movie. Let's have some input fellas,' Blackpool's skipper yelled as the home side's impetus shrivelled and died. The round of gee-ups and clapping that followed his exhortation produced nothing except noise, however. Soon the visitors were edging towards the hundred mark, then past it. It's the sort of gritty percentage cricket the Northern leagues are supposed to be all about, each run bitterly contested. In terms of entertainment it's more chess than *Grand Theft Auto 3*.

St Annes has had its share of top players. Kanhai was at the Warton Ground late on in his career; S. F. Barnes had been the professional at the tender age of sixty-three; Paul Rocca put in five years' service; Jimmy Adams, Eldine Baptiste and Stuart MacGill had also played there. The club's most famous former cricketer, though, is certainly Andrew Flintoff. Freddie Flintoff is hugely popular with the English public. This is not just because he's a fine player, but because he is an archetype. Like Ian Dury's Sweet Gene Vincent, there is one in every northern town.

Several decades ago Dave Edmunds from Rockpile described himself to *NME* as the second best Chuck-Berry-style guitarist in the world. Top of the tree, if I recall correctly, was Keith Richards. I can't now remember where Chuck Berry fitted in the scheme of things, though I like to think he'd been narrowly nudged out of the bronze medal position by Johnny Thunders.

Even in his current knackered state I think we might judge Andrew Flintoff to be the best Freddie-Flintoff-style cricketer in the world. And that is no easy title to hold on to, let me tell you. Because just as at any given moment, in any given settlement across the length of breadth of the known universe you can guarantee that somebody will be twanging out the opening bars of 'Johnny B. Goode', so you can rest assured that on any Saturday or Sunday afternoon at any cricket field in the North of England you will find a Freddie. You will recognise him instantly. He's a bloke with cropped fair hair and ruddy cheeks, built like a nightclub doorman, or possibly just a nightclub door, who rumbles up to wicket and delivers the ball with a mighty bass grunt, powering it into the surface of the strip with the intensity of someone who won't be satisfied until he's got one to bury itself so deep in the wicket the groundsman has to come on and dig it out with a pick and shovel.

The bloke is all might and main, his follow through such a whirl of limbs and dust it seems at first that it will only be halted when he collides with the sightscreen. Instead, via a series of hops and skips, he comes to a juddering stop a few feet from the batsman. If he has not taken a wicket he appears bemused by the cupidity of fate. He smiles ruefully and shakes his head, occasionally making a helpful remark to his adversary such as, 'See that piece of wood you're holding? It's called a bat,' or 'If you're going to drive like that you might want some additional insurance, pal,' before striding back to his mark, huffing and puffing like a water buffalo. His aggression is bottomless. As Neville Cardus wrote of an earlier incarnation of the phenomenon, the giant, barrel-bodied and busy as a bumblebee Bolton and District Association and Lancashire paceman Walter Brearley: 'Every ball was a crisis as far as he was concerned.'

When he comes in to bat the Freddie's approach is simple and robust, recalling the words of one of Brearley's contemporaries Walter Warburton, who played for Eagley in the Bolton and District Association. When asked by a journalist to outline his philosophy of batting, Warburton replied, 'I clout the first ball for four and I keep on clouting.' Local glaziers put money behind the bar for him.

John Kay wrote of Squire Render 'a giant of a man who used to bowl flat out for hours on end for Werneth and slogged his way happily to many a half century', and there have been dozens of others like it before and since. A few years back, sitting on a bench somewhere in the land where cotton was king, the old man sitting next to me said, 'See this lad's about to bowl here? He's a belter, this lad. I tell you summat. He's from Moston, right? That's a right tough area, Moston. I'm from round there myself. I went into a pub one time. It were quiz night. The first question were, "What are you looking at?"' The old man let out a series of snorts and wheezy squeaks and parps. He sounded like a walrus sitting down on a harmonium.

'This lad, though,' the old man said dabbing away the tears of merriment with a handkerchief so well used it looked like a full-colour relief map of the Amazon basin, 'he's good 'un. But he's a bit rough, isn't he? I'm not messing about. When he first come to play here he were wearing an ASBO tag. He'd been playing up the road. Better standard of cricket than this. Much better. Only, a couple of the batters from other teams got restraining orders on him. Wasn't allowed within eight hundred yards of them. Bit of a problem when you're bowling at them that, isn't it? I don't care who you are. Shoaib Aktar, Keith Miller. Doesn't matter. If you're firing it down from half a mile away you're going to struggle. So he come here,' the man said. 'I think they're paying him five thousand a season.'

'I thought the leg spinner was the pro,' I said.

'Oh aye, leggy's the pro,' the old man replied, 'but there's not any decent amateurs round here'll play for less than a hundred and fifty a match.'

The lad in question was indeed a belter. He was also a Freddie. On a pitch as green as a seasick squid he fizzed the ball round the batsmens' chins, bowled unchanged through the innings and finished with 6–42. He came in to bat at number four and struck thirty in next to no time, the ball flying off the middle of his bat with a satisfying *thwock* until he suddenly appeared to hear the voice in his head that whispered 'play yourself in' and was caught at midwicket off a checked hoik. Later he walked around the boundary in his stocking feet, a pint of lager in each hand and a fag in his mouth.

I am not quite sure if the ASBO man was the Keith Richards of Freddie-Flintoff-style cricketers, or even the Dave Edmunds, but he was up around the Wilco Johnson/Mick Jones mark, no doubt about it.

St Annes won by seven wickets. They took the Northern Premier League title. Dinuka Hettiarachchi finished it with a haul of eighty-seven wickets at just over ten apiece. His batting was strictly for connoisseurs of low scores. He managed just 106 runs all season. Blackpool finished ninth. Richard Gleeson ended the season with fifty wickets at 14.10 apiece and was widely praised for his hostility.

Bailing Out the Scorebox

Blackrod

All month people had been complaining about the weather. Not so much at what it has been like, as the fact that the Met Office promised so much more. We were told to expect Mediterranean temperatures and widespread drought. People had layed in emergency supplies of sunblock and barbecue charcoal and repaired all the holes mice had nibbled in the paddling pool. But, though the weather wasn't exactly bad, it wasn't super either. It was just, well, normal. And people were disappointed. They were narked. Collectively they stamped their little feet and said, 'It's not fair. It's not fair. You promised. You promised.'

It had rained on and off all week. The train headed south into the Lake District cocooned in a damp haze. The Eskimos are said to have many words for snow. By now I was running out of ways to describe drizzle. The train was filled with Glaswegians going to Blackpool for a holiday. 'Like Redcar in Glasgow holiday week,' my father used to say to indicate a place seething with drunken menace. Not that Glaswegians are any more menacing than anybody else. It's just the accent. Even when a Glaswegian is paying you a compliment he sounds like he's just caught you in bed with his wife.

Earlier in the week I'd tried to demonstrate a willingness to embrace cricket's thrilling new age by going to a Twenty20 game in County Durham. It didn't excite me. Largely this was because the sight of burly club cricketers striding to the wicket to the accompaniment of 'Eye of the Tiger' blaring from a PA-cum-mobile-disco seemed incongruous in front of a crowd of fifty old men and a few kids in football shirts.

And there was also the fact that the players were wearing the new hi-tech England kit. For those of you who missed it, I should explain that two seasons ago Andrew Strauss and his men tossed aside the traditional cricketers' clothing of mildewed flannels and jumpers that smell of linseed oil and sandwich spread in favour of an exciting cutting-edge garb specially designed by the boffins at Adidas. Like all new sports clothing the kit features a whole range of technological breakthroughs including Formotion™, ClimaCool® and FlowMapping™. Some readers may detect a big whiff of what scientists in my own secret laboratories call Bulshitt™, and I would be tempted to take that line myself, were it not for the fact that ECB chief Giles Clarke assured everybody at the time that this was not just a marketing gimmick. Since nobody in sport would tell the public a fib, we will take his word for it. My only concern about the new gear is that Adidas's website does not say if you can get the grass stains out of the slacks by the traditional method of leaving them in a bucket of soapy water under the bathroom sink until frogs have spawned in it.

The new clothing had caught on remarkably fast. This is because of what I call the Super Alan Effect. This phenomenon is named after an old team mate of mine, Super Alan Smidgen. Super Alan was a man in thrall to sporting technology. At the start of every season he would arrive with a whole bag full of the latest clobber, all of it apparently about to transform his game. Down the years Super Alan had bats with a scoop out of the back, bats with sloping shoulders, bats with two scoops out of the back, bats with powerspots, bats with three scoops out of the back and bats with replaceable edges. None of them did him any good at all. This was not the fault of the equipment. It was the fault of Super Alan. Super Alan was crap. If he'd bought a bat with four middles he'd never have found any of them. His footwork was so leaden it was a brain damage risk to the under-sevens, his timing so off he should have replaced the manufacturer's logo with a notice reading, 'Can you come back on Tuesday?'. On the odd occasions when Super Alan actually struck the ball it made a weird metallic squeak, like somebody pulling a rusty nail from a gatepost with a claw hammer, and dribbled shamefacedly away to backward point.

Standing in stark contrast to Super Alan was Kumar. Kumar was pipe-cleaner thin and always wore a dark blue sun hat. Standing in the field he looked like a garden cane with a plant pot over it. Yet when he stood at the wicket it didn't matter that his limbs were like knotted string and that his bat was a gnarled and worn veteran unmarked save for a barely traceable imprint of the name Herbert Sutcliffe. When he cut his wrists whirred and the ball flew to the boundary like a rocket-propelled grenade. When he drove through the covers the leather struck willow with a *puck* as sweet and soft as love's first kiss. His timing was so perfect he could have used a fence paling and still outscored the rest of us. Kumar was thirteen. Super Alan was forty-seven.

At the time I couldn't understand why Super Alan wasted so much money on kit. Now I am forty-seven myself and I can see that what was going on was a variation of My Dad's First Law of Sports Cars. My Dad's First Law of Sports Cars runs thus: A) When you are young you cannot afford a sports car.

B) When you are middle-aged you can afford a sports car but you can't buy one because the children and dog would not fit in it. C) When you are old you can afford a sports car but your reactions and eyesight are so shot to buggery you can never drive it at more than 37mph. (My Dad's Second Law of Sports Cars, incidentally, states that you will always find yourself stuck behind C) when you are on your way to the airport and late for your flight.)

The older you get the more time ravages your sporting ability and the more cash you have to spend on equipment you think will compensate. My recent preoccupation has been fencing. In the past four years I have invested more money in steel than Lakshmi Mittal. The last épée blade I bought was imported from a village in the Auvergne where it had, if I recall correctly, been forged by a family of ancient smiths in fires of rosemary-scented charcoal, beaten using hammers made from meteorites and tempered by the moist breath of Carmelite nuns at prayer. The blade is as light as a spider's thread, the colour of moonlight. When tapped with a fingernail it emits the keen and joyful note of the ascending lark. Yet strangely even this magical implement cannot transform me from Quasimodo to Scaramouche. The message I am being sent is clear: like Super Alan, I will just have to buy an even more expensive one next time.

As the Twenty20 match wore on through its various power-plays and snatches of 'Another One Bites the Dust' and 'Dreadlock Holiday', the players' wives and girlfriends started to arrive. It's odd how amateur sportsmen imitate the professionals. I'd noticed that the minute the cricketers got off the field they immediately changed into flip flops and shorts, just like Straussy and the boys. The wives and girlfriends seem to be similarly inspired by the example of Mrs Flintoff and Kevin Pietersen's kind-of-pop-star wife. They turn up in turquoise crop tops and white slacks, Reactolite shades balanced on big hair.

To me, it all seems a bit silly. Cricket is often praised as an elegant game, but it's fair to say that not since the days of Ranjitsinji and his billowing silk shirts has the game produced any player who could remotely be described as a fashion leader. These days cricketers do their best to look hip and modern with their shades, baseball caps and tracksuits, but the effect is altogether more Jimmy Savile than Jay-Z.

It's a brave effort but the players are swimming against a sartorial tidal wave. Because let's face it, how cool can you be when your job requires you to wear white polyester slacks? If Blue Note had made similar demands of their musicians even Miles Davis would have looked like a dork.

The problem is the message that's sent out from headquarters. Lord's may not have Royal Ascot's hats, but it has something just as impressive in its own way: the MCC members, a body that is to style what Henry Blofeld is to Futurism.

Every test match morning at nine the Grace Gates swing open to a rolling mass of strident striped blazers, cerise corduroys and panama hats that look like they have been winter home to a herd of hibernating hedgehogs. Anyone who regards fashion as the repressive construct of a metropolitan elite should worship these people as gods.

From a glance around the impressive museum at Lord's, it is clear that right from the off the MCC's aims have actually been threefold: playing cricket, staging cricket matches and waging an all-out terror campaign against the running dogs of haute couture. It all began with the colours. There are two explanations behind the MCC's choice (well, three if you include the rather dull one about the Star & Garter club). One is that the person who came up with them was colour-blind, the other that he was a wicked prankster.

Personally I lean toward the latter theory. I imagine the joker experimenting with fabrics for years until the perfectly clashing shades of cherry and custard had been produced then stitching together a tie, holding the finished product aloft and maliciously chuckling 'Now let's see them find an outfit that will match this vile little bugger!'

Impossible, naturally, but such is the anti-fashion verve of the MCC's membership that most don't even bother to attempt it, opting instead to fling it together with the first thing that comes to hand. A pale blue sleeveless safari suit, perhaps, or a Tattersall check shirt buttoned incorrectly (and this is the sort of little detail that transforms an outfit from one that simply affronts the fashionistas to one that slaps them round the chops with a sand-filled sock) so that one half of the collar curls like a stale sandwich.

Or they might plump for a mint green v-necked pullover displaying considerable evidence of past gastronomic indulgence. Just as scientists can uncover ancient weather patterns by studying the rings of fossilised trees, so future archaeolgists will be able to determine trends in middle-class dining habits by carefully scraping away the layers on an MCC member's jumper. Not, I should say, that the jumper is the product of slovenliness. Far from it. The garment serves an important purpose. The member knows that if ever food supplies run low he has simply to soak his sweater in boiling water to produce a nutritious broth. It is not so much a pullover as a knitted Cup-a-Soup (quite often complete with crunchy croutons).

Under threat from the ever-growing tyranny of style (many members have now abandoned baggy-crotched, straw-coloured corduroy trousers in favour of New Labour chinos) the MCC is now flaunting its colours like never before. The Lord's catalogue offers everything from button-down plaid shirts to boxer shorts in the characteristic septic-boil combo of yellow and red. There is a whole page of pyjamas and night-shirts. A little superfluous, perhaps, since it is clear from their rumpled appearance that most members sleep fully clothed.

There is also a celebration of the heroic resistance in the Lord's museum. In one section a little picnic tableau has been arranged. On the floor a rug is covered with a lavish spread, beside it on a fold-out chair sits a perfect waxwork of an eld-erly, moustachioed MCC member apparently in the act of falling asleep while munching a chicken drumstick. At least, I have always assumed it's a waxwork.

Luckily MCC members rarely venture to the North. A pity, as they'd certainly fit in at Preston station on a Saturday. When I changed trains, Blackpool-bound stag parties had also abandoned fashion and opted instead to dress as seventies tennis players. Crowds of Björn Borgs, John McEnroes and a bearded Chris Evert mixed with little girls in pink rainwear and teenagers with Wonderbra cleavages and surrounding clouds of JLO perfume. I caught a train bound for Manchester Victoria. We plodded through Leyland and Chorley. From the train all towns seem the same. You form an impression of places filled with light industrial units, where the only deco-ration are skips, stacks of pallets and piles of gravel ballast and the only flowers are convolvulus and willowherb.

From Blackrod station I walked up a steep slope to the vil-lage. Blackrod means 'bleak clearing' in Anglo Saxon, and though there are very few trees left these days the name still gives a fair impression of the place, perched on its windswept hill.

I walked past a pub with its own bowling green, a branch of the British Legion, and then on through a large fifties coun-cil estate. In the distance the flag of St George flew from a church. Posters advertising bingo nights at Blackrod Welfare indicated that this was once a pit town. There'd been dozens of collieries here, employing just about everybody of working age in a village of four thousand people. Most had disappeared in the thirties, however, and now most people in Blackrod commute to work in Bolton or Chorley.

It was in Blackrod that the great Australian fast bowler Ted McDonald was killed in a motor accident in July 1937. Tall, lean, dark-haired, brilliant at rugby and soccer and a committed chain smoker, the Tasmanian terrorised England's batsmen in 1921. His action was silky and smooth and it was said by one Australian sportswriter that 'his arms revolved with all the beautiful regularity of a windmill'. The effects of it were altogether more combustive. In the first test he struck his future county team mate Ernest Tyldsley in the face with a bouncer. After scoring seventy-four against him in the same series, C. B. Fry was so covered in bruises he looked like plum. In a test in Cape Town the following winter McDonald produced a ball of such velocity it smashed opener Jack Zulch's bat. Fragments of it flew back and dislodged a bail. The South African was given out hit-wicket. I bet he was glad to go.

In 1922 Nelson, not for the last time, surprised the cricket world when they signed Ted McDonald as the club professional. He took time to acclimatise, but in his second season at Seedhill bagged 112 wickets at 6.67 apiece, including what we might call a ten-for against Burnley. In his third season he picked up ninety-nine more, robbed of another century only by the weather that washed out Nelson's final game. At the end of the season he left Nelson for Old Trafford, his first full-time contract at the age of thirty-four.

McDonald struck 998 times for Lancashire, helping them to four County Championship wins in five seasons. He retired from the first class game aged forty and went back to east

Lancashire to play for Bacup and later joined Blackpool. He remained velvety and venomous. Neville Cardus described him as 'a satanic bowler, menacing, but princely'. He was forty-six when the car struck him.

When I arrived at Vicarage Road cricket ground the sky was dark. An assortment of men in Twenty20 tops – Hong Kong Cricket Academy, one said – were messing about with tarpaulins and a roller wrapped in sponge. Big squares of upholstery foam were soaking up moisture from the bowlers' run-ups.

Inside the clubhouse two elderly men who were probably the umpires sat over long-finished mugs of tea, gazing at a big TV pinioned in a corner to the left of the bar – Sky's coverage of the Ashes test from Edgbaston. 'Any chance of play?' I asked hopefully. In the North-East I wouldn't have bothered. The game would have been abandoned long ago. But this was Lancashire.

'There's a lot of water,' one of the men said without taking his eyes from the action.

I looked at the screen. 'Ian Bell's still in then,' I said.

'It's highlights of yesterday. It's wet down there an' all,' the second man added grumpily.

Blackrod's pavilion and clubhouse is a low brick affair like an old person's bungalow. Along one wall are photos of the landscaping of the ground back in the eighties. One appears to show a bloke bailing water out of the scorebox. I looked out of the window. The scorebox is above the groundsman's shed. There was no evidence of flooding now, but by the time the players had wheeled away the covers and got the tarpaulin halfway across the outfield it had started to spit and they had to put them all back on again.

Both teams trooped into the clubhouse. Soon afterwards,

Blackrod seconds returned from a fruitless trip to Little Hulton listless and grumbling. Somebody switched channels and we got Sky's rundown of the 1995–6 Premiership season, Kevin Keegan blowing up in front of the cameras and all. By the time that was over and the TV had been flicked back to the cricket David Gower was announcing that play at the test had been abandoned for the day. It was half-past two.

Fifteen minutes later the rain stopped at Vicarage Road. A breeze got up, drying the outfield. Blackrod and today's opponents, Little Hulton, were sufficiently close to the top of the Bolton Association to make a game worthwhile, however short, especially since the two teams above them had been forced to give in to the weather. The covers came off again. The sky brightened. 'Play will start in fifteen minutes,' a man in a tracksuit announced from the doorway.

'Fifteen minutes!' one player growled in response. 'Fifteen fucking minutes? We'll play for fifteen fucking minutes. Then it will be fucking tea. Then it will fucking piss down and we'll all fuck off. Get the game fucking on and get fucking on with it. I can't be fucking arsed with this.' It wasn't the sort of speech you could imagine Sir Pelham Warner making, but you could see the fellow's point.

By the time a quarter of an hour had elapsed the pitch was marked out, the boundary rope had been unwound from an ancient iron contraption that looks like a piece of Victorian farm machinery and sawdust piles dumped at the bowlers' marks. Bees were buzzing around clover flowers and an ice-cream van was driving down Vicarage Road playing the tune from *Monty Python's Flying Circus*.

The players were warming up around the boundary, but before they could get on to the field and start to play an old lady in a white blouse and pinny emerged from the clubhouse flapping a hand towel and yelling, 'The teas are ready now lads. Come and have your teas.' So both sets of players trooped back indoors again.

The Bolton and District Cricket Association is the oldest cricket league in Lancashire, and the second oldest on the planet (the oldest is the Birmingham and District League). It was formed in 1888 and at one point featured twenty-four teams, divided into two sections.

In 1929, after prolonged and secret negotiations at Rockwood House in Bradshaw, twelve rebel clubs announced that they were breaking away and forming the Bolton Cricket League. It hardly mattered, though, because there was no shortage of sides around Bolton – a conservative estimate in 1920 put the number at around 250, leading locals to claim that Bolton was the globe's foremost cricket hotbed. That was why I had come to Blackrod, which, if the locals were right about the passion for cricket round these parts, was more or less the Calcutta of the cottonfields.

Many of the clubs were associated with local non-conformist churches, so that fixtures would often seem like a clash of rival theologies with Harwood Primitive Methodists taking on Walkden Wesleyans or Bolton Unitarians battling with Rose Hill Congregational. Given that most of these churches had a long association with the temperance movement it was perhaps not surprising that one of the Bolton and District Association's first major sponsor was Vimto, made just down the road in Wythenshawe.

Blackrod had begun life as Blackrod Parish Church Cricket and Tennis Club. They didn't join the Bolton and District Association until 1985, but made their mark early by winning the league title in 1988, thanks largely to professional Alan Baybutt who took 111 wickets. Little Hulton had an altogether longer and more illustrious history. They'd joined the Association in 1907, hired their first professional, Ralph Tyler the cricket coach at Uppingham School, in 1919 and won the title half a dozen times. The Pakistani test all-rounder Mudassar Nazar had played for them as a teenager and so had Ernie Machin, the barrel-chested Coventry City striker of the early seventies.

The Bolton Association as a whole had produced almost as many Lancashire cricketers as the Bradford League had for Yorkshire. Cardus's old favourite, Walter Brearley, had begun his career in it, so had the man who'd injured Bagger Barnes, Dick Pollard. Charlie Hallows, John Tyldsley and the splendidly named Jimmy Heap were other Old Trafford stalwarts who'd started out playing for the likes of Edgeworth Recreation, Chloride and East Lancashire Paper Mills.

Filled with sandwiches and scones, the players emerged from the pavilion. The game has been shortened by the many delays. At first it seemed it would be thirty-eight overs per side, but then the scorer came out of the box, glanced up, shrugged and disappeared back inside again. A few seconds later the number of overs clicked down to twenty-eight. It was ten to four when play finally started. Take note Ashington, I say.

Limiting innings by overs was a relatively new innovation in the northern leagues. Up until the seventies most games had simply been played out in an allotted time. Games started at half-past one and finished at half-past seven. Initially, the finish time was so rigidly adhered to that when the team batting second passed its target it kept on batting till stumps regardless. If the team batting second was bowled out, then the opposition batted again. When northerners paid to watch a day's cricket they expected to see one, whether there was any point to it or not.

Timing the games had certain advantages. It allowed teams that were struggling to battle for a draw and placed an emphasis on the fielding sides bowling teams out. It was, however, open to abuse.

Bagger Barnes wasn't the only Australian to fall foul of the Lancashire League. Arthur Richardson had a long, thin face and wore wire-rimmed half-moon spectacles. He looked like an insurance clerk, albeit one who you half suspect might have turned up in the pages of the *Daily Sketch* after being charged with an acid-bath murder. Richardson had preceded Barnes as pro at Burnley. In 1932 the Turf Moor team travelled to Rossendale to take on Rawtenstall. Rawtenstall's pro was S. F. Barnes. The great man was nearly sixty, but he was still a force to be reckoned with and proved it by taking 9–20 as Burnley were dismissed for sixty-four. Rain had interrupted play, but even so Rawtenstall were cruising to victory when Richardson decided to intervene.

By constantly messing around with the field arrangements, engaging in lengthy consultations with the bowlers before moving long leg to long off and so on, Richardson managed to waste so much time that with Rawtenstall on 64–5 the umpires removed the bails and declared the game drawn. The Burnley team were booed off the field and a crowd jeered the team bus as it left the town, but Richardson was unperturbed. At the top level of cricket the line between gamesmanship and cheating is a fine one. So fine, in fact, that the people who can pinpoint exactly when an action crosses over it are rarer than photos of Shane Warne with natural hair. Among those who play to the highest standard the watchword is simple: 'Others cheat. I am *professional*.'

The League Committee was not impressed, however, and contacted Richardson to demand a written explanation. The Australian responded with a letter so filled with profanity it was immediately destroyed by the secretary so that future generations would be spared the shock of coming across it.

Richardson somehow got away with it that time, but Burnley later suspended him for swearing at his own captain.

At Vicarage Road an elderly man in a grey blouson came and sat beside me. 'From Little Hulton, are you?' he asked. When I told him I'd come from Northumberland he did a genuine double take. 'Really? Have you had some tea?'

I said I was amazed that there was a game to watch. 'They'd have called it off hours back where I'm from,' I said, still nursing a grievance against Ashington and Stockton. 'Aye well,' the old man replied with a wheezy chuckle, 'umpires round here aren't so fussed about waiting. If it gets past half three they get paid whether there's any play or not.' In Northern cricket it's not just the players who keep an eye on the money.

Blackrod batted and were quickly struggling. Little Hulton's opening bowler Mark Penny is a strapping bloke with cropped fair hair. On a claggy wicket he got the sort of lift normally associated with a Harrier jump jet. At the other end the pro Abir Chippa bowled slow left arm. He's slightly built, fuzzy haired and remorselessly accurate, chugging down fourteen overs with barely a bad ball. Apart from a single dropped catch at mid-on, Little Hulton's fielding was really sharp too; there were a couple of brilliant catches in the deep, the difficulty of them increased by the damp, the grey skies and the backdrop of council houses and hedgerows.

Though the Bolton Association is made up of teams that all come from within a dozen miles of one another, the players on both teams are drawn from all over northern England and some drive up from the Midlands. Many of the most influential are Asian.

Other elderly blokes sauntered over and joined us on the bench at square leg. One said that Alvin Kallicharran, the little baby-faced West Indian who hooked Dennis Lillee repeatedly for sixes during the first World Cup, played a game at Blackrod recently. 'He's old as a tree, but he's still got the footwork.'

Talk turned to the pros of the past. Collis King – a West Indian cricketer in the tradition of Constantine – was once the star of the Bolton Association. Javed Miandad was the pro at Daisy Hill in 1976, the same season Mudassar was at Little Hulton. The two teams met in the final of the Cross Cup that year. Javed scored 111 and took 4–89 with his leg-spinners, but his compatriot finished on the winning side, scoring 105 and picking up three wickets in thirteen overs of accurate medium pace. Ehtesham-ud-Din followed Javed at Daisy Hill. He did so well during the 1982 season he was brought into the Pakistan team for the third test at Leeds. He wasn't the only league pro to be called up in that way. I have strangely vivid memories of wire-haired medium-pacer Mike Whitney making an unlikely appearance for Australia in the fifth Ashes test of 1981 after performing well at Fleetwood in the North Lancashire and Cumberland League. Whitney took four wickets and returned to the Irish Sea fishing port to find celebratory banners draped across the street.

'Best innings I ever saw round here,' one of the men said, 'were when Allan Border were pro-ing for East Lancs. Worsley Cup match. A hot day. The sun were cracking slabs. Border scored 170-odd. Finished on the losing side,' he paused for a moment, then shook his head. 'It's not what it were,' he said. And all the old men nodded and mumbled in agreement.

'It's the bowling that's gone downhill. Batting's still all right' one man said, though there's not much evidence from Blackrod to support that theory. The Sri Lankan pro Asela Jayasinghe, a thirty-five-year-old veteran who made over four thousand first class runs for Colombo, scored eighteen and the team's best performer during the season, Mo Fazil, helped out with seventeen, but with Chippa and Penny bowling unchanged three run-outs in the innings and a couple of chances superbly pouched on the boundary, Blackrod sub-sided to ninety-two all out.

During the changeover a teenage boy emerged from a back-garden fence, sucking on a roll-up. The old men greeted him pleasantly. 'You seen your dad recently?'

'Have I heck.'

'Is he still in Horwich?'

'No idea. He's as much use as a fireman with a wooden leg, that fella.'

Little Hulton's reply did not begin well. The opener Lee (known to one and all as Wee Wee) was bowled off an inside edge by Ahmed in his first over. Jayasinghe, bowling fastish medium pace, opened at the other and beat the bat five times in his first over. Barlow also fell to Ahmed, but then Mark Penny came to the wicket and blasted a quick seventeen. His bowling partner Chippa stuck around to make the highest score of the match – twenty-four not out – and Little Hulton scraped home by three wickets.

Little Hulton finish third in the League and Blackrod fourth. Abir Chippa scored 576 runs, and took sixty-six wickets and seventeen catches.

Dawn of the Blob

Chatburn

When I told them I was writing this book, lots of my friends said, 'I'll come to a game with you.' And then as the summer wore on they all gradually made their excuses. I wasn't surprised. Cricket is a bit like public transport – everyone is pleased it's available, but they just find it rather too much effort to actually use it. Cricket, like buses, takes up more time than most people feel they can really spare. As Philip Larkin so wisely said, 'Unresting death, two forty-over innings, a tea interval and the train ride to Accrington and back nearer now.'

But for the trip to see Chatburn *v* Long Lee in the Mewes Solicitors Craven and District Cricket League, Division 2, I did have company. My friend Dorothy, who hails from Keighley and therefore takes her cricket seriously, had come along. And it was partly for her benefit that I had chosen Chatburn. It wasn't that it was a particulary famous club, but the ground near St Chad's Church looked pretty and it was a convenient distance from her home. Originally we'd been planning to go and see a game in the Bolton League together but it had clashed with me judging the home-made drinks section in a local agricultural show. Oh yes, I live quite the glamorous media life, I can tell you.

*

Chatburn cricket club is perched on a hillside with the church at one end and the village primary school at deep midwicket. A prodigious slope falls so sharply towards the river that any fielder at fine leg or long off is barely visible from the wicket. Occasionally you see what appears to be a hedgehog running across the outfield and realise it's actually somebody's head. Surprisingly, the nets are at the downward-sloping end of the ground. Any bowler with a big follow through is likely to burst out the back of them and carry on until he hits the water.

A council sign at the entrance warns that anybody caught playing golf on the field will be 'escorted from the grounds by a constable' something I'd like to see happen more often. Especially on golf courses. Pleasingly, there's also a tree inside the boundary rope which inevitably calls to mind the great lime that once stood at the St Lawrence Ground, Canterbury, the rules governing the intervention of which were always lovingly outlined by John Arlott because they offered proof of the game's antique eccentricity.

Chatburn had recently cut the ribbon on a swanky new pavilion that looks a bit like an executive show home. It's over in one corner of the field, in a dogleg created by the school, and it's really quite a walk from there to the wicket. In fact, if an estate agent were selling it they'd probably describe it as 'cricket-field fringes'. Any batsman who doesn't get a sprint on could easily be timed out by a vigilant umpire and a cantankerous bowler.

I suspect the cricket pitch must have been moved at some point because there are high nets up protecting a row of houses next to the new pavilion, but they are so far away from the square even Cec Pepper or Bill Alley would have struggled to belt a ball anywhere near them.

The scoreboard is sheltered under the cemetery wall. The

scorer is a young woman with a radio, who keeps the fielders updated on the score from Burnley's match as well as that on the field. She seems normal enough, but the sight of her signalling to the umpires stirs up disturbing memories.

There was a decade of my life when I attended first class or indeed any other form of cricket every chance I got. The eighties were a troubling time in Britain. There was social upheaval, strikes, turmoil and Saint and Greavsie. Some of my friends resorted to heroin. I went to county matches.

I invariably travelled with a workmate who was universally known as The Blob. The Blob was inoffensive enough, but the thought persisted that one day the police would find something nasty under his floorboards and the newspaper reports would say, 'colleagues describe the accused as a quiet man who kept himself to himself'.

The Blob was single, with the narrow shoulders and bulging bottom of an emperor penguin. He smelled much like one too, the result of living off a diet of fish-paste sandwiches. Fish paste comes in a jar that is the olfactory equivalent of the Tardis – it looks tiny from the outside but it houses a pong the size of a galaxy. The Blob's sandwiches were made from bread with the springy texture of disposable nappies and the moisture content of wet wipes. A vein of fish paste ran through the middle of them like self-deprecation through a Waugh family gathering. Luckily The Blob was not a sharer.

The Blob used words like palpable and plethora, referred to Lord's as 'HQ' and of batsmen making hay while the sun shone. I did the same myself. It seemed more or less impossible to speak of county cricket without sounding like *Test Match Special*'s Peter Baxter. Fogey was the lingua franca of what The Blob and I invariably referred to as the Summer Game.

The Blob and I did not talk much during play, I should say.

He was far too busy to converse. He was a compulsive scorer.
The Blob wrote down the details of every batsman's innings
with a sombre gravity – St Peter in man-made fibres.

One Monday, shortly after I had first started working with
The Blob, I asked him if he had enjoyed his weekend.
'Veritably,' he replied. 'I scored the Leicestershire Sunday
League match.'

'You went up to Grace Road?' I asked.

'Oh no, just off the tellygoggin.'

I pictured the scene: the curtains drawn to cut out the glare,
the stale biscuity odour of bachelorhood filling the room, The
Blob, his freshly sharpened pencils lined up neatly on the arm
of his chair, a Thermos of weak tea between his feet, acknowl-
edging the umpires' signals with an upraised hand. It was a
measure of the uncertainty of the times that I found the vision
extremely comforting.

Why did I go to cricket with The Blob? Well, frankly, who
else would go to watch county cricket? Northamptonshire
versus Derbyshire at Bletchley is not an event that attracts a
hip crowd. It is the sporting equivalent of C&A; carp fishing
without the excitement of firing a catapult loaded with live
maggots every few hours. The only thing likely to set your
pulse racing at county cricket is a bolt of static from the bloke
behind you's bri-nylon blouson.

The tiny crowd that assembled was largely the same whether
at Worcester, Basingstoke or Tring. There was a smatter-
ing of elderly ladies in cream macs who would occasionally lay
down the baby jacket or bobble hat they were knitting and call
for Norman Cowans to pitch the ball up, or for Ray East, the
'Clown Prince of Cricket', to amuse us once again by walking
like a chicken.

There was also Mr Pavilion. He was at every cricket ground
I visited, with his binoculars and his cool box. Some people

came to cricket to watch. Mr Pavilion came to talk. Though not actually to anybody.

Mr Pavilion wore a panama hat, terry-cotton shirt, shorts that terminated with turn-ups, fawn socks and sensible sandals. I imagine he and his forbearers had worn this garb since time immemorial or at least since shepherds first hurled balls of wool at one another on the Sussex Downs and Mr Pavilion's ancestor called out 'pitch it up, man' or 'use your feet to the spinners, sir' or whatever other phrase he had plucked at random from *The Golden Treasury of Cricket Wisdom for All Occasions* (abridged from the original Latin by Thos. Carlyle).

A day with Mr Pavilion always passed the same way. The captains appeared. 'A vital toss to win,' Mr Pavilion announced in the general direction of one of the matrons, a vital prop without whom too many of his thoughts would, like desert blooms, blossom and die unknown. 'I'd bat if I were skipper.'

The side which unwillingly followed this course having called wrongly was promptly reduced to eleven for four; a state of affairs which aroused in Mr Pavilion a grave distemper for which he sought physic in nostalgia. 'Hutton and Washbrook would have batted through till tea on this strip . . . Hammond would have torn this attack to shreds . . . Archie MacLaren would have posted his fifty by now.'

As Mr Pavilion railed on and on you noticed that he was retreating further and further back in time, praising cricketers who retired long before he was born. You realised that if he carried on at the rate he was going he would work his way back through Grace and Felix and Alfred Minn and, in a couple of minutes, would be proclaiming: 'Then in this time of shadow came the one they called the run-bringer, the flayer of long-hops; and his name was Beowulf, Prince of the

Scyldings, and he'd have treated this Neil Foster fellow with the contempt he deserves, I can tell you.'

Lunchtime came and Mr Pavilion opened the cool box. From it came a quantity of food such as would have tested the seams of umpire David Shepherd's shirt front: chicken legs, potato salad, coleslaw, ham and paté, hard-boiled eggs, a bottle of Chablis, bags of crisps, punnets of strawberries. It went on endlessly; while I listened to the crunch of crisp lettuce and the slurping of cherry tomatoes, a polythene glass of beer in one hand and a damp carpet tile that was once, allegedly, a sandwich in the other, peevishly damning the idiocy of a man who brings smoked trout to a cricket match.

After lunch, fortified, Mr Pavilion hit a vein of form as thick as Rio Ferdinand's wage packet. 'Four all the way,' he crowed as the batsman mistimed a drive and sent it rolling gently towards mid-on. 'Elegantly done, sir!' as a tail-ender aimed a mighty hoik at a half-volley and sent it skimming over the slips. 'Textbook defensive stroke!' as a number eleven prodded forward and lost his middle stump. This latter event afforded Mr Pavilion the opportunity to make his joke: 'An excellent shot,' he guffawed, 'if only he'd hit the ball.' By mid-afternoon the jollity and the Chablis had taken its toll and Mr Pavilion would fall asleep, jerking awake every once in a while with the startled look of somebody emerging from an erotic dream involving their in-laws

Geoff Millets was another recognisable face in the crowd. With his beige anorak, his taupe sunhat and his pale blue easy-fit trousers Mr Millets appeared indistinguishable from the rest of the crowd but his blandness masked a deadly turn as surely as does the spinner's flight. One minute you were sailing merrily along, the next you were stumped. We went to cricket to watch, Mr Pavilion to talk – Mr Millets went for a good argument.

Mr Millets was a master of his craft. Youngsters watching at home would have been well advised to study his action. As he approached the possible disputation Mr Millets's movements were quick and furtive, his head swayed from side to side as his finely tuned hearing sought an opening. Suddenly his left ear picked up a phrase, 'Knight has got to be . . .' His hawk-like eyes quickly identified the speaker and never left him as he gathers himself ready to deliver, '. . . the best one-day batsman in England.'

That was Mr Millets's cue, 'Cobblers!' he yelped with the strangulated ferocity of a wrist spinner appealing for a bat-pad catch he knows he has no chance of getting. His chosen victim should have shouldered arms and offered no response, but Mr Millets had pushed him on to the back foot and lured him into the corridor of uncertainty. 'Sorry?' he replied.

'With all due respect,' Mr Millets would say, finding his insidious length, 'you are talking a load of rubbish.' With that, he closed in for the kill. And a slow and painful death it was too. An argument with Mr Millets was so long and labyrinthine it makes the average meeting of the Yorkshire committee look like a drag race.

Despite the passing years Mr Millets never lost his focus. He had a resident's parking permit in The Zone and once in the groove he could not be distracted by anything, particularly cricket. Nor would he let his victim relax. A friend of mine missed the whole of Ian Botham's seventy-nine-ball hundred at Old Trafford thanks to an injudicious remark about covered wickets. Another can remember nothing of Shane Warne's first spell of bowling against England except for the vague smell of scampi fries and the phrase 'Actually, I think you'll find . . .' To a third, the very mention of Graham Gooch's three hundred against India causes him to slump forward put his head in his hands and whimper, 'OK, OK, Doug Walters' record in this country was better than people give him credit for' over and over again until he is sedated by a large gin and the talking book of Henry Blofeld's memoirs.

People say that you didn't have to get involved, but the fact of the matter was that when your number came up you couldn't cheat Geoff Millets. You couldn't beat him in an argument either. He had all the facts at his fingertips and he used them to chip away at an adversary: 'In fact it was versus Uttar Pradesh', 'If you check your *Wisden* you'll discover it was 33.72', 'Yes, but D. H. Robins's XI *v* T. N. Pearce's XI wasn't first class'. There was no escape. The best you could do was accept what was happening, sit back and admire one of the game's true artists.

The matrons, Mr Pavilion, Geoff Millets, me and The Blob. A young man in stone-washed jeans and a Freddy Starr Ate My Hamster T-shirt whose social skills were that he could drink twelve pints and still do a passable imitation of a peacock completed the happy multitude.

As the eighties gave way to the nineties I drifted out of The Blob's orbit and, finally wrestling the monkey of county cricket off my back, burned my scorecards and moved on.

Five years ago I met another former workmate. I asked him what had become of The Blob. 'Got married,' the bloke said. 'Got married?' I asked. 'Are you sure?' The bloke nodded. 'Some girl he met at Arundel when Lavinia, Duchess of Norfolk's XI were playing the Australians. Oddly enough her name is Wicket. She's a scorer too. They've got a couple of kids.'

I can picture them now at The Parks or Chesterfield, all in a row, heads down in concentration, the silence broken only by the occasional murmured, 'He must have got the faintest of snicks to that, though it looked like a bye to me.'

The Chatburn opening bowler from the church end was Steve Bowker, a stocky slow left-armer. He wasn't bad at all, and did the spinner thing of looking perplexed after every dot ball, as if trying to unravel some ancient enigma that I'd seen used so well by Carlisle's leg spinner.

At the other end Ashley Bennett, a balding chap with a tuft of hair he scratched like a lachrymose Stan Laurel, bowled medium-paced wobblers. He got the Long Lee opener Stowell caught off a wild slog. A couple of balls later he clean bowled the number three, Butterfield, then had the new batsman Taylor dropped at mid-off. His bowling looked innocuous, but maybe the pitch was devious and deceptive. It was, I noted, more or less the same livid green as the mushy peas we'd had with our mutton pies at lunch.

John Lockley, who'd arrived a bit late, striding up the hill with his cricket bag over his shoulder and a small boy trailing in his wake, soon replaced Bennett. He was a bit quicker, with a slingy action that encouraged the ball to swing away from the right-handers.

For the first time during the summer I'd come to a level of cricket that doesn't run to two umpires. There's a full-time adjudicator who takes the ends, while one of the batting side does square leg duties. I feel that's a fair system. Many years ago I was forced into the invidious position of having to umpire a cricket match when my own team were batting because one of the proper umpires had failed to arrive. At one point I turned down an LBW appeal and, mindful of the fact that I had just given The Wangler, who picked the side, gave me a lift and whose wife made the teas, not out, ventured to suggest by way of mitigation that the ball had pitched outside leg stump. At the end of the over the other umpire, a wily old fellow tanned the colour of a tinker's nut-bag and stooped by years of having dozens of jumpers piled on his shoulders, took me to one side. 'Never give your reasoning,' he said sagely. 'There's many a good decision been spoilt by a bad explanation.'

Bowker continued to bowl with good flight and control. He produced a really nice delivery that pitched on middle and turned to clip the outside of Taylor's off stump. A couple of overs later he did the same again to dismiss Ayrton, a mighty looking chap whose backlift chopped into the crease with a hollow *thwack* like somebody chopping damp logs. Three balls after that another turning delivery dismissed a short left-hander Day who put Dorothy and me in mind of little Harry Pilling, the diminutive Lancashire batsman who'd first come to public attention when he was a teenage Hadfly boy playing at Stayley in the Saddleworth and District League and setting a record for the number of runs scored in a season. (The record stood for twenty-seven years, finally broken by Pilling's Lancashire team mate Barry Wood.)

Long Lee were 40–5 in fifteen overs. It quickly got worse, Bowker claiming his fourth clean bowled to get rid of Robinson. All through this genteel carnage the Long Lee opener Broadley had been blocking gamely away. He reminded me of a chap I once played with who was the brother of an international footballer. The international footballer was one of those seventies mavericks celebrated for their flair, hair and wild lifestyle. The maverick had clearly got all his brother's share of craziness too, because he was the dullest bloke I ever met. When he batted he was almost impossible to dislodge, but since he scored at a rate of about one run a week he didn't benefit our team much either. Once, as if to prove a point, he suddenly and unexpectedly danced down the wicket to a quick West Indian opening bowler from the Cadbury's works side and slammed him straight back over the sight screen for six. Then he went back to his usual game as if nothing had happened. He never ever did it again. His bat wasn't so much dead as cremated and scattered on the wind.

A similar thing happened at Chatburn when Broadley unexpectedly abandoned his blocking and smacked the ball for a steepling six into the trees over mid-on. The blow was impressive but clearly upsets Broadley's equilibrium. He is caught at cover off Lockley in the next over for a battling thirty-two, leaving the visitors in serious bother on 62–7.

At this point, sensing the way things are heading, the Chatburn skipper Mark Braithwaite called for a couple of men on the boundary to 'go into the clubhouse and put the kettle on'. As a piece of gamesmanship it was an impressive effort. 'Put some toast under the grill, love, we'll have this lot skittled out before it's brown.'

He was not far wrong either, as the last two wickets fell in rapid succession and Long Lee were bowled out for sixty-three, Bowker picking up 5–15 in his twelve overs. There's no collection, which is probably just as well as I wasn't sure the crowd would raise enough for a round of drinks. Or even *a* drink. Though, in fairness, Dorothy may be more generous than I am.

While the players had tea, Dorothy and I went off and bought some home-made gooseberry ice cream from the shop across the road and discussed the many and varied problems that have beset Yorkshire cricket over the years. 'They could have kept the Yorkshire-born players only rule and tapped into the local Asian community for players a lot sooner. It would have sent out a positive message,' I said as talk turns to Adil Rashid. 'They might have done that,' Dorothy replied, 'though I think it would have been altogether too logical for Yorkshire.'

The Craven and District League was formed in 1888. Like

the Ribblesdale League it stretches across the Pennines, all the way from Baildon Bottom to Pendle Hill, taking in along the way such places as Ingrow and Foulridge. Chatburn was the most westerly club in it. Long Lee was over near Keighley in Yorkshire. If Settle *v* Clitheroe had been a dwarf roses match, this was a bonsai version.

The Craven and District League didn't have the same prestige as some of the others I'd visited, but it made up for that with its scale, five divisions of cricket featuring just over thirty clubs and sixty teams. Only the Airedale and Wharfedale League, with its nine divisions, was larger. The redoubtable Craven Herald covered both this, the A&W *and* the Ribblesdale League. The summarised match scores and the tables took up an entire broadsheet page.

When we returned to the cricket the sky had started to darken. There was a distinct hint of autumn in the air and not much shelter to be had from a cold, damp wind that whistled in from the Forest of Bowland. I'd wondered if the pitch would prove a factor when Chatburn batted, particularly since they'd been skittled out for eighty-one by Ingrow the previous weekend, but their batsmen made light of the conditions. Braithwaite and Thornber put on fifty-four for the first wicket and the team scampered to victory by eight wickets in just fifteen overs.

The game was over at ten past five. Dorothy and I got mugs of tea and raspberry buns at a café in the long main street and sat outside talking about Johnny Wardle, the slow left-armer who, in the tradition of Bobby Peel, left Yorkshire for the Lancashire League in controversial circumstances. In 1958, during a county match at Sheffield, Yorkshire's secretary had come into the press box and handed out a brief announcement that Wardle's contract had been terminated. The spinner had been in bother with the Yorkshire committee before, but the final straw had been an outburst in which he'd made derogatory comments about Yorkshire's decision to appoint Ronnie Burnet, a thirty-nine-year-old amateur who played for Baildon in the Bradford League, as county skipper. Wardle, as senior professional, had been expected to help Burnet, but instead he complained that his advice was ignored and sniped to the press.

Square-shouldered, fair-haired and hard-faced, Wardle was an attacking spinner and a cavalier late-order batsman. To the public he was a clown and a showman, but he was also tough and awkward, with a sharp tongue he wasn't frightened to use. He'd fought his way up, learning his trade playing for Denaby Colliery and forcing his way into the county side at the expense of the rugged veteran Arthur Booth. As a consequence Wardle harboured a bitter resentment against anyone he felt had been granted an easy passage. In a charity match at Lord's he'd been so irritated by the posturing of Cambridge-educated David Frost that, in contravention of the traditions governing such occasions, he'd deliberately bowled the TV presenter for a first ball duck. Shades of S. F. Barnes.

Wardle was equally intolerant of any failing among his team mates and reputedly gave Ray Illingworth and others such a hard time that his sacking was greeted with relief in some parts of the Yorkshire dressing room. By this time he was thirty-five. He'd played twelve seasons for Yorkshire and twenty-eight times for England. Brian Close called him a 'bowling genius'.

Wardle had been due to tour Australia with the MCC but in light of Yorkshire's actions his place was withdrawn. Unabashed, the spinner went as a reporter instead with the newspaper that had printed his original outburst, apparently earning more money than he would if he'd been playing. When he came back he signed on with Nelson. He played in the Lancashire League for ten seasons and became the fourth-highest wicket-taker in the League's history. Like many other cricket rebels he was happiest in an environment where his bust-ups were tolerated, his egotism could manifest itself as flamboyance and the amateurs did as he told them. Meanwhile, on the other side of the Pennines Yorkshire under Ronnie Burnet won the County Championship for the first time in over a decade.

'It's funny when you think about it,' I said to Dorothy. 'All the players that departed from Yorkshire over the years – Close, Illingworth, Jack Burkinshaw, Brian Bolus – the only one that stopped was Geoff Boycott.'

'Maybe that was why the others went.'

The Chatburn players were leaving the ground and walking home, bats and pads slung over their shoulders as we finished off our tea and buns. 'Well,' Dorothy said, swallowing the last mouthful, 'I can't say the cricket was of the highest standard, but we've certainly done well eating-wise.'

Chatburn finished the season in fourth place, Long Lee in fifth. The divisional title was won by Bingley Congregationals. Despite his fine bowling display against Long Lee, Steve Bowker finished the season with just thirteen wickets.

Tougher Than Cheap Steak

Rawdon

The weather patterns of the summer so far had been reversed. It rained all week and on Saturday all was bright and shiny. When I took the dog out at seven in the morning the sky was blue with vague clouds like whitewash smeared on glass. There was a nip in the air, though, and heavy dew on the grass. The cricket season had just two matches left to run. Soon it would be time to get out the linseed oil and soak away the grass stains.

On the train to Leeds a group of women from Durham were heading to a wedding. 'I wanted to wear my diamond studs, right?' one of them said, 'But the holes in me ears had closed up. I had to ask our Paul to reopen them. I said, "You sterilise the needle and I'll numb my lobes with a couple of frozen chips." Well, he did it. But I tell you what – he had to have a lie down on the bed after. His legs had went.'

Outside Leeds station I caught a double-decker bus bound for Otley. Rawdon is to the north of the city, on the flight path of Leeds Bradford Airport. As we headed past the Leeds Harley-Davidson centre rain spattered the windows. We went through Kirkstall, which seems naked without the words 'Lane End' attached.

I hopped off the bus as soon as I saw the Rawdon road sign

and walked up steeply sloping streets. Rawdon, like Blackrod, is perched on top of a hill. A short way in the distance is Yeadon, another village that had a big impact on Yorkshire cricket.

In Feast Week of 1883 Merritt Preston had killed Albert Luty with a fast rising delivery at the Swan Ground, home of Yeadon Cricket Club, these days of the Bradford League. The two men are buried in the village churchyard. The graves are twenty-two yards apart. The cemetery is also the resting place of eight men from Yeadon who played for Yorkshire, among them Ted Peate, the first of the county's great slow left-armers, who made his debut in first class cricket in 1879.

Peate's first engagement as a professional cricketer was with future Bradford League club Manningham. He'd been making a living from the game before that, though. As a teenager he was a member of an unlikely sounding circus act called Treloar's Clown Cricketers. The troupe mixed slapstick and low-grade buffoonery with a game of cricket – so not that different from the Yorkshire county side of the seventies, really.

Peate was a high-class bowler who claimed to have located a length that was unplayable by any batsman, the spinner's equivalent of the philosopher's stone. He certainly took lots of wickets: 819 for Yorkshire alone. Yet his biggest influence on the game came with the bat. It was Peate's wild slog that presented Australia with victory in the 1882 Oval Test and so gave rise to the Ashes. Questioned as to why he produced his rash stroke when one of the greatest amateur batsmen of the era, Charles Studd, was at the other end, Peate memorably responded, 'I was all right myself, but I couldn't trust Mr Studd.' Studd was a southern gentleman strokemaker who wore a hooped cap; what true Northerner could have put any faith in him?

*

Rawdon's Larkfield Road ground is a steep haul up several flights of steps from the main road, tucked away behind a big pub called the Emmott Arms. I'm pretty sure it's not named after Emmott Robinson, but it really ought to be. Robinson was one of the great characters of Yorkshire cricket, though he hadn't actually made his debut for the county side until he was thirty-five. Before that he'd spent his time as a professional in the leagues, at Keighley, Eccleshill and Littleborough, where his coaching in particular was highly valued.

Robinson was diminutive, scruffy, with the bowed legs of an occasional table. In photos he looks like something carved out of wood, roughly. Robinson was the physical embodiment of Yorkshire cricket – not pretty, but bloody effective. So remorseless was his dourness it turned into comedy. 'Never take a risk if you can win without one' was his catchphrase. He batted doggedly, bowled diligently and fielded suicidally close to the wicket at short-leg, silly mid-off and silly mid-on. When a batsman from Cambridge University expressed concern about his safety Robinson didn't blink. 'You just take care of yourself. I'll take care of me.'

There's a clubhouse at one end of Larkfield. A long straight row of trees at the other masks a sixties housing estate. Drystone walls painted white ring the field, just as they do at Bacup and Settle.

There was a distinct tingle in the air as I entered the ground, and it wasn't just the easterly wind either. Police bollards were out on the road to restrict parking and there was a photographer from the *Craven Herald* on duty with a tripod and a bag full of lenses. Rawdon were second in the Airedale and Wharfedale Cricket League, Divison One, and today's visitors Beckwithshaw were top. There were just seven points between them. A good win for the home side and that situation would be reversed with just one game to play. A win for

Beckwithshaw, meanwhile, would clinch the title for them. I had no idea where Beckwithshaw was, but on the front of the *Yorkshire Post* property section there was a house for sale there at a price of £1.25 million, which led me to believe that it was probably near Harrogate (the Monte Carlo of the North). And I was right.

The start was delayed by fifty minutes, the innings reduced from fifty overs to forty-seven per side. The umpires walked out to the middle. One was grizzled, with a face like a pickled walnut. He looked like the sort of club comic who'd talk with a fag in his mouth and say, 'Take my wife . . . No, *please*, take my wife.'

His colleague looked like Jack Hampshire, which is more or less compulsory in Yorkshire. J. H. Hampshire had been a fixture of the Tykes team for most of my childhood and adolescence. My father didn't rate him and claimed that Hampshire batted 'like the village butcher'. My father was born in Lancashire and was predisposed to see weakness in Yorkshire cricketers, while completely ignoring exactly the same flaws in, say, Frank Hayes or David Lloyd.

Jack Hampshire scored lots of runs at county level, but despite bagging a century in his debut test (like Frank Hayes) never quite made it at international level. My dad was being a bit unfair to him, really, though there was some merit in the butcher comparison. When some batsmen hit the ball it smacked off the willow with a sound like a popping champagne cork. When Hampshire belted one it gave off an altogether different noise, a big thwack, like somebody tenderising beef with a meat mallet.

Beckwithshaw won the toss and opted to bat. Rawdon's opening bowlers were an Australian, Dean Morgan, who plays grade cricket in Geelong, and a local known simply as Beast. The bowling was quick and tight and batting conditions were far from easy, largely because the minute play started the field had been enveloped in a moist mist. The visitors' opening pair, John Inglis and Phil Critchley, struggled to get going. It took them twelve overs to reach twenty.

Morgan had a big shout for caught at the wicket, but the Hampshire-looking umpire turned it down despite the fact that just about everybody in the ground had heard the snick. Rawdon's skipper, Stewart Smith, hurled his cap down in disgust when the official waved away the appeal. 'Get a bloody deaf aid, umpire,' an angry man sitting near me bellowed at volume even a lamp-post could hear. He was the first example of the once-ubiquitous Yorkshire barracker I had come across on my travels. When I was younger there was always a crowd of them in any ground in the county, yapping away at the opposition and the officials like terriers. At Headingley in the mid-seventies two blokes sitting in front of my father and I had spent the whole day baiting the Australian wicketkeeper Rodney Marsh until, half an hour before the close, he'd finally cracked and flicked a v-sign in their direction, an act they greeted with the satisfaction of men whose hard work has paid off. 'There is in Yorkshire crowds something that is lacking from the crowds of the south,' the great Australian cricketer and writer Jack Fingleton noted in *Brightly Fades the Don*. 'Yorkshire crowds are like our Australian ones. They are part and parcel of the game.'

'You want to go and get your bloody ears syringed,' the man continued. To make matters worse the batsman hit the next two balls through the covers for fours. 'That's eight bloody runs you owe us,' the angry man called as the umpire retreated to square leg. 'That's ten, now,' when the next ball was squeezed for a couple.

In the next over Rawdon's captain exorcised his frustrations by chasing a ball to the boundary with such fierce gusto he cannoned back on to the field off an advertising hoarding. The noise of the collision made everybody in the ground wince, but the skipper just bounced to his feet as if he'd hit nothing more solid than a freshly buttered crumpet. They breed them tough in Rawdon. This, after all, is the home village of Brian Close, who was turning out for the Rawdon first team at the age of eleven.

Close was a sort of sporting West Riding version of Leonardo da Vinci, so good at so many games he never quite seemed focused on the one he was actually playing. He captained Yorkshire and England at cricket, played professional football for Leeds United and Arsenal, was a single-figure handicap golfer playing right-handed and a single-figure handicap golfer playing left-handed, a county standard tennis and squash player and no slouch at snooker either. Frankly, it's a bit of a relief to discover that when it came to bridge Ray Illingworth usually got the better of him.

Close was a shrewd and inspirational skipper, a dashing batsman and cunning bowler, but what most people remember about him was his hardness. As I mentioned way back in the introduction, Close's autobiography is called *I Don't Bruise Easily*. A more accurate title would have been *I Bruise Just as Easily as Anybody Else but I Don't Give a Stuff*. Though I suppose that wouldn't have fitted on the cover so easily. When it came to hitting a cricket ball there were many who could match Brian Close, but when it came to being hit by a cricket ball he was in a league all of his own. He fielded even closer to the wicket than Emmott Robinson. Sometimes the ball cracked off his head and was caught in the slips, on other occasions it was blasted into his shins so often and with such force the blood flowed down his leg into his boots and bubbled up through the lace holes.

Against the West Indies on the final day of the Lord's test

in 1963 Close took the extraordinary decision to minimise his
risk of being caught by simply allowing the short-pitched
deliveries of Wes Hall and Charlie Griffith to strike him on
the chest. The next day he travelled up to Bradford to play for
Yorkshire. Before play local pressmen photographed his
injuries. He was so badly marked his ribcage looked like a
painting by Francis Bacon. Yet he went out on to the field and
bowled twenty-two overs. As Peter Cook's fictional football
manager Alan Latchley might have said, Close was somebody
who could look at himself in the mirror and say, 'That . . . is
a man.'

The rain that had been swirling in the air now started to fall,
but the players stayed out regardless. Beckwithshaw had
reached thirty-four off fourteen overs when Inglis, the more
attack-minded of the openers, slashed a ball to point. It
dropped invitingly just in front of the fielder. He got his fingers under it but spilled it as he fell to his knees. The game has
been tight and tense, the sort of cricket the Northern leagues
were built on, and every chance has to be worked for. The
fielder knew it. He remained on his knees, staring at the turf,
hands held out before him, cap on the ground a few feet in
front like some sort of offering to the gods.

    An off-spinner, Andrew Doidge came on at the football
pitch end and extracted plenty of bounce and turn. Doidge
once played for Pudsey St Lawrence in the Bradford League
but has been struck down by knee injuries. 'He's been waiting
for the operation for months,' a smart-looking chap in a flat
cap informed me. At the other end the elderly but still influential West Indian Denis Rack, replaced Morgan and bowled
whippy medium pace. A stumping chance was missed off
Critchley and the score crept slowly, painfully, patiently up to
seventy for no wicket.

The name Rawdon means 'rough valley', but the raw might as well refer to the wind. 'It's the coldest place in the world is this,' the smart chap tells me as I announce my intention to go into the clubhouse in search of a hot drink to warm my hands.

Inside, cheery women in tabards were busying themselves cutting sandwiches and lining up sausage rolls. There are photos along the top of the bar of Close, Bryan Stott – a former Rawdon player who hit seventeen centuries for Yorkshire and helped Ronnie Burnet's side win the title – and Hedley Verity. Verity came from Rawdon. He'd started his career at Larkfield Road and played his final match in England here too, skittling out Darby single-handedly. I looked at the picture. The great spin bowler was by all accounts a man of quiet good humour, but there seemed to me to be a sad and distant look in his eyes in all the photos I'd seen of him, as if somehow he'd been able to see the Nazi bullets that would cut him down as he led his Green Howards platoon through that cornfield in Sicily.

Back out in the middle there was finally a breakthrough for the home side as Inglis tried for a quick single, was sent back and slipped on the greasy turf. In the next over the excellent Doidge bowls his replacement, a left-hander, round his legs. 71–2 with twenty-eight overs bowled.

There was another run out shortly afterwards, this time the number four getting over eager. Critchley traded his helmet for a cap and, as if to celebrate, jumped down the wicket and smashed a mighty six straight over the pub roof.

As the overs tick down things began to accelerate. Doidge got one to bite and jump and had Critchley caught at short leg. The pacey Morgan returned. He took a wicket almost straight away, the batter caught at square leg off a misjudged hook, then a couple of balls later clean bowled the new man.

At the other end a hard-hitting middle-order batsman laid into the off-spinner. He had one smacked drive palmed over the boundary for a six, and pounded another over the wall and on to the roof of the football changing room in the next field. When he faced the Australian Morgan he took a mighty swing across the line and sent the ball hurtling so far over the Emmott Arms it may still be bouncing down the hill as you read this.

Morgan responded by digging one in short, the batsman went to pull it but didn't connect cleanly and was caught at cow corner. His replacement lasted only a couple of balls before the Aussie knocked back his off stump. Doidge – who was not rattled by the brutal assault – got a tail-ender caught at long on and trapped the last man LBW. Beckwithshaw had gone from 71–0 to 163 all out in the space of twenty overs. Morgan and Doidge both claimed four wickets apiece. 163 didn't seem like a big score, but in the conditions and with the sky darkening it certainly wouldn't be easy for Rawdon.

The Airdale and Wharfedale League was originally one section of the Yorkshire Cricket Conference, a sprawling league that also included the robustly named Heavy Woollen District. In 1936 the Airedale and Wharfedale clubs resigned from the Conference en masse and set up on their own. Rawdon had been a member since the start, but Beckwithshaw had begun life in the Nidderdale League, graduated to the Harrogate and District League and finally pitched up in the Airedale and Wharfedale League in 1977.

The club was ambitious, though. You could tell that by the amount of noise they made when Rawdon's innings began. Every time the ball went through the air the wicketkeeper yelled, 'Catch it!'. I have never understood the point of that. It's like shouting 'Save it!' at a goalkeeper when a striker is running up to take a penalty. What does the person think the fielder will do if he doesn't shout? Spit at the ball? Sing it a few bars of the theme from *Love Story*? Has anybody ever plucked one out of the air at mid-off and then, as they are being congratulated, said, 'Don't pat my back, Keith's the one to thank. If he hadn't told me to catch it I'd just have stood there and watched it whiz past my head'?

The wicketkeeper is not alone, it should be said. Beckwithshaw are easily the most voluble team I have come across all season, and frankly that is saying something.

Recently a friend of mine was put in charge of a local under-tens football team. My friend has for decades planned to revolutionise grassroots football with his innovative tactical schemes, now at last his chance had come. His radical formation for the under-tens was based on two wingers and a pair of deep lying attackers breaking late into the penalty area. Five minutes into the first match he recognised a flaw in his masterplan: the wingers couldn't kick the ball hard enough to get it into the box.

My friend had to make immediate changes from the sidelines. Unable to effect anything too complex he was forced to fall back on the tried and tested methods of primary school football coaches the length and breadth of our sceptred isle: telling the players to hoof it as far as they could in the direction of the opposition goal and then all run after it yelping like terriers. The thought that he was behind the resulting unaesthetic tumult was very upsetting to a football purist such as my friend.

Even more disturbing for him was the opposition coach. At the lower levels of football you often find people in charge of teams whose sole qualification for the job is their ability to bellow a few likely sounding phrases at a volume that drowns out the sound of passing juggernauts. 'Channels, channels!' they roar. Or, 'Tuck in, tuck in!' Or, 'Work the line, work the line!'

Nobody knows exactly what these instructions mean, though anybody who has made a study of parks football might form the opinion that 'channels' translates as 'boot him', 'tuck in' as 'hack him down' and 'work the line' as 'hack him down and then boot him'.

In my friend's case, the opposition coach had clearly combined the study of the *Big Boys' Book of Shouty Football Phrases* with regular visits to a relationship counsellor because he kept urging his players to talk to one another. 'It's too quiet,' he beseeched. 'We're not talking. Let's talk to one another, lads.'

My friend found this increasingly irritating. After an initial attempt to get his point across by counter-attacking with shouts of 'Let's suppress it! Let's bottle it up!' he finally cracked.

'We've gone silent. Communicate with one another. Communicate,' the opposition coach shouted. My friend stomped over to him. 'They're English. They're male,' he barked, 'they're not supposed to fucking communicate.' He has now been relieved of his duties, which is probably just as well, all things considered.

My friend was clearly wrong, of course. English men do communicate. It's just that its rare to hear a centre-half noisily extolling the virtues of his new Dremel power tool to his midfield, or a goalkeeper keeping his defence organised by yelling, 'What was the name of that actor in *The Brittas Empire?*' By and large, however, he has my sympathy, because it has to be said that these days there is far too much communicating going on across the playing fields of Britain. Team mates shout at one another, individual sportsmen bellow at themselves. Just about the only sports people who have so far failed to pump their fists and cry 'One hundred per cent, right now!' are boxers. And that's only because they're fearful the other bloke will seize the opportunity and knock their teeth out.

There was a time when a trip to the cricket offered the opportunity for quiet contemplation, the chance to catch up on some reading and take the odd nap. In those days the only thing that disturbed the gentle atmosphere of a county match was the occasional belch and every so often the wicketkeeper banging his gloves together and muttering, 'bowled, Bob,' into the collar of his shirt. Woe betide anyone who threatened the peace. Once at a match in Scarborough several decades back a series of vehement appeals from Yorkshire medium pacer Arthur 'Rocker' Robinson so incensed one white-haired spectator that he rose slowly to his feet and yelled, 'Will you shut up, Arthur? Some of us are trying to get some kip.' He spoke for the majority. Cricket was a place of calm. Not any more. Nowadays it is impossible to concentrate on the quick crossword for the infernal clamour of the players.

A cricket match has come to resemble that moment at a children's party when all the eleven-year-old boys, hyper with sugar and E-numbers, start shrieking out their favourite catchphrases from *Little Britain*. 'Come on, to the end!' mid-off calls clapping his hands. 'Heads up, lads!' exhorts midwicket. 'I am liking those areas, Nobby!' first slip cries to the bowler. 'Toes, boys, toes!' fine leg exclaims 'Let's keep squeezing!' point hollers. 'I'm a lady!' yelps extra cover.

This happens after every ball. 'Focus!' the skipper shouts. 'Intensity!' I should add that intensity and focus is the key to modern sporting success. You must be intense and you must be focused. However, I would advise against focusing intensely as that is likely to make you go cross-eyed, never a good idea when you are facing Brett Lee.

A long time ago I played cricket for a team in Middlesex captained by a former Guards officer. The former Guards officer had intensity all right. When it came to old-fashioned attitudes to discipline he made Douglas Jardine look like Haringey Council.

One time the opposition batsmen attempted to scamper a second run and the bowler, who was new to the team, bawled 'My end!' to the fielder who had gathered the ball. The fielder obliged. The batsman was run out. As we gathered near the wicket the captain marched up and stared icily at the bowler. 'For future reference,' he snapped, 'if there's shouting to be done on the field, I will be the one that does it.' At the time I considered him to be a tight-arsed Southern git, but over the course of the season I must confess I've started to come round to his way of thinking.

'If we're going to win this we'll need a good start,' the man sitting next to me said as Rawdon's opening pair took guard. Beckwithshaw's two pacemen are clearly determined to prevent that. James Lilley, the bowler from the football pitch end, is young with the vague look of an indie band bass player. He bowls left-arm fast-medium with a hunch-shouldered run up, hands down by his sides, like somebody doing an impression of Bob Willis. He had Rawdon's opener caught at the wicket for a duck. 0–1. 'Great scoreboard guys,' the Beckwithshaw captain Ben Quick cried, clapping his hands.

At the other end Stuart Hudson, a big burly man signed in June from Kirkstall Educational, bowled with incredible hostility. His first ball hammered the number two right in the guts, the next struck his thigh pad with a sound like somebody beating a carpet. The fourth flew off the splice and dropped just short of silly mid-on.

In his next over Hudson had the Rawdon number two caught behind off a really quick one. Two balls later the new man tried to withdraw his bat at the last minute, failed and nicked it to the wicketkeeper. Two runs on the board and three wickets down, any chance of a good start doomed.

The left-armer bowled a maiden and the glowering Hudson returned. He was hurtling in now like Mr Rochester chasing a madwoman, and sent another Rawdon batsman back to the hutch clean bowled with his second ball. The new batsman was smacked on the thigh with his first delivery and caught off the glove with the next. 2–5.

'I'm loving this scoreboard, boys,' Ben Quick shouted. 'Their number nine is already padding up. All of us, all the way, lads.'

Rawdon's skipper, Smith, clipped a couple off Lilley, but thick-edged the next straight up into the air and was caught by the cover fielder. At the other end Hudson struck Rack on the pad. Rack responded with a wild cross-batted slog designed to send the ball bouncing off the Mir space station. Unfortunately he was beaten by the pace and succeeded only in spooning the ball back to the bowler. Rawdon were now seven wickets down for four runs. The rampant Hudson had five wickets and around the pavilion people were looking up the record lowest total for the League, which turns out to be seven by Knaresborough.

As I walked around the boundary a bloke who was watching from over the pub car park wall indicated the scoreboard and said, 'What's the proper score?' When I told him that the scoreboard was correct he raises his eyebrows. 'Bloody hell. I thought it must be brock.'

The lowest total was passed, more by luck than judgement, before Hudson trapped another Rawdon batsman LBW. 12–8. There was a brief revival as the ninth wicket put on twenty-eight runs, but then The Hud claimed his seventh wicket at 40–9 and Lilley wrapped up the innings and the title two overs later. As Beckwithshaw celebrated with high fives and motivational slogans I wandered down the hill and got the bus back to Leeds.

On the top deck a young woman talking on her mobile said, 'What? And were you, like, totally naked? Not even a bra, or owt? Well, I know you've got a bad neck . . .'

This is Hardcore

Tonge

Autumn was close. In the mornings there was dew on the grass and condensation on the windows. Cylindrical hay bales littered the fields like the droppings of some gigantic rabbit. On Friday evening, when I took the dog out at a quarter to nine it was nearly dark, the sky a creamy mauve colour like blackcurrant jam stirred into semolina pudding. During the week the weather was beautiful and for once it carried on into the weekend.

I caught the five past nine train to Carlisle. It was the last day of the cricket season and I was heading for Tonge. Tonge is a small town north of Bolton that forms part of the parish of Prestwich-cum-Oldham. The nearest station to Tonge's ground is Hall i' th' Wood. It's actually spelled like that on the signs, with the apostrophes, which makes it impossible to say it without adopting a Northern accent, even if doing so makes you sound like Celia Johnson auditioning for a part in *Hobson's Choice*.

'Return t' Arl I' thee wood,' I said at the ticket office in Bolton station. 'Arl I' thee wood?' the ticketman said. 'Aye, Arl I' thee wood,' I retorted, fighting off the urge to add, 'and a couple of them barmcakes for us tea, chuck.'

Hall i' th' Wood is a fabulous Jacobean manor house. It was in the outbuildings of this house that Samuel Crompton perfected his spinning mule, one of the cranks that drove the Industrial Revolution. Crompton's spinning mule was so successful that by 1811 it was estimated that seven hundred thousand people were using them to spin cotton. The road that runs from Hall i' th' Wood station and Tonge cricket ground is named after him. It seems more or less impossible to get any more Lancastrian than that. I imagine that if you stood in Crompton Way, Tonge, near Hall i' th' Wood eating a hot pot pie and singing Gracie Fields's 'Sally' you'd create a critical mass of Lancastrianism that would cause a massive explosion.

I had taken the train from Preston to Bolton, past the now familiar avenues of carpet warehouses, sports centres, laminate flooring specialists, driving ranges and go-kart tracks. 'Lancashire – A Place Where Everyone Matters' reads a banner on a council building in Chorley, as we chugged on into an area of wooded hills, fanciful seventies haciendas and golf courses.

Bolton covered market proved to be the best source of food I found all summer. There were stalls selling brown barmcakes, fresh ovenbottoms and a bewildering variety of pies. The fish stall looked like something from Barcelona. You could buy twelve varieties of Lancashire cheese. I settled for two, some genuinely home-made meat and potato pasties, a flatcake (like an Eccles cake but not from Eccles) and a paradise slice.

Outside, tall Somali women in hijabs queued for Carr's pasty shop and a West African man bought a bed linen set for £11.40. 'It's duvet cover, sheet, pillowcase, the lot, is that,' the stallholder said in an accent that recalled Bernard Manning, though he's Asian.

Tonge's ground is across Crompton Way, an apparently unstoppable four lanes of traffic. As I stood waiting for the lights to change a BMW rolled past emitting the sort of rhythmic thudding that was either a powerful sound system or a gang rival desperately trying to escape from the boot.

The Castle Hill ground is a big oval with allotments at one end. The long brick social club has a Shell garage directly behind it to which the waiting batters nipped out periodically for ice creams and Lucozade. On the other side of the thoroughfare from the ground, what was once a cinema is now a cut-price supermarket. There's a high, wide expanse of net at this side of Castle Hill to keep cricket balls from flying out on to the highway.

It failed in its duties on one occasion and everybody waited for the thunk of a dented bonnet. None came, but even if it did there's nothing the owner could do about it. 'That fence is legal height,' one committee man said. 'If the ball goes over it we're covered. There's no legal regress. We get people coming in with their windscreens gone and that, but it's their look out. Mind, I tend to scoot past cricket grounds pretty fast myself nowadays.'

Tonge were batting when I arrived and the sun was pleasantly warm. The vistors in today's Bolton League clash are Farnworth, whose opening attack is two spinners. One is a little Asian, Mo Adnan, who bowls slow left arm around the wicket varying his pace and flight subtly. The other, Lee Sutton, is a tall, upright, balding man with a passing resemblance to P. H. Edmonds (Middlesex), though he's bowling off breaks.

'Come on now, the spin twins!' the Farnworth skipper urged after every other ball. The pair clearly relished the encouragement. Tonge's opener Nigel Partington hit a fifty, but the rest of the batsmen struggled to get going on a pitch that was clearly turning. A grey-haired Aussie at first slip took three blinding catches off Adnan, who finished with seven wickets. There was nothing that could really be called a collapse, though, and Tonge struggled through to 153 all out.

Farnworth's pro at the start of the season had been Aaron Redmond, a veteran New Zealander who'd played seven tests for the Kiwis and made a name for himself as a sturdy all-rounder with Canterbury and then Otago. He'd started the season in blistering fashion, smashing 145 in a league match. Maybe that was what caught the eye of the New Zealand selectors, because they'd surprisingly called him up for the World Twenty20. Redmond had repaid the favour by blasting the Kiwis to victory over Ireland. Since then he didn't seem to have returned to Bolton. Tonge's pro is a young Englishman, Adam Street, who's on Derbyshire's books and plays grade cricket in Australia during the winter.

Learic Constantine had turned out for Farnworth on his off-days from Windhill, and the club had also fielded Brad Hodge and current England bowling coach Otis Gibson. Sonny Ramadhin had played for Tonge and so had Vinoo Mankad and Manoj Prabhakar. One of the club's first pros had been Cec Parkin, who'd helped the Castle Hill side lift their first Bolton League title in 1932 with a club record of 112 wickets in the season.

Like S. F. Barnes and Learie Constantine, Parkin was a Northern cricket legend. Born in Egglescliffe on the banks of the River Tees, he was six feet tall but weighed just nine stone, hit the ball hard with a modicum of grace and bowled medium fast with such variety it was said that an over from him was the next best thing to watching the circus. His speciality was a lethal donkey drop that sailed up to a great height and clipped the top of the bails full toss.

Batsmen were either disoriented by Parkin's enigmatic

variations, or took offence and thrashed him all over the place. Whatever, entertainment was guaranteed. The bowler himself claimed to have perfected many of his more outlandish deliveries by bowling indoors at his long suffering wife, who frequently had bruised fingers as a consequence. His son later dismissed this explanation wearily as 'another one of Father's tales'.

Parkin had been the professional at Church in the Lancashire League before the Great War and played for Undercliffe in the Bradford League during it, but he really came into his own when he signed for Rochdale in the Central Lancashire League in 1919.

The Rochdale president at that time was a local showbiz impresario, Jimmy White, a big, brash man. On one memorable occasion White had offended the members at Lord's by turning up in the pavilion during the Gentlemen v Players match and, after watching for twenty minutes or so, bawling out, 'So which of this lot are the Gentlemen, then?' In CLL matches he employed the Stephen Potter-esque trick of distracting opposing fielders by having his most attractive actresses and showgirls parade around the boundary exposing their ankles while Rochdale were batting.

When Parkin came for his job interview, White asked what his terms were. 'I replied, "Well, I will consider fifteen pounds a week",' Parkin recalled in his memoir *Cricket Triumphs and Troubles* 'I was asked if I would sign there and then, but the thought struck me that I had asked for too little, and the best thing to do was to say, "I will consider it.". Asked how long I needed to do so, I replied, "A week.". In my mind I knew I was going to sign for Rochdale, and I said, "If you will give me a five-pound note I will promise not be interviewed by anyone else until I have seen you again.". I was very much in need of a fiver at the time.'

The money was a sound investment. Parkin's showmanship and joie de vivre transformed Rochdale. Soon the team was winning and the gate receipts had risen from thirty pounds per match to over three hundred.

If S. F. Barnes was a grim Northern archetype, Parkin was his exact opposite – the chirpy, cheeky chancer. Robertson-Glasgow described him as 'a man who loved cricket from top to toe and expected some fun in return'. One thing the two players had in common – apart from both being called directly from league cricket into the England test side – was their ability to get up the noses of the people in charge.

At the height of his fame Parkin had the temerity to write a newspaper article suggesting that England might do well to appoint a professional as captain. In the thirties the very notion of such a thing was so shocking he received a stiff rebuke from Lord's and was told he would never be asked to play for the MCC again.

Parkin had already experienced the singular mindset of cricket's ruling elite. He had played a single match for Yorkshire as a young man, but then Lord Hawke had discovered that the all-rounder had been born on the north bank of the Tees and therefore in County Durham. His Lordship told Parkin that because of the county's strict Yorkshire-born only qualification he could not play for them again. Lord Hawke was born in Lincolnshire, but that didn't concern him in the least. He, after all, was Lord Hawke, and Cec Parkin wasn't.

Tonge's heavy roller is painted in the club colours of yellow and deep red. I noticed this because the groundsman started it up, fastened the accelerator down using a plank of wood and allowed it to trundle out to the square all on its own, like an obedient old horse, while he rushed about collecting up his pitch-marking gear. By the time the roller has reached the wicket he had run over and jumped aboard. I like to think that one day he might get distracted by something, and the roller will make its break for freedom, rumbling across the square, up the bank, over the players' four-wheel drives, smash through the fence and escape through the allotments.

Farnworth's innings began. The Tonge opening bowlers are both left-armers. The younger one from the Crompton Way end is Adam Street, the club pro. He's quick, coached at county level by Karl Krikken, who began his career in the Bolton League. The other bowler is a tubby fellow who bowls medium-medium, rolling his wrist over the ball. 'Nice areas, Cheddar,' the fielders shouted. Tonge picked up four quick wickets as Farnworth struggled to get into double figures. It looked like Rawdon all over again. I'd have to say though that the surroundings were altogether less tweedy than they'd been in the Airedale and Wharfedale League.

When I'd told a friend of mine who'd played a lot of league cricket that I was coming down to watch Bolton League he'd said, 'Oh, it'll be real hardcore down there, all right.' He was quite correct, too. The standard is as high as you'd expect in a league that nurtured Steve O'Shaughnessy, Mike Watkinson, Rod Estwick and David Hughes – the Lancastrian all-rounder who seemed to specialise in late evening big-hitting in Gillette Cup ties of the seventies. But anybody who thinks cricket is a middle-class game should pop along to Tonge and have their prejudices smashed to bits with a lump hammer.

Pink roses and strident chrysanthemums peer over garden walls, the boundary is marked with white painted kerb stones, the pitch set in a natural bowl with raised banking on which are set pots of red and pink pelargoniums. There are white-painted benches and plenty of spectators, deck chairs and iceboxes, lots of families sheltering from the sun under beach umbrellas. There are also tattooed youths with rearing bull terriers standing outside the clubhouse supping superlager, and dire warnings about drug dealing in the toilets. I didn't meet with anything other than friendliness but a feeling persisted that if you stepped out of line, just once, you'd get what was coming.

A little after five, lads started arriving back from the second team game, which had ended early. They whizzed round the gravel drive to the car park in their low-slung and alloyed XR3s, tooting horns and yelling out of the windows. Their noisy arrival seemed to intensify the atmosphere out on the field. Tonge's appealing became more vociferous and aggression started to simmer.

Clearly there was some other stuff going on as well. Every once in a while the batsmen would turn and address remarks to the slips and there was backchat with the bowlers and between the non-striker and mid-on. It was hard to tell if this is just normal byplay, part and parcel of the rough-and-tumble blood-and-guts cricket Roy Genders had enjoyed.

A mate of mine who played most of his formative cricket round Leeds moved down to Gloucestershire later in life and played for the team in his village. 'I'll tell you the difference,' he said. 'The first game, we were away and the lads in the team said, "You'll have to watch their wicketkeeper. Their wicketkeeper is terrible. He's a right bastard." Well, I went out to bat. I scored about forty or so. And I thought the wicketkeeper seemed like a good lad. I thought the nasty wicketkeeper must be ill, or something, and this was his replacement. Then when I go back to the pavilion, the rest of the team are going, "You see what we mean about that wicketkeeper. He's a total disgrace, sledging like that." I said to myself, Bloody hell. Because if they got their knickers in a twist about him, if they'd played in West Yorkshire they'd have shat themselves.'

All things are relative, though. Cec Pepper might, or might not, have invented sledging, but in recent years it has become such an integral part of cricket that before the 1999 World Cup Scotland felt moved to call in Australian David Boon as a sledging advisor after the chunky batsman had upset a Scottish bowler with a few choice remarks during a practice game. Part of Boon's role must surely have been to explain the arcane etiquette that apparently governs insults on the cricket field.

The existence of an unwritten Sledgers' Code came to light back in the nineties when England's Craig White complained that Ruchira Perera of Sri Lanka had transgressed it. White grew up in Australia, if not the birthplace of sledging then certainly its alma mater. 'I don't think we sledge,' Australian skipper Steve Waugh famously remarked recently. 'I would prefer to call it mental disintegration.' (Presumably he meant of the opposition, though some may say that Brett Lee's hairstyle points at a certain amount of collateral damage.)

Experienced in this rugged environment, White said that while he had no objection to abuse generally, the taunts levelled at him by the Sri Lankan had gone beyond the bounds of acceptability. The exact nature of the insults was never made public.

An insight into the usual insults was given by former Australian rules footballer Barry Stoneham. Talking about sledging, the Geelong Cats veteran said that he felt it was all par for the course in a red-blooded game, but 'you can't slander people with personal remarks about their lifestyle'.

Whatever the unwritten law is, it's clear that at Castle Hill somebody crossed the line in the sand. When the fifth wicket fell, the batsman given out caught at the wicket after a long debate between the two umpires did not go quietly. Instead he removed his helmet, pointed his bat at the celebrating fielders and bellowed, 'You ever mention my fucking sister again and I will fucking kill you.' He was escorted away by one of the more conciliatory fielders, twisting and turning to get a good stare at those who'd offended him.

I wondered for a few moments if there'd be a fracas. In the seventies and eighties Lancashire League games had often been marred by crowd trouble. Unlike at football this frequently involved the players too. In a game between Todmorden and Church even one of the scorers had been censured for his behaviour. At Tonge, however, things calmed down again fairly quickly, despite the noisy intervention of several spectators.

Another wicket fell to Street, but this time without incident and Farnworth were struggling at 34–6. Their wicketkeeper, Booth, then did what wicketkeepers have a habit of doing: producing a slightly eccentric but effective innings, full of chips and flicks and shuffling footwork. Briefly he rescued them. At the other end a tall batsman took a more direct route, hammering the ball straight for a couple of sixes until he chanced his arm once too often and was caught on the cover boundary.

Booth continued on his merry way. A short man, he is best off the back foot. At one point he shifted his weight onto his rear leg and forced a shortish ball from Street through point for four. The old man at Windhill would have nodded in approval at that one.

Tonge changed bowlers at both ends. From the allotment end came a tall blond-haired fellow who sprang to the wicket like Jacques Tati imitating Tony Greig. He beat the bat every other ball and had a big shout for LBW turned aside.

At the other end the skipper, a square-shouldered Asian, came on. He bowled what at first appeared innocuous medium pace, but in his second over clean bowled Booth for twenty-nine. Sensing victory, the second eleven and the bull terrier boys greet the returning batter with a chorus of 'Na Na Hey Hey Wave Goodbye'.

Street returned and finished the innings off with 7–56 as Tonge ran out winners by thirty-three runs. The defeat meant Farnworth missed the chance to finish in second place. Tonge, who'd begun the season poorly, were pleased to end up ninth.

I'd enjoyed the games at Lascelles, Carlisle, Settle and Bacup. The matches at Blackpool and Rawdon had been good ones, competitive and hard-edged, but this one had been the best. It was rough and rude and shaven-headed, certainly, but it was also high quality, furuulous and unique. It was the cricket Roy Genders had written about half a century ago. Unrefined, unadorned, it was cricket with the crusts still on.

'Well at least it passed off without further incident,' I said to the man sitting on the next bench as the players trooped off. He chuckled slightly, 'You should come when we play Walkden,' he said. 'They bring a coach load of fans. Things can get a bit messy'. 'Really?' I asked. 'Oh aye,' the man replied. 'They're from Bury.'

The sun was shining brightly as I waited on the platform at Hall i' th' Wood. People were out in their gardens, the windows of the houses open. There was the sound of radios, kids playing and a couple arguing over whose responsibility it was to make sure there was always some beer chilling in the fridge.

Bolton station was crowded with Manchester City fans. I waited for the train north. A very old man with a sunken face and a curled and protruding tongue sat down next to me. I'd seen him on the train earlier in the day, on the way up to Tonge. He was crook-backed and rheumy-eyed and looked like a relic of an older, crueller age.

'All right, cock?' the man said, twisting to look at me. 'Beautiful weather, intit? I've been up to Blackburn, me, for a ride out on train.'

'I've been to Tonge to watch the cricket,' I said.

He looked at me with his head tilted slightly, 'Have you, now?' he asked, 'Were it all right?'

I told him it was good.

'Good eh?' he said with a flinching nod. 'Well now, we've both had a lovely time then, haven't we?'

The train for Wigan pulled in and he doddered over and got on, waving back to me as he slipped through the doors.